*Unloose My Heart*

# Unloose My Heart

A Personal Reckoning with the
Twisted Roots of My Southern Family Tree

......................

Marcia Edwina Herman-Giddens

The University of Alabama Press
*Tuscaloosa*

The University of Alabama Press
Tuscaloosa, Alabama 35487-0380
uapress.ua.edu

Hardcover edition published 2023.
Paperback edition published 2024.
eBook edition published 2023.

Typeface: Garamond Premier Pro

Cover image: iStock.com/Vizerskaya
Cover design: Lori Lynch

Paperback ISBN: 978-0-8173-6166-2

A previous edition of this book has been cataloged by the Library of Congress.
ISBN: 978-0-8173-2145-1 (cloth)
E-ISBN: 978-0-8173-9431-8

This book is dedicated to my children, grandchildren, great-grandchildren, and all who come after. I wrote this for you because I want you to know the truth.

I also dedicate this book to all the people enslaved by our ancestors and their offspring, named and unnamed: kidnapped, bought, sold, and born into slavery, always held against their will.

Below are the names of my ancestors' and relatives' enslaved people mentioned by name, often with a price, found while I was researching my forebears. These names appear in wills, deeds of sale, succession papers, occasional letters, advertisements, and historical documents. Many are children. There are so many more unnamed and unfound.

1734
Mimbo, Pegg, Hannah, Ireland, Judith

1740
Peter, Crump, Stephen

1743
Mingo, Judah, Mou, Agge, James, Randol

1775
Sam, Aggy, Black Simon

1791
Osbon, Fillis

1799
Dye, Infant Dye, Thamer, Mary, Phoebe, Pompey

1800
Mariah, Tona, Harper, Susannah, Daniel, Sarah, Miner, Sipio, Sharp, Jane, Pina, Caesar

1803

Lucy, Tom, Dick, Venus, Cate, Siczha, Tom Brown, his wife,
child Rachel, child Cate, Moses, Flowra, Jacob, Lucy, Alek,
Peter, Titus, Joe, Jack, Venus, Bethy, Nelly, Nelly's child 1,
Nelly's child 2, Ben, Dol, Aban, Sigh, Cirles, Ned

1807

Petter, Jean, Lucy, Tim, Tee

1810

Selah, Sarah, Philip, Lydia, Daniel, Amos, Demsey, Abilley, Rose Lastly

1818

Joe, Dilcy, Lucinda, Wallace, David, Stephen, Dolly, Zilphy, Burwell

1830

Efraim, Isaac, Lelah, her child Bob, Jack, Ellen, Harbored, Elizabeth,
Harriet, Weigum, Barry, Clarissa, Ralph, Willie, Joe, Mark

1836

Prudence

1842

Winny, Andrew, Ferely, Seaborn

1844

Armistead, Patty, Louisa, Amerias, Tuskiah, Anthorn, Terry,
Rachel, Siccilly, Thomas, Billy, Linis, Nelson, Maria, Clairinia,
Siccilly the 2nd, Terry, Ridley, Clarissa, David, Lisa, George,
Henry, Peter, Harriet, Lewis, Lavinia, Amelia, Nelom

1845

Margaret, Zilda, Winny plus four children, Simon, Wesley, Riley, C___
plus child, W___, Catherine, M___, ___ [mother], John, Eli, April

1850

Burk, Thomas, Charles, Betsey and two
children, Cornelia, Mariah, Casey

## 1851

Dido, Sophia, Maurice, Tom, Mosley, Quanimo, Mintas, Millians, Mary, Toney, Eliza, Ned, Amy, Andrew, Leanon, Tom, Alfred, Lewis, Caroline, Damon, Esther, Jerry, Juliana, her child Jobe, Madlin, Quash, Sarah

## 1852

Jack Barnes, Lucy, Westley, Alfred, Adolph, Louisa, Frank, Nancy, Mary, Lucy, Mahala, Virginia, Yellow Andrew, Mary, Robert, Violet, Jackson, Ephrains, Big Caroline, Sarah, Tom, Justin, Little Jack, Rose, Ruben, Nat, Ben Burton, Alec, William, Nancy, Alec Jesse, Billy, Amanda, Holland, Kimbell infant, Ted, Aspasie, Millie, Israel, Henry, Justin, Richard, Alec, Ellen, Black Andrew, Rosetta, Black Lucinda, Cyrella, Jane, Ellen, Charlotte, Oscar, Amaka, John, Joshua, Henrietta, Adeline, Sam, Sarah, Sarah, Rhoda, Sarah, Susan, Andrew, Clarisse, Charles, Maria, Thom, Jim, Matilda, Moses, Nelson, Jenny, Francis, Elizabeth, Henry, Isaiah, Joe, Betsy, crippled infant, Easter, Phyllis with her child, Rosanna, Lucinda, Carolyn, Cora, Dary, Bill

## 1857

Peter, Judy, Lucinda, Willie, Harriet, Amos, Arthur, Henry, Mary Ann, Adam, Landy, Mary, Jane, Benjamin, Albert Jr., Young Henry, Betsy, Betsy's child Laddy, Catherine, Lucinda, Solomon, Littleton, Sarah Ann, Risanah, July, Winny, Winny's child, Pompey, Nelly, George, John, Celick, Garry, Hannah, Abram, Ralph, Britton, James, Robert, Riole, Albert, Mary, Mary's child Reuben, Sarah Jane, Lucy, Clarissa, Andrew, Cyprus, Sindy, Morris, Eliza, Jane, Allen, Philip, William, Hampton, Renah, Eliza

## 1860

Carson, Judy, Pandy, Mary, Jane, Ben, Albert, Jim, woman and child Peter, Dan, Sarah, Patsy, Brodus, Sally, Dick, September, George

## 1863
Ben

## 1865

Fillis, Osbon, Fuller, Joseph, Prince, Randal, Peter, Margaret, Toney, Bacchus, Riley, Jim, Sylvia, Charles, Alick, Bella, Venno, Caesar, Albert, Oliver, Louis, Bunyon, Hester, Ann, Lindy, Sarah, Hanner, Dana, Patty, Grace, Bob, Judy, Jane, Shep

# Contents

## Part I. Early Childhood

## Part II. Coming of Age

## Part III. "Bombingham"

## ~ Contents ~

# Figures

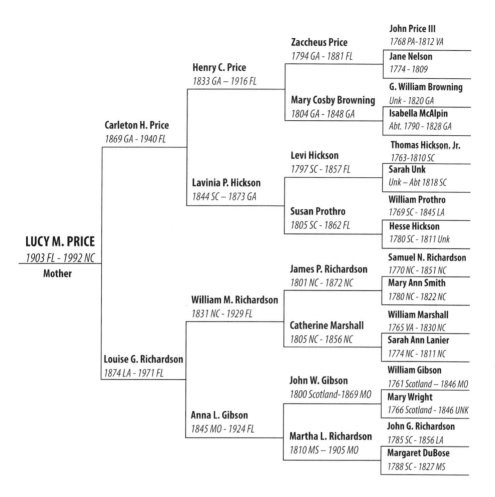

**LUCY M. PRICE**
*1903 FL - 1992 NC*
**Mother**

**Carleton H. Price**
*1869 GA - 1940 FL*

**Henry C. Price**
*1833 GA – 1916 FL*

**Zaccheus Price**
*1794 GA - 1881 FL*

**John Price III**
*1768 PA-1812 VA*

**Jane Nelson**
*1774 - 1809*

**Mary Cosby Browning**
*1804 GA - 1848 GA*

**G. William Browning**
*Unk - 1820 GA*

**Isabella McAlpin**
*Abt. 1790 - 1828 GA*

**Lavinia P. Hickson**
*1844 SC – 1873 GA*

**Levi Hickson**
*1797 SC - 1857 FL*

**Thomas Hickson, Jr.**
*1763-1810 SC*

**Sarah Unk**
*Unk – Abt 1818 SC*

**Susan Prothro**
*1805 SC - 1862 FL*

**William Prothro**
*1769 SC - 1845 LA*

**Hesse Hickson**
*1780 SC - 1811 Unk*

**Louise G. Richardson**
*1874 LA - 1971 FL*

**William M. Richardson**
*1831 NC - 1929 FL*

**James P. Richardson**
*1801 NC - 1872 NC*

**Samuel N. Richardson**
*1770 NC - 1851 NC*

**Mary Ann Smith**
*1780 NC - 1822 NC*

**Catherine Marshall**
*1805 NC - 1856 NC*

**William Marshall**
*1765 VA - 1830 NC*

**Sarah Ann Lanier**
*1774 NC - 1811 NC*

**Anna L. Gibson**
*1845 MO - 1924 FL*

**John W. Gibson**
*1800 Scotland-1869 MO*

**William Gibson**
*1761 Scotland – 1846 MO*

**Mary Wright**
*1766 Scotland - 1846 UNK*

**Martha L. Richardson**
*1810 MS – 1905 MO*

**John G. Richardson**
*1785 SC - 1856 LA*

**Margaret DuBose**
*1788 SC - 1827 MS*

| Paternal Generation 6 | Maternal Generation 6 |
|---|---|
| **John Price II** | **Col. James Richardson** |
| *1728 PA–1782 VA* | *1734 CT–1810 NC* |
| **Sarah Jenkins** | **Elizabeth Neal** |
| *1731 PA–unk* | *1727 Barbados or NJ–1808 NC* |
| **William Nelson** | **Samuel Smith** |
| *1754 VA–1813 VA* | *1715 unk–1786 NC* |
| **Mary H. Taliaferro** | **Sophie Roots** |
| *1760 VA–1786 VA* | *c. 1755 NC–1786 unk* |

| | |
|---|---|
| **Joshua Browning** | **James M. Marshall** |
| *1758 VA–1807 GA* | *1735 VA–1818 NC* |
| **Margaret Rankin** | **Anne Harrison** |
| *1754 NC–1842 GA* | *1742 VA–1793 VA* |
| **Robert McAlpin Sr.** | **Burwell Lanier** |
| *1757 SC–1804 MS* | *1741 VA–1812 NC* |
| **Mary Cosby** | **Elizabeth Hill** |
| *1754 VA–1827 AL* | *1740 VA–1792 NC* |
| **Thomas Hickson Sr.** | **William Gibson** |
| *unk* | *1740 Scotland–unk Scotland* |
| **Wife** | **Wife** |
| *unk* | *unk* |
| **Evan R. Prothro** | **George Wright** |
| *1742 PA–1822 GA* | *Scotland unk* |
| **Elizabeth Morgan** | **Elizabeth** |
| *1748 SC–1817 GA* | *Scotland unk* |
| **Thomas Hickson Jr.** | **Francis Richardson** |
| *c. 1763–1810 SC* | *1763 SC–1820 MS* |
| **Sarah** | **Martha Gaulden** |
| *unk–1818 SC* | *1765 VA–1832 MS* |
| | **Daniel DuBose** |
| | *1737 SC–1800 SC* |
| | **Mary Nettles** |
| | *1760 SC–1821 MS* |

*Figure 1.* My mother's Price family tree. Note: Thomas Hickson Jr. appears twice because of uncle-niece marriages.

# Preface

We went searching for our maid, Jessie, who had gone missing. At home, her presence made me feel safe. Her strong, brown hands glowed with a comforting warmth. The door we stood before tentatively opened, and a frightened, dark face peered out from dim light inside. I clutched my father's hand tighter. That is how I learned in Jim Crow Birmingham there was Black fear, and it swam in the streams of white fear. I was ten years old.

I grew up there, under the smog of steel mills, carrying the weight of being an only child born to two disparate people. After several years in a New York City suburb, we moved to Birmingham, not knowing anyone or having

*Figure 2.* Me, age six, with my parents, Lucy Marshall
Price Herman and Edwin Parker Herman.

any contacts, just before I started the first grade. Somehow, the move was supposed to help my mother's asthma.

Little did I know that the young Birmingham, an industrial transplant to Alabama rather than part of the "Old South," was the most segregated city in the country. I doubt I even knew what segregation was, but I soon found out. By my teens, Birmingham had acquired its shameful nickname "Bombingham." I could occasionally hear dynamite blowing up Black people's homes and churches (in the vernacular of the day I would have said "colored people," that being the then-polite designation for African Americans). I didn't know about the Ku Klux Klan, nor did I ever see the Klan at its evil work, but they couldn't hide their loud bomb blasts that traveled down the valley.

Added to the smog was a sorrowful vapor clinging to me at home. My mother had her own struggles functioning. In those days, there was little help for mental health issues. Proud of her "blue blood" and ashamed of my father's descent from simple Lancaster County farmers and millers of Brethren and Mennonite persuasion, she had come from well-to-do enslavers. She would unashamedly tell me stories about "how good they were to their slaves" and how "happy the darkies were." She didn't see I had my own reasons to feel outcast and trod on; thus, I identified with these trampled invisible people from the past as my sorrow increased. All my mother's white supremacist talk—"Whites are the superior race, colored people are childlike, they need us to tell them what to do"—never sat right with me.

Until I was well grown, a heavy cloak of shyness kept expanding, nourished by my clotted unhappiness. Growing into racial awareness in a dual atmosphere of racism at home and in my community, I searched for my moral compass as I came of age. Identifying with the persecuted, I noticed when others were persecuted. Two events involving a Black woman seared me to my core: one when I was ten years old, the other at seventeen.

Somewhere along the rumpled course of my teen and young adult years, I met activists, white and Black, who protested the evils in Birmingham, and I joined their journey. That took me places I could never have imagined. Some were dangerous.

Dozens of books have been written about the appalling events in Birmingham. I do not need to repeat these. I have my own civil rights stories. I was no hero, just a minor figure.

For almost fourscore years, I have allowed my personal ghosts to remain unexamined. What else happened in Birmingham? Which of my ancestors were enslavers? How many? How did this affect my life? After a rocky start, my life became happy and rich and demanding: filled with raising children, going back to school, and eventually having a rewarding career in medicine and public health. Passing years gifted me with a growing number of grandchildren and, just recently, great-grandchildren. I was busy, and I was having fun.

~

Christmas 2017 found me sad because our holiday plans had to be postponed as several of us were ailing. Not being a TV watcher, I was idly searching topics with my laptop to take my mind off my misery. Related to my 2015 solo Big Road Trip, as I had dubbed it, which took me from North Carolina to just west of the Mississippi, I learned later I had crossed paths with the ghost of a fourth great-grandfather on the Natchez Trace. After I learned about his murder on the Trace, to see what more I could find, I would occasionally Google his name. This time, information appeared that shocked me, catapulting me into doing more than just reading and thinking. I needed to enter my own history, my ancestors' history, Birmingham's history: find out what I didn't know, what I had forgotten, see how it all wove together, and how I had navigated my growing up.

As I considered what to do, in early 2018 I was lucky enough to be introduced to William Ferris, then associate director of the Center for the Study of the American South at the University of North Carolina. When I told him some of my stories (surprised to find tears brimming in my eyes), he gave a name to my angst that I had not thought of myself. He said, "Your history is haunting you." He was right. He encouraged me to write it down.

So, I wrote this book step by step, discovery by discovery, with all the shocks, sordidness, and unexpected pleasures along the way. I am no historian; my writing background is in science. What is in this book is what only I can do: tell some family stories and my own stories. Some of my stories involving public events have never been told as far as I know.

This book is an odd composite. There are my own stories, from early childhood on through young adulthood as I came into awareness of the complex social divisions, sharp as knives, for Birmingham's class, racial, and ethnic groups. Crossing boundaries could hurt or kill. Then there is a story in a place I had never heard of, one that intersects with mine. For that, I thank a fortuitous meeting, first online and then in Natchitoches Parish, Louisiana, with a newspaperman named Robert Gentry. A reporting assignment sixty years prior had led to his lifelong inquiry into a disturbing local legend. It involved a plantation owner who turned out to be my third great-granduncle.

This and other research have added further disturbing dimensions to the grim history of my many slaveholding relatives and ancestors. Some go back to 1639. One goal, albeit painful, has been to expose what my family and I have never fully known: illuminate the ghosts. Certainly, the romantic tales I grew up with were not all there was. How can one understand what one doesn't see? Forgive what one doesn't know?

So, to ease my haunting and to satisfy my growing need to uncover the forgotten and secreted past from which I came, this book grew and sprouted tendrils. Daily news reports show us that racial problems in our society are far from over. Those of us who look white seem to have only just started to examine our existential angst of "whiteness." I hope that sharing my stories and my family's history may help others as it has me. For years, I have also pondered whether my social standing, my social capital, is due, in part, to my family's history as slaveholders. I now know it is.

—

Herein is my pilgrimage and my quest and how I ended up on adventures I never could have imagined and with a rainbow of new friends and cousins.

*Unloose My Heart*

*Part I*

# Early Childhood

# Chapter 1

# A Hybrid Self

Here is my beginning.

—

I am an only child who grew up bisected by the separate cultures of my parents, one southern, the other northern, born when they were almost forty. My southern childhood was filled with sharp edges shadowed by Birmingham's smog. My northern childhood was crisp and clean and safe. My parents fought bitterly with occasional violence. They loved me fiercely.

I would have drowned in fear and despair but for the odd vortices that would spit me out from time to time. I sought solace in nature, which my father taught me. Seven years old, tears on my cheeks, I discovered the breezes whispering to dandelion seeds. I walked down the alley below my bedroom window collecting broken shards of blue glass, jewels settled in the coal ash gravel. At the age of eight, I saw a field of glowing daisies looking to heaven while hiking with my father. I kept that vision for times I couldn't sleep. I sought more private treasures and held them tightly. And, luckily, I found myself with a double handful of adults who appeared at just the right times to keep me afloat.

My northern childhood comprised parts of summers spent with my father and his favorite sister, my beloved Aunt Mary, in Lancaster County, Pennsylvania. It was a protected place of beauty and rolling farmlands, Amish and Mennonite horse-drawn buggies swaying on ribbons of road, woods and clear creeks, fields of ruby-red tomatoes, and lots of shoofly pie. There were other times and northern places: weeks with my mother's sister Beth and her family, when I needed care that my mother, sick, could not give; and later, northern visits with them. There were two summers with them on an island

*Figure 3.* My mother, Lucy Marshall Price Herman, in a park
in Washington, DC, in 1938, three years before I was born.

off the coast of Maine, where we kids had absolute freedom to roam on land
and water. When I was staying in the North, I was teased for having a southern accent. When I was at school in Birmingham, I was called a Yankee for
my northern accent.

My parents were an unlikely couple. Living through the Great Depression, neither had been married before their 1939 wedding in a church they
had never been to before and never saw again. No family attended. My petite
mother wore a black eyelet dress. Slim and brought up to have good posture,
she probably looked taller than her five feet two inches. She often referenced
her olive skin, which I also inherited. Her dark brown hair matched eyes that
sat above high cheekbones. There are no photographs. Maybe she looked
happy. I hope so. Growing up with her often-scolding face and unhappy demeanor makes it hard to imagine.

As couples did in those days, my parents had saved enough to make a
down payment on a bungalow in Arlington, Virginia, and to buy some furniture. They had met in Washington, DC, where each worked as a government

clerk, my father in the Treasury Department and my mother in the Department of Agriculture. I came along two years later. In one more year, we moved to New Hyde Park, New York. My father, in a new job, commuted into the city to work in the just-opened Social Security office.

—

Papa was born in 1904 on a farm in Lancaster County near Ephrata, the second youngest of the seven who lived to grow up. None of them were tall. He didn't seem short to me because of his strength and stocky build, until I overtook him by one inch in my adolescence. I stopped growing at five feet seven inches. He already had a bald circle atop his head by the time I was born. What hair he had was straight and almost black. He was handsome, with full lips, hazel eyes, and a dimple in his chin. Those last three traits I inherited from him, whereas my eye and head shape are from my mother.

Papa grew up thinking most of his people had come from Germany about three generations earlier. After his sudden death in 1972, I resolved to find out more about his heritage. I was stunned to learn they were largely Swiss Anabaptists. Seeking to escape persecution, the Herman line reached this country in 1710 and went straight to Lancaster County. There they farmed for two hundred years, none leaving the county until the 1900s.

I have little detail about his people except from a few wills and deeds. His ancestors were uneducated, many illiterate. There are no letters. The only photographs are a few of his mother, one of her mother, and one of his father. My father told me once that his father used to say people should live in little houses that had wheels so they could move easily. No wonder my grandfather felt that way. He frequently uprooted the family to try yet another occupation and location in the county.

Papa's parents often spoke German, the Pennsylvania German dialect. They struggled to make ends meet, but the children had shoofly pie and a pitcher of milk waiting for them after school and at least one pair of shoes even if they were hand-me-downs. An 1823 locally crafted grandfather clock made of black walnut stood in the corner of their dining room. My oldest child now has that clock. It turned out to be my sole inheritance from Papa. Why that happened and why it was never in our house when I was growing up is a story about two wills my father wrote twenty years apart and Papa's youngest brother. That story must wait for another time.

At age six, my father learned to swear from his older brothers as he struggled to keep up with them on their several miles' walk to school. His temper

*Figure 4.* My father, Edwin Parker Herman, in the 1928 senior annual of Ephrata College, thirteen years before I was born.

must have started then, too, as he grappled with trying to get those hand-me-down shoes on his feet. Already too small for him, they kept him from catching up. Papa was the first in his whole long line from 1710 to finish high school, much less college. He realized that to get anywhere, in addition to obtaining an education, he needed to learn proper grammar, so he bought a book and studied hard. By the time I came along, no one could tell his background by his speech. He was kind and gentle except when he lost his temper at my mother, who would drive anyone crazy. In turn, I learned to swear from him. I adored him.

My mother was the fourth of six; five reached adulthood. She was the last baby delivered by her mother's father, William Marshall Richardson, a physician then in partial retirement and struggling to grow oranges in the middle of Florida. It was eight years after the area's grim setback from the Great

Freeze of 1895. He and my great-grandmother had built a home called Hill-crest on a knoll in the middle of the grove. They could see Orange Lake from the piazzas across its two stories. Both of their daughters would arrive from south Florida when it was time for the delivery of their latest baby.

Mother's delivery was as difficult as her infancy. She filled the house with unrelenting howls from severe colic. My grandmother, the older of the Richardsons' two daughters, did not like my mother. Whether because of the near-fatal birthing, the colic, or other reasons, I will never know. I knew this and a lot more that I should never have heard. Before school age, I had already become my mother's confidant because no one else liked her much either. Even as a child I could see how much my mother was harmed by my grandmother's not liking her.

Mother loved her brothers and sisters though she had her conflicts with them, often due to her criticisms. Because she liked to see them often, I got to know them well. I called them by Aunt and Uncle and my grandmother M'Wese, short for Mother Louise. Right after M'Wese died, in 1971, my mother had her own gravestone erected beside my grandmother's. She did not want her younger sister, Beth, whom she felt her mother adored, to get there first. There it stood in the West Palm Beach cemetery, waiting for the final date to be engraved, until Mother died in 1992.

My mother's parents were proud of their family lineage and taught her to be. They had good blood, good educations, good grammar, good manners, and refined looks as my mother would say. They also held many people in bondage on both sides. Even she did not know how many. M'Wese was the only living grandparent I had. My grandfather, Carleton Hickson Price, had died just a year before I was born, from an almost lifelong struggle with tuberculosis.

I am told that my grandfather was a warm, friendly man. He was definitely a supporter of southern ways, friendly or not. After his father's death, he carried on the family effort to get the US government to pay his father's estate back for cotton "stolen" from him by Union forces during the Civil War. The box of what we cousins call "The Cotton Papers" sits waiting for me to glean its offering for this book.

After six children and my grandfather's inability to earn enough to support the family, M'Wese sent him packing as a means of birth control. At least that is how I interpreted his having to leave and the subsequent stories of his sickly, peripatetic life. He and my grandmother never divorced, continuing a cordial relationship until his death. My mother, born in 1903, was followed by Beth in 1907 and a brother in 1908. Having the last two so close in age was too much for M'Wese, so she sent Beth of the gravestone competition to Miami to be raised by my grandfather's father, the one of "The Cotton Papers," and his second wife. They were "Miami pioneers."

My grandmother was ambitious and worked hard to support her family. She became the first licensed female real estate agent in Florida, developing part of West Palm Beach. She was also a good artist. Our summer visits are linked in my mind to the smell of her painting. Her easel and palette with its thumbhole fascinated me. Half-squeezed oil tubes lay in her artist box. The odor of the oils and the mystery of colors appearing from mixing them became a Florida part of me, along with exotic fruits and tropical vegetation, beaches, afternoon rains, huge roaches, and occasional scorpions.

I was slightly frightened of M'Wese. Though short like my mother, she seemed formidable. She had become somewhat stout by the time I knew her. Rather than risk any jiggles, she wore a corset. On one occasion, having been too near the shower when she emerged, I had the job to pull her corset's laces taut over her plump, still-damp skin and tie them. She considered herself a blue blood, which meant the entire family was. All of us grandchildren had to meet high standards for appearance and behavior.

My name was suggested by M'Wese. She wanted Mother to name me for her father, which, of course, Mother did. My grandmother also proclaimed that "Marsha" should be spelled "Marcia" even though her father's middle name was Marshall, his mother's maiden name. That makes me named after a long line of enslavers.

The spelling choice for my name has always perplexed me (never having gotten an answer as to why) and still causes confusion. This great-grandfather had a sad and heavy history. My knowledge of him was expanded by letters he wrote that came into my possession not long ago. Being named after him I carried a muffled sadness that linked him with me. He was born in North Carolina in 1831 and died in Florida in 1929, twelve years before I was born. There is more about him later.

I have no memories of hugs from M'Wese or feelings of comfort. My cousins' memories for her are warmer. Perhaps her distance from my mother was carried over to me. My mother spent her life trying to be loved by her mother. On occasion Mother wrote desperate, needy letters to M'Wese that I would read when she left them on her desk. She also compulsively wrote in journals and left numerous notes on envelopes and any scrap of paper that was available. Sometimes she would write up and down the side margins after she had filled a sheet of paper with horizontal lines.

My mother's many journals now hide in a corner of a closet in my house along with a few Nazi and Ku Klux Klan publications I found after she died. I had thought of reading the journals to aid my lacuna-filled memory. After glancing at one started when she was pregnant with me, I could not go on. The first pages detailed her efforts to get an abortion when she found herself pregnant with me. This shocked me since, from the time I was young, she frequently told me she married my father, even though she did not love him, because she wanted a child before she got too old. I later saw this confirmed in letters to her younger brother. The journal pages bled into others about cold-water enemas she gave me as a toddler. Those were the days when people were preoccupied with their bowels. My mother took bowel activity on as an obsession. Sometime in my sixth year, I was finally big enough to refuse her further access to my body. She still examined the toilet after I used it, sometimes moving the contents with a stick to have a proper look and count the pieces of toilet paper I had used. I was allowed only three.

So, filled with horror, I put the journals away and decided not to look at them further.

———

Not until much older did I realize that my parents' disparate heritage contributed to the desperate loneliness of my early years. Born to parents of different cultures and classes, with no nearby family, and their marriage growing more contentious by the day, they had no shared traditions to draw on and carry out in family life. Buffeted by no foundation and swirling undercurrents, I grasped for anything solid I could find. This forced me, though shy, to reach out more, which was a good thing.

As for what I remember about my life, the whole of it feels like the scattered butterfly wings I see on my garden paths, their edges frayed yet still bright with color. In between are huge gaps. I know how frail memory is, mine especially. If anyone should have kept journals, I should have. Other than those I wrote in periodically for special trips and my gardening journals, I never did.

On many occasions I have contacted my children's father when desperate to retrieve some long-ago happening that occurred when we were together. For those years, from 1958 to 1993, he is my memory bank when I am floundering. I am grateful for his help. So, what I do remember must have long settled into safe little spots.

My severe myopia probably helped configure my lack of memory. Abuse doesn't help. I have always focused on close-up details. My clearest memories are things like the place where I saw my first wild black-eyed Susan, the first time I had real butter, a laden apricot tree behind an ancient European wall. I have great gaps for bigger things such as kindergarten (no memory of it at all), large chunks of elementary school, my learning to drive a car, even the years significant events occurred.

—

*Apologies to my mother.* At some point as a young child, I became aware that my primary emotion about my mother was fear. Alone with her I never felt safe. By the time I was an adolescent, I realized she struggled with severe depression, paranoia, and other mental health issues. Although that did not help me with survival strategies, it was the beginning of my trajectory through many years to get to a place of forgiveness. As an adult, I have consulted from time to time with mental health professionals without being able to learn much since my mother was not available. With increased insight, especially in that she surely felt abandonment, along with yet another recent consult with a professional, a likely diagnosis at last emerges, that of a personality disorder, probably borderline personality disorder. It is illuminating to me to know this.

As my story unfolds, I recount harmful things that my mother said and did to me and to others in addition to her racism. I came to dislike her intensely, even to hate her. Now, with some wisdom that comes with old age, I realize she did the best she could. I know she loved me and cared deeply that I grew up well. In recent years I have found forgiveness and now even think of her with compassion and tenderness. I know her life was hard.

There were some good things I learned from her. They were likely due to her peculiarities rather than good judgment, but nonetheless they became strengths I absorbed from our relationship. One was that she was a woman without fears. She was not afraid to try new things. She had no squeamishness about confronting spiders, traveling alone, or knocking on a stranger's door, or any other of the common inhibitions or fears that many women have. Hence, I did not grow up with learned phobias or limitations in behavior because I was female. Coupled with my father's entire lack of expectations of roles due to my being a girl, this gave me a rare freedom for that time. I played with dolls, but I introduced them to bugs and snakes, cap pistols, and my miniature metal cars and toy soldiers.

As I got older, I learned to lie if it could get me out of trouble. Why I would incur my mother's wrath, I mostly do not know. There was one understandable time when I spilled mercurochrome on the rug under our five-foot-wide oak dining room table. I liked to play between two of the lion-clawed legs. I was pretending my doll had been cut and was painting the cut with the disinfectant. Maybe I was working out my own being cut with the metal edge of a measuring stick Mother would hit me with. Little strips of blood would appear on my underwear. I learned to hide that ruler, the back brush, and other objects she used on me and pretend I did not know where they were. I learned to be sneaky. And when I was able to read, I learned that by perusing her journals, I could glean what she had in store for me and sometimes take measures to protect myself.

Thus, I learned to survive. I had to be strong, and that strength has stayed with me. My learned hypervigilance is part of it. I have read about the quality of resilience that some children seem to be born with. Many are not. I was fortunate to be one of the former.

---

I know she loved me. She cared about me and did the best she could. In the end, it all turned out well.

## Chapter 2

# Moving to Birmingham

I am a white girl of Jim Crow Birmingham and, yes, echoes of bombings still whisper in the deep crannies of my mind. My parents and I moved there in 1946. The city was thick with Jim Crow, thicker even than its smog. I didn't know what Jim Crow represented when I first arrived and how it would weigh on me and change the course of my early life. My only memory of the move is seeing a jumble of boxes and furniture and watching a man bring in my wicker doll carriage. School started in a few weeks, and I was still five years old. About a month later I turned six and was walking the three-fourths of a mile each way by myself to the first grade at Lakeview Elementary School. Birmingham did not have school buses.

Moving that summer was not the best timing or circumstance for me, a painfully shy and unhappy child who had to soon start school and get used to a thirteen-room house. Plus, I was left-handed, which was to cause me trouble later. My mother planned to rent the five extra bedrooms as an income source. I never did like that house. After it filled with strange men coming in and out at all hours, I hated it.

—

During my first year, we lived in Arlington, Virginia. My father went to night school to obtain the law degree required for his position with the Social Security Administration. Soon he was transferred to New York City. We lived in a Cape Cod cottage in New Hyde Park, Long Island. When I was around three my mother almost died from an asthma attack. I was sent to Alexandria while she recovered so Aunt Beth could care for me while my father worked. Cousin Marion, four months older, and I must have had fun together as we still do. Her brother, Toby, was a baby. I remember nothing about that time.

Back on Long Island, sometimes Mother took me into the city for shopping. I liked the end car of the subway so I could watch the water dripping from the top of the tunnel as it went under the river. When I was older, she would tell me about the subway doors closing on me when I was only halfway inside. Men sprang to the doors to pull them partly open as the train had started moving, others pulled on my arm. Mother complained that my dress got ruined because the rubber on the doors' edges marked it with permanent black streaks. It always seemed she was more upset about the dress than any danger I was in or trauma I might have had from the experience. So, it seems, the pattern of my life with her had begun.

In another two years, the move south happened. For my asthmatic mother, I realized later, Birmingham seemed an odd choice since it was one of the most polluted cities in the country at that time. Her doctors had recommended she move south. Because of my father's Social Security position, the choices were either Atlanta or Birmingham.

My parents left me with Aunt Beth and her family again this time when they investigated the two cities. My uncle worked at the Pentagon. They lived on a pigeon-filled cobblestoned street in Alexandria, Virginia, in a house built in 1792, beautifully furnished with antiques. I was in another world there.

My aunt and uncle were very kind to me. My aunt was pretty in a cute sort of way. She and my mother had enough features in common that one could tell they were sisters, though Beth's skin was very fair. Aunt Beth never raised her voice at me nor hit me. This aunt is the same one who created the family tree books in the 1930s. She bought five blank genealogy books and filled in the information with India ink, still legible today. How she found so much data I have no idea. In my research now, I find that most of it is correct.

Aunt Beth couldn't have known how my mother's copy of this book would become a thread through my life: a pull from the past and a tug to the future. The book enchanted me. I began studying it as soon as I could read. From the center, the pages to the right were the maternal branch, the left, paternal. There were cutouts on every page that allowed access to further pages for the female lineages. I could stick my finger into the openings, carefully, which allowed a direct turn to that branch of the family.

Uncle Ken seemed almost magical. His trim body reminded me of a lamppost. His thin face gleamed when he grinned, as though the lamp had been lit. He pulled pennies out of our ears. He had a studio where he made silver jewelry, did artwork, and tooled leather. I love the smell of leather to this day. Cousin Marion and I skipped along the cobblestones scaring away pigeons. My life was suddenly different and enriched; the household was harmonious. I relaxed. My mother picked Birmingham.

—

In 1946, Birmingham had laws designating where Black people could live and how they should live.[1] The city began where two rail lines crossed, near some of the world's richest deposits of iron ore, limestone, and coal. This confluence assured a steel industry, thus its being named after Birmingham, England. The formerly enslaved flocked to the growing city to fill the needed cheap labor demand.

One of the southernmost valleys of the Appalachian chain, Jones Valley nestled between the northern West Red Mountain and the southern Red Mountain like a long and flattened snake. The city grew in the flatland, with the white residential areas primarily on the low mountains on either side of the valley. Over Red Mountain were Shades Valley and Mountain Brook, where the very affluent lived. The top of Red Mountain was marked by the largest cast-iron statue in the world, Vulcan, the bare-bottomed Roman god of the forge, placed in 1938. At the time, he held a neon torch that flashed green if there were no traffic fatalities and red if there were. Growing up under that torch cast another dreary pall. It became almost an obsession every night to look and see whether anyone was killed in a wreck that day.

Of course, when I was little, I did not know all this history. I did see that

*Figure 5.* The house on Milner Crescent in Birmingham where I grew up.

my entire universe was suddenly whiter than ever. The only times I saw Black people was when riding city buses and watching maids enter white homes. The population when I moved there was 270,000 and 40 percent African American. By the time I became a young mother it had grown to 371,000, with about the same proportion of Black people.

My parents picked a house in what was then called Southside. It was the first one on the east side of a street named Milner Crescent.[2] The street sloped gently up the edge of Red Mountain in a curve that befit its name. A walk of only a few steepish blocks brought one out to a view across the entire valley on a clear day. I always assumed Milner must have been one of the founders of Birmingham. It turns out I grew up on a street named after a vicious, greed-driven slaver who figured out how he could continue forced Black labor at no cost despite the 1865 Thirteenth Amendment.[3]

Smog and soot from the steel mills were so bad that clothing hung out to dry sometimes ended up with gray blotches. After I married and lived on the next street above us, sometimes even the houses across the street could not be seen.[4]

Our 1914 house, built into a slight bank, was two stories in the front and three in the back. The base was yellow brick, the rest covered by shingles. The basement smelled of coal dust and damp earth. The huge furnace's air ducts flailed out like an octopus. I would go down there with my father to watch the hopper twist coal into the fire, which raged like the devil's inferno. It was compelling. Another wing of the basement, the only part with a floor, held his workshop. Off that was the inside entrance into the old servant quarters, comprising a small bedroom and grungy bathroom. The entire place was spooky.

The front door opened straight into a large living room with a seldom-used fireplace on the left end. My bedroom was behind that wall; my sleep was punctuated by the mantel clock, which chimed every fifteen minutes. I hated that, too, especially when it tracked my frequent insomnia. My parents' bedroom was beside mine, but they did not stay in the same room for long. Upstairs were bedrooms no. 1 through no. 5 as my mother called them. We shared the hall bath with the roomers. I disliked that more than all the rest of the things about the house. I did like the little closet and its window under the winding back stairs. Its corner shelves held balls of string, ever growing from pieces tied onto the last by my Depression-era parents, along with other curious odds and ends. Those included the cellulose smallpox vaccination cover that had been placed on my upper arm when I was three years old.

The renters, mostly single men, entered our front door and crossed the living room to the stairs to their rooms. The exception was the basement servant quarters, room no. 6. Its entrance was off the backyard. When my parents and I needed to take a bath, we had to wait for the inside roomers to vacate the bathroom, then use the tub they had just gotten out of. They usually did not clean after themselves. I found it disgusting.

In those years it was not uncommon for people to rent rooms. Perhaps it had to do with being soon after World War II. It always seemed peculiar that my mother would rent rooms because it didn't seem aristocratic to me. She must have wanted the money even more than status. She kept all the rental money. After a while, she started buying lots on the outskirts of Birmingham.

No Black people lived anywhere near us, not even on little back streets. So, I grew up not having any experiences with African American people but for buses and from afar. The one exception was the only maid that my mother ever employed, who came by bus once a week for several years. The bus stopped along Highland Avenue. Near Milner Crescent, the avenue, rimmed with elegant houses, was a tree-lined double boulevard and very pretty.

—

Mother loved to swim and wanted me to learn. Soon after our move she sought out an indoor pool. The only options were the Young Women's Christian Association and the Young Men's Hebrew Association. My mother didn't like Jews. She made that clear, but I was too young to understand specifics. Nonetheless, she chose the YMHA because it cost less.

Often, I had to go alone to swimming lessons at the YMHA, taking the bus to downtown Birmingham, even when I was only six years old. My parents did not buy a car until I was ten, so we depended on buses, our feet, and, for me, a bicycle. Between my mother's criticism of Jews and my having to learn the curious requirement to board buses only through the front door and to sit in the front, I soon realized there were rules about what sort of people one was supposed to like and be like. I don't remember being aware of African American people as being any different when we lived in New York. Birmingham taught me differently.

To board a bus, the "colored" people had to climb the front steps, pay their fare, turn around, get off, and go to the back door to board. The bars across the seat tops had two holes to accommodate pegs that held signs lettered "White" on one side and "Colored" on the other. They were moved to accommodate the changing proportions of white and Black passengers. Sometimes I would sit in my white section surrounded by empty seats and watch the "colored" people crowd into the smaller area behind the "Colored" sign. I felt uncomfortable and confused. It was against the unspoken rules for Black people to move a sign.

The swimming pool was in the dank, windowless basement of the Young Men's Hebrew Association. One of the curiosities of the women's dressing room was a contraption variously known as a fat melting jiggle machine, a massage belt, or an exercise belt. Picture my six-year-old eyes watching nude women, some of huge proportions, enormous breasts hanging to their waists, getting on that machine, struggling to get the belt around their hips. Once they turned on the switch, the sight became more astonishing. Even my slim mother would use it on her hips. She was proud of her nice figure and intended to keep it that way.

I already knew my mother could be a danger. I soon learned other people could also do me harm. Elementary school girls made up my swimming class. When it was my turn to have a lesson on front floating, the male swimming teacher put one hand under my belly to hold me up; the other pulled aside the elastic crotch of my bathing suit and began probing and pushing. I can feel his fingers to this day. I know I wriggled away. I told my mother. The swimming lessons ended. It is to her credit that she believed me.

I was exposed to another stress there about how different people can be. Men and women had separate times for swimming. When the girls and women were slow to vacate the pool, loud pounding and deep-voiced shouting would emanate from a door on the far end. We would hurriedly scuttle out, dripping all the way into the dressing room. The men were impatient, angry, and frightening. Finally, it was explained to me that they swam naked, so their pool door was kept locked until we were gone. I confirmed not long ago that was true: the men swam naked, but the women did not.

In school, the first-grade readers did not sit well with me. Jane seemed a shadow figure, a background for Dick and his escapades. Confused, I became resentful. Was I, a girl, not a human being of equal stature? Dick and Jane nudged me on a path of rebellion. Quiet rebellion, because when one is shy, one is muted.

School had other challenges. Mother usually didn't arise until midmorning, leaving me alone to dress, prepare for school, and eat the breakfast my father left for me. Out the door with my book satchel, I walked, still alone, to school. When I was late and had to enter the room with everyone staring at me, my misery was shriveling. Walking in the winter was often painful as girls were not allowed to wear pants; if leggings existed, I had none. One time I was so cold I climbed in a car with a man who offered to take me to school. I knew I shouldn't and kept my hand on the door handle. When he countered my directions and took a wrong turn, I managed to get away.

I was not an early reader. When I learned to print, a mirror was required to read it. That led to another school issue that caused resentment, thus adding to my growing questioning of the status quo. In the second grade when we started adding and subtracting double-digit numbers, I saw them as reversed, so my answer was reversed as well. My teachers knew what was happening. I still got marked wrong. Overall, I was a good student. Fortunately, I mostly grew out of my reversal predilection. To this day, if I am tired or stressed, I still occasionally reverse digits or letters.

One good thing that happened in the first grade was that my parents were told via a note from my teacher to take me to an optometrist. Outside after I was fitted for my first glasses, the jolt I received from being able to see the curb and the distance down I needed to step is still with me. I know because I still start breathing faster when that experience comes to mind. I looked up and saw leaves on trees. Leaves! When we got home, even though I knew it could not be true, I asked my father whether he had repainted the entire house.

Two years ago, when I was being evaluated for cataract surgery, the ophthalmologist asked me how old I was when I was still seeing well. This made me realize I may never have seen well. Even with glasses, my vision soon could not be corrected to twenty-twenty. Now it makes sense that my memories are replete with intense detail of objects. Thus, I remember swaying grasses gone to seed, grooves down the backs of beetles, my little toy cars inside village walls made of tree roots.

I was fortunate that there were children in the neighborhood. I was teased and picked on at times, but that was better than not having playmates. Otherwise, I would have been even lonelier. We mostly had free rein from dawn to dusk and were in and out of one another's houses grabbing peanut butter sandwiches when hungry. I noticed that the children almost never came to my house. There were four or five of us girls who were fast companions. We seldom played with the few boys in the neighborhood.

A block down from my house was an appealing park even though it had no play equipment. On the Highland Avenue side, it was basin shaped. We would scavenge large pieces of cardboard and make sleds, taking turns pushing one another down the steep slopes. When it rained hard, the drain at that corner of Highland Avenue would stop up, creating a pond seemingly just for us. Our bare feet disappeared in the Alabama red clay water. We played and splashed, especially happy when it was a hot summer day. No parents ever seemed to be concerned.

When my family and I first moved to Milner Crescent, there were wooded lots on both sides of the street between us and Highland Avenue. The one just across the alley under my bedroom window became our Land of Tarzan. On Saturdays, some of us would walk a mile each way with dimes in our pocket to see the latest Tarzan movie. The racism must have gone over my head. All we cared about was pretending to swing on vines and hide behind trees.

When that lot was cleared to build a church, we turned to climbing all over the structure, until walls went up, leaving nothing to grasp onto. A recurring dream I had for several years ceased the moment the clearing began. My dream, rather like "Little Red Riding Hood," was of a wolf chasing me. I was caught and gobbled down. As I was fighting and kicking inside his stomach, he would finally throw me up. I ran away fast and was safe. This transcendent dream nourished me. I felt like something was taken from me when it stopped.

A tree-covered vacant lot was off the alley behind our house. We discovered mysterious piles of enchanting, hollow, terra-cotta blocks embossed with various designs. We made clubhouses with them, hid things in their hollow areas, and imagined we were soldiers from an exotic land. By the time this lot was cleared for church parking, we had about outgrown that kind of play. Nonetheless, I missed those trees and their green canopy terribly. I was never able to find the source of the terra-cotta blocks.

The one exception about seldom playing with the boys applied only to me. He was Jimmy Steeves and lived directly across the street, in a stately sandstone home with a broad covered porch. His parents were compassionate and gentle and welcomed me warmly. By the time I was a teenager, I had bounded up the two dozen steps to their front door countless times to savor the quiet and explore treasures with Jimmy. The air inside held a gossamer quality. It must have been from the blending of their huge collection of American Indian artifacts, the thousands of preserved insects in the attic, and the orchids in their greenhouse. His father, an architect, an orchid breeder, and an amateur entomologist, had discovered several new insect species. He taught Jimmy and me how to properly collect and mount butterflies and to examine flowers. We learned to be delicate and careful.

Jimmy was three years younger than I. He never played with the other neighborhood kids. I always assumed that his mother was overly protective, but maybe it was just that he was so much younger. I didn't mind. He was the only child I remember often being in my house. After a few years, his family bought a little cabin on the Coosa River and frequently took me along on weekends. I swam in that river and felt like a water sprite. I wafted through thermals in their meadow and dreamed. I marveled at the magic of a getaway place.

Visiting another friend had been fun until it turned into a terror. On one of my visits to Mary, no one was home except her father. He invited me in to wait, saying Mary would return soon. That was a lie. As we were standing in the living room, he grabbed me. Breathing heavily, he pressed me against his huge belly and started groping. His belt had a brass buckle that knocked off my glasses as I struggled. I don't remember picking them up, but I must have. His weight prevented him from catching me as I ran into their bathroom and locked the door. It seemed like forever before anyone came home. I counted the black and white tiles on the floor and studied their patterns. I can still see them. I never told my parents. I couldn't afford to not have free rein of the neighborhood.

Much of the time I was by myself. I played with my tiny lead soldiers, building forts for them with dominoes. I took my metal cars outside and made little roads in the dirt between tree roots. When I finally learned to read, I read a lot. I loved fairy tales where wicked witches got their comeuppance. I had started to think of my mother as a mean witch, so "Hansel and Gretel" was my favorite. When I was around the age of eight, my grandmother gave me *The Book of Knowledge: The Children's Encyclopedia*, published by the Grolier Society. The set still keeps my other books company, taking up a foot and a half on a top shelf in my library.

I consumed those volumes, learning everything from science to cultures around the world to literature. With their garnet-red covers, some still with tattered blue dust jackets, these books were friends, always there when I needed them. Researching *The Book of Knowledge* now, I learned it was originally written by a British man, Arthur Mee, from the era of white superiority and British imperialism. He wanted to impart patriotism and high morals to his readers. Mine was the US version. Curious, I looked up *slavery* in the index. A partial list of entries includes "among ants, among Bors, in Rome, in the United States, cost of abolition in British territory." In this last entry, a "widening sense of the brotherhood of all men" is mentioned, along with the checking of "certain evils," this referring to vast economic disparities in England, not slavery. Rereading the section on the Civil War, I am struck at its lack of arguments against slavery.[5]

Weekends were happier times for me. My father was home, and I felt safer. Papa soon began a pattern of taking me on hikes on Saturdays. I think he wanted to get away from my mother as much as I did. It is hard to describe how intrusive she was, how critical, how she could heckle and torment anyone. And how her unhappiness glommed onto us like quicksand. Even without the need to get away, hiking was fun, and he wanted to teach me all that he knew about botany. We would pack a lunch and set out on foot through a residential section that halted when the mountainsides became too steep for building. Soon, we were in sloping woods, where he taught me to identify trees, to chew on the stem of a sassafras leaf if I got thirsty, and to look at the patterns of moss growing on tree trunks to help with directions.

I would often develop a stitch in my side trying to keep up with him and was soon calling "Papa, Papa, please slow down." Then he would show me the tiny things, different types of acorns, rocks, insects, and fungi. One time, we passed a walled garden, and over the fence I saw a small field of daisies. I had never seen daisies before. They seemed the purist, prettiest, and most cheerful creation I had ever beheld. I have always kept that moment with me. It became my vision of glory.

# Chapter 3

# Searching for Jessie Robinson

How my parents allowed me to have the precious bundle of gray fur that was my dog I will never understand. I named her Dingy. She came into my life not long before Jessie Robinson did. Jessie was the maid hired by my mother to help her clean and change linens for the men renting rooms. As soon as I was old enough, that task mostly fell to me. Dingy was one of a litter of toy terriers born up the street. When I got her, her tail was already lopped off to a stub, causing her to wag her entire bottom when she was happy, which she usually was. I was eight and under instructions to keep her clean and out of the house. I gave her a bath and was astonished to see a coat of gleaming white fur with large beige spots emerge. By the next day, she was solid gray again. Though the opposite of her personality, Dingy seemed the only suitable name. I thought Birmingham's persistent soot and grime were normal.

Dingy was on the top step of our porch waiting for me every day after school. I poured out my troubles and sorrows to her, and she listened with a cocked head, soft eyes, and her sloppy little triangle-shaped ears. I loved her with all my heart, and she loved me. When we played together, all ten pounds of her wriggled so vigorously I could hardly pick her up.

These were the days of no leash laws or efforts to get owners to control their pets' reproduction. This meant that occasionally, even though Dingy had been spayed, I found myself pulling a male dog off her. In fact, this was my first lesson about sex. It was common to see a male dog seeking a female in heat, his shockingly crimson penis emerging as he mounted whatever female he could grasp. That lesson was augmented by my finding a new, carefully wrapped condom in our next-door neighbor's yard. They had several almost grown sons, and I soon partly understood the connection between them and my mysterious find. I showed it to my friends. Somehow, we figured out what

*Figure 6.* Me at home, about age ten, with my beloved dog, Dingy.

it was. No one ever explained sex to me, and partially informed explanations from older children weren't that helpful. I eventually figured it out, but not with any help from my parents, unless you count the anatomical details I found in an old "marriage" book that I discovered in their Victorian glass-doored Big Bookcase.

Neighborhood life in those days had events that introduced a comforting pattern to my life, except for the telegrams. The free-roaming dogs ignored the black produce truck that came a few times a week. A tiny house on wheels, it was full of vegetables in neatly partitioned bins on either side of a narrow aisle. A special bin held candy and, on a shelf above, a few loaves of bread. Housewives would come out of their homes and make their purchases. Few mothers worked in those days. The truck charmed me. I looked forward to climbing inside, clutching a few pennies for candies. We also had a milkman. It seemed both normal and exciting to find the bottles, wet with condensation, beside our front door three times a week. The postman brought mail twice a day, postmarked with a legible time and place. Occasionally a telegram arrived, announced by the doorbell. This prompted anxiety even though the news was sometimes happy, like a new baby announcement. Notices of deaths or serious illness were the usual.

The mail deliveries I looked forward to were the small boxes from Canada that came several times a year. My mother still had trouble with asthma and had heard a stranger talking about a curative remedy. The boxes' contents were intriguing: various-sized medicine bottles with liquids of different colors, droppers, and a vial for measurements. By now, I was old enough to read labels. The only ingredient I remember on the label was arsenic. I understood arsenic was poisonous and secretly hoped it would do my mother in. Her asthma ceased in a few years and never returned. Decades later, I told this story, leaving out my wishes for her demise, to an allergist who was a colleague. He said that small doses of arsenic were known from ancient times to be helpful for asthma.

When my parents had one of their terrible fights, my mother would leave, taking me with her. Papa must have taken care of Dingy. I have memories of dark, gloomy sleeping quarters in rooming houses far drearier than our house. Not enough food to eat. No paper on which to do my homework. Terrified of being alone with my mother. Having to walk a new and longer route to school. I only understood that we were all hurting. When Mother knew Papa would be at work, she would take me back to our house to pick up things we needed. The kitchen table would have a pile of money waiting for her and notes that I could see started with "Dear Blossom." I was never able to read them. Blossom was Papa's pet name for Mother. As the years went on, he used it less and less.

One of their worst fights occurred when I was nine years old. Papa was out of town at one of his rare work conferences. He arrived home to find me in my bed, very sick, my room darkened. Day after day I had lain in the dark not eating and almost too weak to move. My mother, who was in a Christian Science religious phase, would read Mary Baker Eddy to me several times a day. Since illness was supposed to be an illusion, I suppose she hoped I would absorb this from the readings and get well. She did not want me to know what was wrong with me. Forbidding me to leave the room, she even provided a chamber pot. I finally sneaked into our first-floor half bath. One look in the mirror told me I had measles. Back then, measles was so common even children knew the rash. Returning home, my father exploded when he saw how sick I was and immediately took me to a doctor. In the middle of their yelling, weak and trembling with fear, I feared I might die.

When I got better, my forced attendance at the Christian Science church continued. My mother was usually too depressed or constipated to get out of bed in time so we could go together. I had to walk the mile each way alone.

Sunday school was held in a big open room. The table where my class met was under a huge painting of Jesus holding his hand toward little children who were surrounding him. Lambs frolicked in the background. The caption, which I read over and over to myself, was "Suffer little children to come unto me." I would think how much I suffered and wonder why Jesus never helped me.

I never talked to my father about my mother's treatment of me or about their fights. I felt I could understand those. She would needle him and criticize, complain, and fuss until he snapped. He had a vicious temper once unleashed. He would swear at her and call her ugly names. I was more afraid to leave these scenes than to stay. The fights were fairly frequent. Afterward, she would write long letters to her younger brother about how horrible my father was and how she had never loved him.

I could not understand his care for her and still don't, but I believe he loved her. I will never know why he did not intervene more to protect me. He must have been aware to some extent of her abuse. I don't think he ever knew about the rulers, the sticks, or the back brushes she would strike me with. When I was a little older, I began to hide whatever she had taken to hitting me with and stayed out of her way as much as I could. Papa never saw the half-moon marks that she would make with her long fingernails squeezing into my upper arm, sometimes bleeding, and taking hours to fade. He never saw her counting how many times I used a tissue when I had a cold, threatening punishment if I did not get at least twelve blows on each. Nor did he hear her criticizing me year after year for everything from my looks, my weight, and my posture to how I did things. Perhaps, he could not stand the fights that would be a sure result. Perhaps, he knew that as a father in the 1940s he would never be allowed to have custody if he left her. I never doubted that he loved me with all his heart. He, too, must have done the best he could.

Over the years Mother continued leaving Papa periodically. Twice she had him served with divorce papers. Papa worked a year after he could have retired so the larger pension would ensure plenty for her old age. He knew he would die long before she did, "dropping dead" before he was old. That is exactly what happened, as it had with his brothers. I was thirty years old, he sixty-seven. My grief pierced my world sharply and deeply. The ripples spread far and touch me yet at unexpected moments.

~

Around the age of eight I discovered the Birmingham Public Library. It sat beside the courthouse downtown. I took myself there by bus. It was a grand, three-story neoclassical building of Indiana limestone built in 1927. I spent my time in the children's room and, when older, the entire library. The children's room was palatial with its beautiful dark wood shelves full of books and, above these, grand murals depicting fairy tales. A mezzanine overlooked the main adult reading room, with its murals on world mythology. Even the ceilings had paintings blended with elegant borders. The only ladies' room was on the mezzanine, just opposite a brass sculpture of Romulus and Remus. I loved that sculpture almost as much as I did the children's room. The twin boys on their haunches stretched their mouths toward the she-wolf's teats. I studied it over and over and decided that if babies cared for by a wolf could survive, I could too. I was already friends with a wolf, the one in my dreams. In 2019, I visited the library, now the Linn-Henley Research Library, to do some research for this book. I went straight to that corner. There the statue sat. My heart glowed.

I knew I never saw any Black people in the library, but I did not know they were forbidden by law to use it even though their tax money was helping support it. The first library African Americans had in Birmingham was in the Colored Masonic Temple building, supported with their own money. Their second library, a 1939 branch of the Birmingham Public Library, opened after much effort and money-raising by the African American community. It was named Slossfield Branch Library. I suppose it was time that the Sloss name stood for something nurturing rather than exploitation and high death rates.

There were books at home, too, treasured storybooks I looked at repeatedly as I did the genealogy book, which was titled "Ancestral Tablets" in gold letters across an olive-green cover. The spine was covered by a wide strip of brown leather. I thought it elegant. It seemed so old, but with a publication date of 1936 it was only about thirteen years older than I was when I began to study it so intently. Had it not been for the intriguing picture of the McAlpin coat of arms, I probably would never have focused so much on that name. Because McAlpin was in my grandfather's maternal line it did not show up on the center page. I had to turn to it through an open box to the lineage for my grandfather's grandmother, Isabella McAlpin. There I would look at what Aunt Beth had for Isabella's parents' names. After that there was nothing, leaving me to wonder.

—

Around this time, my mother hired Jessie Robinson to come once a week. She called my mother Mrs. Herman; we called her Jessie. She was a kind and

*Figure 7.* Jessie Robinson in the 1950s. She came once a
week for several years to help my mother clean.

gentle woman who, to my young eyes, seemed older than she probably was. I
remember her hands, so beautiful and strong, their skin ridged with tendons
and a few wrinkles, the smooth places in between gleaming like burnished
chestnuts. When I gaze now at the sole photograph I have of her, she appears
to be around fifty years of age.

In those days, Black people were expected to go to back doors, but that
wasn't possible at my house since it was at the basement level and had no
doorbell. Jessie did not wear the typical uniform of most maids, gray, with
white aprons. Jessie must have brought her own food. At lunchtime, she sat
at our kitchen table, where we always ate. Sometimes Mother and I joined
her. Oddly, my mother didn't have a problem eating together. At the end
of Jessie's workday, my mother would hand her three one-dollar bills and
a quarter for bus fare. After my parents bought their first car when I was

ten, on rare occasions we gave Jessie a ride home. That is how we had some idea about where she lived. Of course, she had no phone. I don't remember whether we knew anything else about her life.

After several years of Jessie's faithful one-day-a-week appearance, a week arrived when she did not arrive. After another few weeks with still no Jessie, we were worried. Finally, my father decided he and I would look for her. I realized even then, after the first house we stopped at, he took me along to appear less threatening. I was beginning to understand why. We knew her house was in an area down Twentieth Street that ran eastward along the valley, the "colored" section comprising many blocks of small, run-down dwellings. We parked on a street in the general location we remembered and began knocking on doors.

Little did I know, this search was to be a pivotal moment in my life, a hunt that scorched my very being. We stepped onto the tiny porch of the first house and knocked. We repeated this for quite a few houses as no one opened their door, even when we could tell someone was there. Finally, a door opened slightly, and a dark face peered at us. Even though I was only ten years old, the fear on that person's face was so palpable it punctured my heart. It was then I began to understand the ugly truth wrought by this brutally segregated city. To this day, when I think of searching for Jessie, my heart quickens, my eyes moisten, and my breathing becomes shallow and fast. Now, thinking back, I know the anguish of that experience set me alight, helping me see my way to my later principles and actions. We continued to other houses. Occasionally, through a cracked door, someone would say they had no idea who Jessie was. At the last house, before we gave up searching, a woman opened her door wide enough that I could see inside. I was shocked. The room, its walls unpainted beadboard darkened with age, was faintly lit by one light bulb hanging naked from the ceiling by a frayed wire. The almost bare room was neat and clean as best as I could see in the dimness. A tattered sofa was on the right wall. A picture hung on another. Those are the only details that have stayed with me over these years. What has never left is the way the weak gray light struck into me as though it had been a blinding flash. Even though tightly gripping my father's strong hand, I was confused and afraid. I filled with a sorrow that has never left me.

I had never seen the living quarters of any Black person. Though aware a range of money and material goods existed, I never imagined the extent. In the fourth grade, I had been surprised when the teacher asked students whether their family had a telephone. About a third of the class raised their hands. Some students had clothes that had been patched and darned. One of my friends lived in a tiny apartment with plain, utilitarian furniture. Another lived in a grand house with elegant furnishings. Even so, I had no idea people could be so poor. All I knew was that something was wrong.

Jessie Robinson returned to our house in another week or so after our search. We never did know the cause of her absence. Now I can only wonder whether it was related, though unlikely I suppose, to some horror perpetrated by Birmingham's white supremacists. To this day, I dislike being in a room lit only by a ceiling light, no matter how bright it is.

—

After writing this much about Jessie, I knew I wanted to find out more about her. Here is my search for Jessie Robinson, now sixty-five years later. How could I know so little, nothing really, about this gentle person who, for four or five years, was an intimate part of our household and made me feel safer? Somehow, she was able to endure working with my mother.

I had her name, a guess at her age from the photograph, and the approximate area where she lived. So, I searched Birmingham censuses and city directories. Nothing showed up in the directories for the 1950s, except several men named Jesse Robinson. I turned to the latest available census, which was 1940. Again, most Jesse Robinsons were men, both Black and white. I finally found a Black female, Jessie Robinson, who was thirty-nine years of age at her last birthday and whose address fit my memory of where she had lived. Because there were no others that came even close to these specifications, she must be right person. It excites and pleases me to at last be able to know something more.

Jessie was born in Alabama. Her age suggests that her grandparents were probably enslaved. Her address was listed as 2618½ Alley B South. She was widowed and living in the same duplex that she had lived in for the last five years. Losing a husband at such a young age must have been hard. I could picture her duplex, having often passed the humble run-down houses that populated the sections where poorer Black people were required to live.

It may be that she never had children since none were listed with her. Or maybe they were already on their own. Her cousin Frank Jones had moved in with her within the last five years. Perhaps he helped financially at first, but in 1940 he was out of work. In 1939 he had worked only eighteen weeks, a truck driver for a seed company. Now, he was not even seeking employment. At age forty, he may have had health problems or injuries. He had only a third-grade education and was unmarried. At least Jessie had someone there to keep her company and help with chores around the place.

Jessie Robinson was listed as head of household, renting their duplex for $6 a month. She told the census taker she had earned $206 in 1939, which is equal to about $3,630 in 2019. She further stated she worked seventy hours a week most of that year. Since the hours she worked and the annual income she reported don't seem to add up, I looked at other census pages. I still don't know about the long hours. The amount that women listed as "household maids" stated as their annual income ranged from $150 to $260, so hers fit. To get a perspective on salaries, I looked up the father of my friend Jimmy, across the street, in the same census. At that time, he had had five years of post–high school education and was a draftsman in an architectural firm for $1,800 per year. That would be about $31,700 now.

The education column by Jessie's name is the real puzzle. It indicates that she had three years of college. No other African Americans in her neighborhood for the several census pages before and after her listing were recorded as having any college. I must wonder whether it was a mistake. The code was C3. Perhaps it should have been just 3 for third grade. If she really did attend college, why she was working as a maid remains an unsolvable mystery.

Later, in the Birmingham City Archives, I found her in the 1948 city directory, listed as a maid. Amazingly, one of the archivists located a 1960 photograph of her rented duplex taken by the Board of Equalization for tax purposes. As I was looking at the photograph and those nearby, the irony of the name of the tax assessors' entity was remarkable. Equalization, indeed. I tried to find a death certificate but did not have enough information to make a request.

The census taker visited Mrs. Robinson and Mr. Jones on Friday, April 5, 1940. Franklin D. Roosevelt was president. I feel better that I was able to find out something about her, but I will not stop wishing I could know more.

—

As I approached the fifth grade, my life was not all bleakness and sadness. The hikes with my father, the library, my books, my growing number of hobbies, days spent playing with my friends (excepting the bullying) brought me times of happiness. My mother had some good moments. One time, she made a sundress with sewn-in panties for my favorite doll. The material was white with blue stripes. I was thrilled and astonished. Sometimes she would make paste out of flour and water so I could cut paper shapes and glue them together. I loved playing with paper dolls and would use old Sears and Roebuck catalogs to make my own. Occasionally, when she was in a good mood, she would call me by a pet name, "Mar'cha." I always had a happy feeling when that happened. And then, there was ice cream.

Mother had begun looking at land for investments. Her agent was a dowdy bachelor about her age whose clothes were often covered with spots of food. If my father had looked like that it would have been hell. Mr. Winn's appearance was acceptable, perhaps, because he had gone to Harvard. While they were off tromping through property, I was left in the back seat of his car with an ice cream cone. He was her only consistent friend. Some years later, Mr. Winn choked to death in front of my mother at a Chinese restaurant. When she told me about it, her main regret seemed to be that the ambulance personnel insisted she come with them. Mother had wanted to finish her meal.

Mostly, though, I was miserable. I couldn't know that when I grew up, I would occasionally experience moments of swelling joy, sometimes brimming ecstasy. Now, these moments come in no particular pattern, for no particular reason, and ascend into me on a glorious piercing ray traveling from I know not where. A few have been so full that I thought I would fracture into pieces and simply become part of the universe. These moments show me I am part of something so much greater than myself, part of the great mystery. Then the twinkling moments sneak quietly away, leaving me covered with a sublime gauze and a memory of awe and feeling of gratitude. Many times, I have been tempted to ask others whether they have such moments but have never been able to get myself to do so. These episodes mute my voice. There is a sacredness about them. It seems I can write about them but cannot speak of them.

In early 2019, after writing this, I saw where Rebecca Solnit in her *The Faraway Nearby* had posited, "Writing is saying to no one and to everyone the things it is not possible to say to someone."[1]

—

Around this time, I was getting increasingly curious about the McAlpin branch in the genealogy book. Astonishingly, it has taken until 2020 to really delve into it. It turned out it was not what I expected.

# Chapter 4

# The McAlpins Expand

In grade school, I would from time to time take the genealogy book Aunt Beth had made into my room to study it. First, I would feel the gold letters on the front, then, carefully open it to the middle. I would examine the McAlpin coat of arms over and over. Even though Mother was proud of our McAlpin ancestry she knew little about it. That frustrated me since the coat of arms took hold of my imagination and sent it sprawling into wild adventures. This clan seemed exotic and exciting. I made up Scottish adventures for them. Now, I know the progenitor was Alexander McAlpin, who came from Scotland around the late 1740s, settling in the Carolinas.

As I delved into researching my McAlpin line, in all my fantastical daydreams, what happened surpassed them all. A lifetime later, I would find myself one of the knots on threads from fifth great-grandfather Alexander McAlpin to a fourth great-granddaughter on one line and a fifth great-granddaughter on another, neither of whom he may have wanted to know about. They are Black, and we are Alabama and Florida cousins, and we have embraced.

—

Here is the backstory.

After I had my DNA analyzed some years ago, my next major encounter with the McAlpin name occurred when I uploaded my raw DNA in 2018 to a site called GEDmatch. Unlike Ancestry, GED uses real emails. I glanced down the list of my matches and saw a Christopher MacAlpine-Belton. (I refer to various family branches by the spelling they use.) It turned out both he and his mother, PJ, were on the site. She and I are fourth cousins, meaning we share the same ancestor several generations back. My eyes opened a bit

*Figure 8.* The McAlpin coat of arms in the genealogy
book I studied so much as a child.

wider when I saw on another source that they were African American. Via
email, PJ and Christopher generously shared information with me. We know
exactly how we are related.

Though Alexander Sr. is my fifth great-grandfather, he is PJ's fourth,
even though she is a generation younger than I.[1] Her ancestors were a good
bit older than mine when the relevant children in our lineages were born.
One of Alexander's many grandchildren was Jefferson Carruthers McAlpin,
an enslaver, father of eleven children with two wives, and the father of more
with his enslaved woman named Jane. McAlpin, with his power to violate
Jane, may have had more than one child by her. The known child was Francis
Percy MacAlpine, born August 1, 1866, in Forkland, Alabama. After the war,
Jane married twice and probably had several more children. She died in Alabama in 1888. She founded a remarkable line of descendants. Francis is PJ's
grandfather. We are still trying to learn more about Jane.

Two years ago, DNA linked me with another cousin, Kathleen Lanoix. She turned out to likely be my first cousin once removed. Her lineage extends from McAlpin through my Price line. My curiosity piqued, I wrote her immediately and heard nothing for months. I had just given up hope when she called to invite me to her ninetieth birthday celebration in January 2019. When my phone rang, I happened to be standing near the North Rim of the Grand Canyon, which I decided was prescient. The mystery of our connection is still not completely solved, but mutual DNA matches point to my great-grandfather Henry Choice Price or one of his brothers being her grandfather. His maternal grandmother was a McAlpin. Photographs of Kathleen's father and my great-grandfather look almost identical. Figuring out this perplexing relationship has been and is still a great deal of work, work that resulted in my being rewarded with a whole new enormous family headed by this tough and lovable matriarch.

Conveniently, both cousins live in New York City, so, when the year turned to 2019, I found myself planning a trip to the Big Apple.

—

PJ MacAlpine and I had arranged to meet for a cup of coffee on my first morning in the city. Our meeting spot was in a crowded restaurant on the corner of Thirty-Fourth Street and Seventh Avenue. By design, I had worn a red coat so she could spot me. I was anxious and apprehensive, given how it was that we were related. While I waited for her, it seemed the steam from my coffee was mimicking the cacophony of expectations swirling in my mind as they finally settled into musing about her singing. I had found a photo of her online at a microphone, her powerful, confident face thrown back in song. Halfway through my first cup of coffee, I spotted her bouncing through the café door. We gave each other a sliver of a tentative hug. How could I have known I would hear her sing at the end of a most unusual day in a most unusual setting?

Once we both had food and drink in front of us, I took in her smooth café au lait skin, her pretty face with a strong square jaw, and her long, thin fingers and small ears with tiny lobes that looked so much like mine. She spoke and then spoke more. Her dark eyes threw sparkles when she laughed; they danced across her long eyelashes and drank in the world even when she turned to matters of pain.

Now, trying to describe my emotions and wonderment as I sat with this newfound cousin who, before DNA matching, I would likely never have met and come to know, I find I am not up to this task. The words swim on my tears, blurry and unformed. I feel the threads, the dark history that binds us together from that cotton plantation in Alabama. I am in awe of this beautiful, vibrant woman and her accomplished complex family and the way they thrived, coming so soon from slavery. There is too much unsettled past, too much raw racial divide in America, too much violence, too much shame, too much depth in all this to put my white words around it. I want to thank her for the great gift she has given me. And, later, I want to thank her son, as well, but I am too timid and afraid to express my gratitude.

I had planned to spend the rest of that day at a museum. PJ had the sense to call and learned it was closed because of another government shutdown, the second one in little more than a year. This one, under the Trump administration, was the longest in US history thus far. Congress fails to fund the government, and all "nonessential" services shut down. Hence, no open public museums. Though the reason was different, it reminded me of the parks closed by the Birmingham city government in the early 1960s to preserve segregation.

The museum option out, the next thing I knew, PJ swept me into the subway to emerge in Lower Manhattan and meet up with her son, Christopher, and share lunch. He is a sturdy, handsome man with strong features and thick, tightly curled dark brown hair, gently mannered with carefully spoken words. He paces himself with care. I have so many questions. They bear with me. Christopher must return to work. Suddenly, I hear PJ asking me whether I have ever been inside the New York Stock Exchange. I have not.

It turns out, until the previous week, she had worked there. The exchange is an elegant edifice built in 1903 on Broadway. Security is tight. I am photographed and pass the procedures. Inside, because I am with her, I find myself treated as a VIP. I am introduced all around, surrounded by the bright lights, hundreds of flashing computer screens, and people scurrying around. PJ is hugged over and over by people who clearly love her. We stay for the four o'clock bell ringing ceremony, which marks the market's daily closing.

By then, we have been joined by her good friend John Wilson, who is an EMT for the city and state of New York and provides training to the security guards and others at the exchange in CPR, first aid, and related services. He is also analyst of floor operations at the exchange. John is a tall friendly man with a warm manner who exudes strength and competence. His complexion is dark and his features rugged.

The time has come for us to part. A plan is made for John to walk me to my subway since PJ lives in a different direction. We are about to go when she suddenly says, "Wait! I want to sing for you." And there I am, with PJ's back against the exchange's marble walls, oblivious to the cleaning people sweeping papers from the floor, listening to "Bonnie Annie Laurie" being sung in the clearest, sweetest voice with the most beautiful vibrato I have ever heard. Suddenly I was in a magic land with a flock of canaries, our ancestors' plantations far behind, and the enslaved Jane is somewhere listening. Alchemy in the staid Stock Exchange. It is a thing of poetry to perceive the hard and ugly past and the healing grace these cousins have brought.

—

As a child, all I knew about the McAlpins was that they became family when Isabella McAlpin married my mother's great-great-grandfather, William Browning, in Georgia around 1800. Now, my childhood nostalgia and romanticism about them is fractured and heavy, in the knowledge that they held so many men, women, and children in bondage over many generations. Whatever else they did as enslavers, the McAlpin "masters" and their sons, since "masters" had absolute authority, ordered their captive female people into sexual relationships or, worse, used violence if they resisted. Either way, it was rape. It appears from the number of genetic matches with African Americans in my Price/McAlpin line as well as my other lines that these occurrences were not infrequent. When I sent my sample off for DNA analysis those years ago it never occurred to me that such violence by my ancestors would be unveiled. Certainly, my mother and her siblings would never have believed it. They are all gone now and won't have to cope with this raw truth.

Little did my mother know when we lived in Alabama that it had been full of McAlpin enslaving ancestors, including my fourth great-grandmother Mary Cosby, who married the father of my infamous third great-granduncle Robert McAlpin Jr.[2] Mostly from Hale and Greene Counties, their Black and white and mixed descendants continue today, now spread widely.

—

My thoughts drift back to that January trip in 2019. It turned out to be a trip that has enriched and changed my life. The day after meeting PJ MacAlpine, I took a taxi past the Met to the apartment of my other new cousin, Kathy Lanoix. After all, I had a ninetieth birthday party to attend. She welcomed me with a warm hug as though she had known me for years. She lives alone in a third-floor apartment in a building on a side street on the Upper West

Side, just around the corner from Amsterdam, with her children nearby. She is a feisty and firm woman who knows what she wants and doesn't hold back in her opinions. Despite this, she calls everyone dear, my love, or darling. Her four grandchildren call her M'Mere. Her smile is quick and bright, her face round with full cheeks, her hair gray and curly, her skin the color of caramel, and her personality just as sticky and stubborn. She is not a complainer. She tells me life must be taken and embraced as it is, tragedies and challenges notwithstanding.

Her daughter, Evelyn Lanoix, arriving soon after I did, was as warm and friendly as her mother. We immediately started discussing how we might be related. We sat in Kathy's bedroom as she has no furnished living room just now. She had been planning to move permanently to Grand Turk, where she was born, so recently sold most of her furniture. Her daughter and I plied Kathy with questions. Some of the information seemed to be new to her daughter. No matter how many questions we asked, her mysterious father, whom we decided must be the link to our relationship, remained beyond our grasp and, still, many months later, remains evermore cryptic.

Kathy is the youngest of at least forty-two known children and the last one alive. Yes, forty-two, and there may be more. Her father, Clarence Benjamin Selver, had three wives, all from Grand Turk, and, as is obvious, had more children with other women. Kathy's mother had three children with Clarence. Kathy, the youngest, was only ten years old when he died, but her memories of him as a warm and loving father are strong yet. Evelyn turned to me, "Thank goodness you are family, I don't have to be embarrassed that there were so many children."

Kathy described her father as white. From the two photographs I have of him now, one as a young man, the other a bit older, he does look either white or a light mixture. Kathy's mother had a dark complexion, though her twin sister was lighter. The family story is that her father was from "London or Portugal." No one in the family knows the names of his parents or where they were born, much less where Clarence was born. Unfortunately, research is made more challenging by maybe several male children named after this roving man, who, it hits me, I am also related to. Closely: likely my half great-uncle. As for his livelihood, Kathy described him as "a businessman." She says he owned farms, dry good stores, even liquor stores (although he didn't drink), all in the Caribbean. I am still trying to find out who he was.

Kathy and her two children now live in New York City. Her husband, a diplomat in Haiti, died in the early 1960s at the hands of the François "Papa

Doc" Duvalier regime. Kathy fled with her two very small children to New York City, where she had some relatives. Times were hard at first. Later, at her birthday party, I was to hear her children laud her for her strength and determined inventiveness as she struggled to support them through their childhood. They are both medical professionals.

The ninetieth birthday party was on a Saturday evening in the social hall of the Catholic Church a few doors down the street from her building. Since I was staying with her, it was decided I would walk her to the church. Hand in hand, to be sure she didn't fall in the gently falling snow, we entered the hall. She was beautiful in her gorgeous pink lace gown, hair put up just so to meet her strict standards. Here I was, a perfect stranger moments before, leading the guest of honor into the party. My emotions swayed like the party balloons floating on a surreal ocean. The circumstances were extraordinary, that much was clear.

Kathy's children had spent Friday decorating the hall with a pink-and-white theme, pink being her second-favorite color, the first is blue. There were balloons, silk flowers on every table, and an enormous vase of lilies, peonies, roses, and white hydrangeas on a side table beside an equally enormous cake. Food was plentiful and good. Beverages ranged from fancy waters to hard liquor. I soon found out the guest list was large and included her neighbors, but Kathy did have her limits. She told me there was one neighbor she did not invite, because of reasons known only to her. Yet, I couldn't help thinking to myself, here she invited me, unknown in person to the family until one day before. Surely, this story shows the power of sharing blood.

After dinner, her children, nieces and nephews, and friends and neighbors gave eloquent and loving tributes to her. Her handsome son reminisced about sometimes having to do his homework in a hall because their electricity had been cut off and eating johnnycakes when there was no other food. He was proud of how his mother managed to survive and support them, creating a life where they could thrive. Kathy worked hard and took classes to get marketable skills. She already knew how to sew. She became a foster parent, raising sixty foster children. Several attended, adding their tributes and stories in turn. Photos scrolled by on a large screen as guests spoke.

The crowd was large and would have been bigger but for the prediction of three to six inches of snow. Everyone clearly loved her. Chatting with the neighbors, I heard many stories about how her activism had improved their lives. The kin, many now my kin, too, all embraced me and welcomed me into their family. They come in all colors, with professions from teaching to engineering to nursing and medicine and more, from many different countries, and among them speaking several languages.

The party wound down. As Kathy and I left, I saw that someone had invited in two Hispanic men they had found on the street. Snow was still on their shoulders. They were sitting at an empty table at the far end of the room, eating like they hadn't for a while. Their gratitude radiated around them. I could feel it.

The morning I was to leave Kathy told me she prayed it would snow more so I would have to stay longer, even though she was to go back to her beloved island within the week. There, in the biggest city, Providenciales, she stays busy making things to sell in her small business and visiting family and friends. I am still in a state of wonderment at this family's openness, their friendliness, the fluidity of all the shades of their skin and professions and cultures flowing into one huge, remarkable clan. If only the world could be like these people. How fortunate I was to experience this. Another wonderous, healing experience. I wished I could have stayed longer, snow or no snow.

—

Sometime before the New York trip, I had discovered that a definitive history of my McAlpin line had been written: *McAlpin(e) Genealogies, 1730–1990*. Now out of print, it was authored in 1990 by a white distant cousin of mine who died in 2015, Doris McAlpin Russell. Progenitor Alexander Sr. had six sons and six daughters between two wives. The first two were Robert, my fourth great-grandfather, then Solomon five years later. In two generations, Alexander Sr.'s descendants were in the hundreds, many staying in Alabama's Greene County area. Robert's daughter Isabella is my third great-grandmother. In a later chapter, I take up the story of Robert's youngest son, Robert Jr., whose 2017 discovery shocked me and helped jump-start this book.

I spent some time looking at McAlpin records. Learning they held so many enslaved people and fathered so many children with their white wives and unknown numbers with their Black enslaved women was blenching. Later, friends said, "It is not your fault that your ancestors had slaves, why should it bother you so much." I agreed I was not responsible for my ancestors' behavior, but I am responsible for my behavior now. The McAlpins in Russell's book are white. If Russell knew about any children the McAlpins sired by women they held in bondage, she kept that to herself. I am driven to acknowledge them, not keep them hidden. I kept researching.

I tried to write more about what I was finding, but my mind shut down. As it was late autumn, the oak trees over my house rained torrents of acorns upon the slightest breeze. They crashed and plinked off the tin roof. They felt like the recent words I had struggled to put down, words that previously tumbled forth in fits and starts like the acorns, but that had yet sprung forth. Now, my mind was frozen, the tree bare. There were rapes, and there must have been brutality: overseers with their lashes and more. Perhaps there were even Black women assigned to the house, nursing their enslavers' babies while their own cried from hunger. The close spacing of some of the McAlpin children would suggest this possibility. I took a deep breath and went out to the garden to plant some tulip bulbs, hoping that connecting with the ground would clear my head. I returned to my desk and continued researching the McAlpins.

The flow I experience now is not words but the blood of these enslaved people, our lineages mingled through their suffering. One group stolen and kept in bondage, the other the enslavers I came from. I see the enslaved people's blood oozing into the ground where they have labored and been beaten and violated, blood soaking into the rags their companions place on one another's wounds, seeping into the rude graves they create for their family and friends.

This is how it was. I have been studying accounts of slavery both by those formerly enslaved and by historians. I know now. The unspeakable brutality they suffered too often remains unspeakable. It must be spoken. We cannot forget. Perhaps not every person in bondage experienced harsh brutality, but records show most did in various degrees. Some were even shot, beaten to death, hanged, or burned at the stake. Some committed suicide out of desperation. They all experienced captivity, exploitation, and severe constrictions on their lives. So many tried to run to freedom. They rebelled. Remarkably, so many not only survived but thrived.

—

I continue reading the Russell book. More surprises await. One took me back to my 2015 solo road trip, where I had unexpectedly found myself traveling on the Natchez Trace. That experience became disturbing, causing me to change my route and leave the Trace. And I didn't even know at that time that thousands of enslaved people in coffles were forced to march to their Deep South destiny on this trail. I reread *My Solo Road Trip* blog, where I had recorded learning that the Trace is a narrow, 444-mile-long national park credited to local Daughters of the American Revolution ladies in the early 1900s who wanted to preserve the disappearing ancient pathway from Natchez to Nashville. This American Indian trail had been in use for thousands of years before modern highways made it obsolete.

I well remember how I walked solemnly on a part of the original Trace. I considered the courage and fortitude it must have taken to walk on this long path, whether for trading, for war, for mail delivery (after the white people took over), for transport of enslaved people, or for general travel. I began to feel heavy and sad, despite it being a perfect early autumn day. Finally, I could take no more and decided to leave the Trace and focus on beauty and happy things as much as possible.

What I later learned in Russell's book was that Robert McAlpin had been murdered by robbers on July 30, 1804, on the Natchez Trace, probably not far from where I had been. Whether that added to my dreary, unsettled feeling the day I was driving the Trace depends on mysteries we humans cannot know. Robert had left his home in Georgia with his oldest son, Alexander, then twenty-four years old, both on horseback, to purchase a large tract of land on the Cane River, in Natchitoches Parish, Louisiana.

Why he wanted to buy this land was probably related to Thomas Jefferson's decision to allow enslaved people in the newly acquired Louisiana Purchase. Robert, like all the McAlpins, was an enslaver. According to Henry Wiencek's book on Jefferson, Congress knew that attracting men with cash and enslaved laborers was the only way to quickly establish plantations.[3] Land must have been inexpensive. So off Robert went, leaving behind his wife and seven children, the youngest only four. That youngest child and the land Robert purchased led me to a long and horrifying story, if it is to be believed.

This great-great-great-great-grandfather Robert fought in the Revolutionary War as did most or all of my maternal distant great-grandfathers who lived at that time and were the right age. His father, Alexander Sr., served as well. Alexander was given 575 acres for his service, which he passed down to Robert. This added to other land parcels Robert eventually owned. Robert, for his own service, was issued fifty-three pounds, five shillings sterling, a value in 2019 of about $12,000. Thus, as a young man he already had land and money. Robert probably migrated south from South Carolina along with other McAlpins during the 1780s. According to records, he was a farmer and a saddler and served as a justice of inferior court in Greene County, Georgia.

When I read the accounts of his murder in Russell's book, I thought of the horror and sadness this young Alexander must have experienced witnessing his father's murder, helpless to prevent it, having to bury him and then make his way home alone across hundreds of miles back to Georgia. He surely feared the same fate as he rode mile after mile, grieving the loss of his father. This fourth great-uncle matured to marry his first cousin Nancy McAlpin in 1813. They had twelve children. He soon became one of the largest enslavers of people in Alabama.

Alexander had a heavy role with his father dead, helping his mother and being guardian to his baby brother, Robert McAlpin Jr. I will call him by his title of colonel, to distinguish him from his uncle Alexander Jr. or his grandfather Alexander Sr. By the time he died in 1858 his ninety or more enslaved people and property in Alabama were worth about $785,000 in today's money. What did it take to do that? He certainly suffered tragedy. Did he learn compassion? He outlived his wife and all twelve children.

Evidently, all the tragedy did not slow him down. Alexander took twelve of the people he had enslaved to the land his father had purchased near Natchitoches, Louisiana. The 1820 census suggests he had his baby brother, Robert Jr., with him. Back in Alabama he laid out a village called Troy, later known as Greensboro. He dealt in land and served as a commanding officer in the Alabama militia. A widower after his wife's 1837 death, he erected a grand plantation house, no doubt built by people he had enslaved. The house is said to be still standing, but when I went looking for it in 2019, I could not find it. I did find something else though, a white McAlpin cousin. There are still African American McAlpins in the area.

Looking at more on Colonel Alexander, it surprised me to see my great-granduncle John Wesley Price (1823–91), son of my great-great-grandfather Zaccheus Price, mentioned by Doris McAlpin Russell. I knew about Zaccheus and his son John Wesley as a child. I recently found a photograph of Zaccheus, so this story becomes tangible. Zaccheus is my mother's great-grandfather.

Of the visit Russell writes (her spelling of McAlpin changes throughout):

> Dr. John Wesley Price, when he first began to practice medicine, spent a summer in Greene Co., Ala., in the home of his great-uncle, Col. Alexander McAlpin, who was the son of Robert McAlpin. In his memoirs,

"Reminiscences," Dr. Price relates: "Col. McAlpine was a fine old man and very humorous for one of his age. One could see fun in his very eyes. He was the most polite man I ever saw. The custom of the McAlpines was to remain in bed in the mornings until breakfast was announced, and that was not early—no one on the place was seen until then. Col. McAlpine always had his coffee in bed before arising, later would have a saddle horse brought to him and he rode over his plantations. The McAlpine family and their visitors all had their attendants and nothing to do but make known their wishes. The young ladies had waiting maids to accompany them whenever they went out in their carriages."[4]

Here is the story Dr. Price told about Robert's murder:

Robert McAlpin and his son Alexander McAlpin, then living in Greene County, Georgia, made a trip to Louisiana. . . . On return, in Mississippi, Robert was waylaid and attacked by robbers. . . . Before he could draw his weapon, he was ruthlessly shot from his horse and his son was ordered away. Alexander rode off a short distance. . . . He returned and found that the robbers had [missed finding] his belt of money. Alexander McAlpin had to travel 30 miles . . . to get someone to help with [burying] his father.[5]

In April 2019, I drove back to Alabama on a cloud of pine pollen, entering Birmingham from the north. I had research to do, and I wanted to visit Greensboro, where I had never been. Birmingham was first, then Montgomery and its civil rights museums, Selma (where I retraced a 1965 march and walked on the Pettus Bridge), and finally the haunts of the McAlpins.

In Greensboro, the town librarian directed me to an old-time southern lawyer who served as the town historian. He and his office were straight out of Faulkner. After graciously answering all my questions, he said, "You know, you have a cousin here in town. She is a very peculiar woman." This new cousin was waiting for me in her electric-powered chair at the door of her slightly moldering house. Neuropathy was only one of her problems. A large woman in height and weight and with prominent features, she was dressed in an old T-shirt and sweatpants. Her unencumbered breasts hung melonlike to her waist, resting on either side of her chest.

Inviting me to sit, she announced that white people should get reparations for Civil War losses. By way of introducing myself, I told her I was a fourth great-granddaughter of Robert McAlpin Sr. "So am I," she said, holding out a cane capped in gleaming gold. "This is his cane." His name shown in the engraved script. This ancestor, murdered on the Trace 215 years ago, the father of Robert McAlpin Jr., on whom I had done so much research, suddenly became real. I was holding his cane. Sure enough, I was in the heart of McAlpin land.

This cousin is the third great-granddaughter of Colonel Alexander. She bragged that he had one thousand in bondage, which I know is not true. More stories followed. Looking at me as though she expected a surprise, she told me, "You know the Colonel had a few children with his slaves." She still has contact with some of those descendants. She claimed one had become a major figure at NASA. I looked him up. He was there. His photo showed a striking older man with café au lait skin. Evidently, not all her tales grew tall.

As I edged out the door to leave, I asked her a question based on the first remark she had made to me. "Did the white McAlpins ever recover their losses from the Civil War?" "No," she said, "from then on we were struggling."

—

More gloomy days have gone by as I work on all this. A year has passed since I made my disturbing discovery about Colonel Alexander's baby brother, Robert McAlpin Jr., and many months since I began working on this chapter. Thinking about how these McAlpins became part of my family line via my third great-grandmother Isabella McAlpin, I was suddenly beset with the idea of expanding her life as best I could using Doris Russell's book, censuses, maps, and wills to gain more understanding of these people.[6] In the end, it didn't help except to tell me that she must have been made of sturdy stuff and that even that far back, the practice of enslaving people had already been in the family for at least several generations.

I have visited the graves of several of these Prices a number of times, long settled in the beautiful old town cemetery in Micanopy, Florida. Even their gravestones, sheltered by live oak trees and soothed by the wind as it teases the Spanish moss, look like they are trying to return to the earth, so lichen and moss covered, broken, and old are they.

## Chapter 5

# Summers North

My memory, which turned out to be distorted, took hold of me last night as I was trying to sleep. Suddenly, the image of one of my favorite childhood books, *The Little Lame Prince*, flooded into a space in my mind where my adventures find their nestling place. I could see the poor little boy with his withered legs perched on his magic carpet, floating above the world as he visited exotic places. My love of adventure must have been ignited by his adventures and flown with him. The Persian carpet was knotted with wool of rich colors and intricate patterns. Only it wasn't.

Searching the internet from my office this morning, I found the version I had seventy-plus years ago. I reconnected with a good friend, even though the plain green carpet on the cover gave my recollection a jolt. The power of the book remains unaffected, nonetheless. I was the little lame prince in my own story as almost every summer from the age of five I went north with my father and south with my mother. My parents realized during my early years that traveling together didn't work. They had too much conflict. My father's relatives didn't particularly like my mother, and her relatives seemed to like him better, which understandably did not sit well with her. It turned out that for me to have separate trips was just what I needed.

Before my parents bought a car, we took trains. I still love riding trains. I tingled with excitement and anticipation, hearing the whistle and rumble as the train pulled into the station. The kindly porters and conductors, with their warm chocolate skin and strong arms, helped us and our luggage aboard. Soon we would hear the deep cry, "All aboard!" and be on our way. I nestled down in my seat, arranged my things, and happily took in the stir of people getting settled, the slow start of the departing train, and the porters creating order.

In the dining car how I loved to sit by the window as the scenery raced by, enjoying a meal on a crisp white tablecloth, seeing my reflection all crazy in the contours of the silver coffee service, and listening to whichever parent I was with having conversation with the other passengers at our table. It was new to hear my parents talk with other adults. Bedtime competed with mealtime on my list of train-riding favorites. The porter came, pulled down the upper bunk, and made up the bed, and soon I was snuggled in, looking out my own little window, being rocked like a baby. The clickety-clack

*Figure 9.* Papa and me at Aunt Mary and Uncle Harvey's Washington Boro home, Lancaster County, Pennsylvania, about 1946. This is my favorite photo of me with my father. He visited his sister Mary Herman Eshleman, his favorite, every year, always taking me with him until I was almost grown. Photographer likely Aunt Mary.

soothed me to sleep. In the morning, I would be in either Pennsylvania or southern Florida.

The first time I remember traveling with Papa was to visit his favorite sister, my Aunt Mary, in Washington Boro, Lancaster County, Pennsylvania. I was five years old. If I had to pick one photograph of myself as a child, it would be the one taken on one of these early trips. I am standing beside my father on a wet winter day holding my favorite doll. We both look happy. He is wearing a suit and tie and is already quite bald. My legs are bare except for my socks drooped to different heights and my little knees showing under the gathered skirt of my dress. I have on a warm-looking jacket. We are on the back stoop of Aunt Mary and Uncle Harvey's house, a favorite sitting spot when the weather was warm. Peas from their backyard garden were shelled there. Conversation thrived. Water was pumped into the trough that sat on a concrete pad a step down from the porch. The handle is barely visible in the picture. I loved to pump the deep water, so cold and delicious. The door behind us leads into the kitchen where my aunt canned produce from her garden, baked many pies, and made Pennsylvania German dishes.

Later, after we got a car and drove, our route took Papa and me across the Susquehanna River. The beautiful old bridge over that broad, rippling river had a nobleness to it. It occurs to me now, as I write these words, that there in Lancaster County, I saw Majesty. Even if one does not believe in God, I think most people would find they could not keep the phrase "God's green earth" out of their minds each time they saw the swelling verdant land, the huge silos, the patches of woods aside crystalline creeks, the emerald fields of corn, and, especially, earth the hue of dark chocolate stirred by a straw-hatted Amish man on a harrow commanding a team of four horses.

———

Mary and Harvey Eshleman bought their two-story home just before they married in 1921 at ages twenty-one and twenty-eight. I loved their house and both of them. They and the house became one of the foundations of my life. White clapboard (a nineteenth-century Gothic vernacular), it had a porch across the front, simple gingerbread trim in the sharp V's of the roof line, and windows framed with dark green shutters. White hydrangeas bloomed below the porch in the summertime. The attic steps were piled with old curiosities, and the basement step sides were lined with gleaming jars of canned fruit, vegetables, and jam. Behind the house the summer garden was always full of vegetables and flowers. One day, having discovered that I loved tomatoes, I followed a nearby row eating every ripe one I spotted. Much to the adults' amusement and some embarrassment, it turned out that row did not belong to my aunt and uncle.

In the early spring, self-seeded pink, purple, and white larkspur bloomed along the fence aside the alley by the house. I keep larkspur in my garden in memory of my dear Aunt Mary. As with hers and my love of her, it faithfully reseeds year after year.

The Eshlemans' house faced a road descending two blocks to intersect with another that followed the Susquehanna River. Luckily for me, a boy about my age, Lee King, lived just across the side street. Also an only child, he was my buddy every summer. We took pennies and straight pins to the train tracks that ran along the river road. We put our ears on the track to see whether the train was rumbling toward us, left the pennies and pins crossed like scissors, and returned later, hoping to find them flattened. Sometimes we were successful.

After the Kings got a mule, Lee and I would climb on bareback, him in front holding the reins and me behind holding his waist. We went riding wherever we wanted. One of my favorite places was a dirt side road to a patch of woods. The trees hid the bubbling creek we splashed in. Any group of trees was a relief from the endless miles of openness, a result of generations farming the rich Lancaster County loam. Washington Boro had only one little store, which was on the riverfront. The store had those huge glass candy jars, the tilted kind with metal covers. For a while, my favorite candy was the pale orange fake peanuts. One penny each. I still have a sadness when I think of that store. Later it and all the houses on either side were torn down due to flooding.

One summer, when I was still little, bored, I implored my father to take me there to buy some crayons. I remember walking hand in hand back up the road, so happy to be with him and my aunt and uncle, looking forward to drawing when we returned. It was very hot. When he pulled the box out of his pocket to hand it to me, the waxy sticks had gotten soft and fused with their neighbors, rendering them unusable. My feelings all melted together just like the crayons. I didn't know which I felt worse about: the fact that I couldn't use the crayons, or my father's effort and wasted money because of me. I was pretty sure it was the latter.

Just about everyone had gardens. Neat food stands stood in front yards holding vegetables, fruit, jams, and shoofly pies for sale. Aunt Mary discovered that I loved shoofly pies. Papa's mother, who had died shortly before I was born, made them for her children as a snack when they returned from school. Aunt Mary took care to have a fresh pie for me when we came to visit. When I was in my teens, I got her to teach me how to make them. Now my younger son makes a better one than I do, a happy tradition passing through the generations.

Uncle Harvey, slender with a rugged face and strong broad hands, was kind and sweet. He had a number of jobs in his lifetime and was handy with cars despite or because he was only able to finish eight years of schooling. Every morning he had a bowl of Wheaties for breakfast, no matter what else he had. That is the way it was there. The house always looked the same, there was always a bowl of M&M's on the sideboard in the dining room, the garden was always bountiful, and Aunt Mary always kept her long hair twisted up in a bun in the back, which suited her slightly plump stature. I never saw her with her hair down.

Papa took me to see where he had disobeyed his parents as a child, crawling to the edge of a bank to look down on Roma people camping. He knew them as "gypsies." Papa showed me the Amish farms, taught me about the Amish and Mennonites, told me how he gathered chestnuts and raised geese to make pocket money, and introduced me to so many other things. When we took walks, Papa told me stories about having to attend his father's Dunkard church. A monitor walked up and down the aisle with a long stick and rapped the hands of inattentive children. After that, Papa was never big on churches. He took me places where he lived in his youth. Everywhere was usually lushly green, but at the right time of year golden fields of wheat brushed the sky. I felt like I'd been placed in the midst of a sweet melody.

Every so often, we would walk down toward the river, turn right past the little store with its big candy jars, and walk a few more blocks to the post office. It took up part of a large old clapboard house fronted with a long porch. It, too, eventually became a victim of rising river waters. Just past the post office, aside a little creek, was a historical marker. Large letters declared 40TH PARALLEL, below which was small text that finished with the sentence, "This boundary acquired national fame as the Mason and Dixon line." Still there, it looks the same. The boundary was surveyed in the 1760s. The nuances of its history were over my head but I did understand it had to do with separating the North and South, and no slavery and slavery. It sat hard on me that a line that wasn't real could have such an effect. It became a marker in my own life and thoughts. No slavery above that line.

My father died at Aunt Mary's in 1972. I know the room into which he took his last steps. He was way too young to die. It was sudden, a heart attack. I was only thirty years old. My children barely remember him. They never got to benefit from his stories and wisdom. At least he was with his beloved sister. And, he had just been digging in his beloved Lancaster County dirt. For that, I am grateful.

~

Widowed in 1974, Aunt Mary had a marriage proposal in the 1980s. Her suitor came over every day in warm weather to help in the garden and share a lunch. When I asked her why she wouldn't marry him, she simply said, "I'm too old to get married again." So, that settled it. She was firm about everything. When she made up her mind, everyone knew that was that. Aunt Mary died in 1993, just one month after her daughter, Lorna, and son-in-law brought her to North Carolina to visit. She was ninety-five years old. By then, Lorna and her husband had built a wing on their house for her to live in, having decided she shouldn't live alone anymore. She had lived in her wonderful house for more than seventy years.

Lorna, Mary and Harvey's only child, was twenty years older than I and already married to a handsome and gentle man when I was still a little girl. Dick's claim to fame, aside from having excellent character and serving in World War II, was modeling in some *Life* magazine advertisements. They soon had four children. I wasn't much older than the oldest. They lived fifteen minutes away from Aunt Mary's. Visiting them was another thing I looked forward to every summer.

Frequent visits to Lorna and Dick's gave me experience with a family whose parents were harmonious and who had friends and four happy children. Lorna died a few years ago. Dick departed his full life at ninety-eight, as handsome and kind as ever. They showed me what a stable, loving family was like.

Thus, Lancaster County was and is another home for me. The lanes running between farms were a path that showed me another way to live. The clip-clop of horses pulling Amish buggies gave rhythm to my life as I was growing up. Visiting Lancaster County every summer is still a lifeline and a joy, albeit now tinged with sadness at all the losses. The roadside signs for homegrown strawberries in the spring and for pumpkins and squash in the fall punctuate my experiences as they did when I was a child. The other variety of signs that hang below the mailboxes of Mennonite and Amish families—"Oh, wicked man, thou shalt surely die," or "The Lord is judging you"—make me smile. They sit comfortably with me as a reminder to try to do some good in the world.

~

When I got to be older, I occasionally visited Aunt Beth and her family. I especially remember two visits at ages twelve and fourteen. By then, living in Shaker Heights, Ohio, my maternal aunt's family had settled into a pattern of vacationing on a tiny island off the coast of Maine for a month every summer. Aunt Beth and Uncle Ken Breeze were kind enough to invite me along. The car trips from Cleveland with them and my cousins Marion and Toby were memorable between the absence of parental fights and frequent stops at antique shops. At a restaurant during the first trip, I had my first-ever taste of homemade bread. That probably underlies my making most of my bread for the last fifty years.

We took the lobster/mail boat to the little island and pushed our belongings in a wheelbarrow the half mile to the cabin. No roads and no electricity made for part of the island's wonderment. Waves broke on beaches that comprised round pebbles and huge granite boulders. Lobster buoys speckled the waters like multicolored confetti. Abandoned houses dotted the interior. We kids went inside the houses to explore at will and stood in awe at the furniture, books, and dishes left as though someone had recently gone on an errand. I could never quite comprehend what force would make families leave so abruptly, especially when leaving meant abandoning their homes and much of their contents. The reason was, supposedly, that they wanted electricity. I still wonder. Maybe the story is correct. There is still no electricity.

For expeditions we walked the island's circumference, which required a lot of clambering over rocks to avoid getting too wet from breaking waves. The island being only four miles around and there being no way to get lost, we had complete freedom. My aunt and uncle did not seem to worry that we could drown even when we took a rowboat out fishing and had difficulty returning against the outgoing tide, or when all of us would jump into ice-cold rushing seawater to ride currents created by an incoming tide.

We picked blueberries and were rewarded with pies made by Beth. We fetched lobsters for dinners from the old man, Monty Gott, who lived alone year-round on the island. Our peanut butter and jelly sandwich snacks we fixed ourselves. Thus fortified, we would head out to romp and explore again. The mosses on the forest's floor were fairy lands peopled with tiny mushrooms under baby spruce trees. On a sunny day, the taller trees seemed to commandeer shafts of sunlight and beam them into our enchanted woodland. On foggy days, more frequent than we would like, we saw nothing but murk as our feet clung to a path. When the fog was too thick, we took to the cabin and played endless games of cards.

Those two summers live on in my mind. I have never wanted to return to the little island. Its enchantment stays with me, and I want no reality to change it.

## Chapter 6

# Summers South

Before 1951, my parents and I would take the train to West Palm Beach, where my grandmother lived. Borrowing relatives' cars, we made the requisite trips to my hermit uncle in his orange grove near Fort Pierce and traveled to Miami to visit my mother's older sister, my Aunt Dorothy Pherigo; her younger brother, my Uncle Bedford Price; and their families. My father returned home before Mother and I did to get back to work. Before long, my mother had made it clear she did not like him along. Plus, traveling together exacerbated their challenges in getting along. One of the biggest issues was around time. My father was very punctual; my mother was always late, sometimes very late.

By the early 1940s, my widowed grandmother was living alone, which she was accustomed to as she and my grandfather had lived separately for decades. Her two-story, porchless house was one-half block from a city cemetery studded by enormous banyan trees interspersed with mysterious crypts and ordinary gravestones. The trees' aerial roots clambered earthward from overreaching branches seeking sand to take hold in. The process created enchanting chambers where I, without children to play with, developed an imaginary life in these root-rooms, pretending to do anything I wanted. Several of my ancestors are buried there. When I was older, I would stand in front of their graves and ponder their lives. Over the years more have joined: my grandmother, mother, older and younger uncles, and others. By the age of ten, I was walking downtown alone, exploring other places of interest.

Working on this chapter now in 2019, I looked at forgotten photographs to jog my memory. In the process, I found an old travel notebook with notes from taking my mother on a trip prior to moving her to Chapel Hill in 1982. She had developed signs of Alzheimer's disease, and I needed to move her close by. When I read these notes, it struck me that I must have always been looking for family qualities I couldn't see. On March 14 in Jacksonville, Florida, I wrote:

> I realized one reason I have been intrigued with . . . was that Mr. Burry's stories [an acquaintance of my mother] depicted the Prices and Hicksons as less austere and more fun-loving than M'Wese's side.
>
> Having known only one grandparent, M'Wese, a Richardson, having spent many childhood summers at her side subjected to her stern and proud ways, her criticisms against any violation of high character, her social values, I saw how my mother was destroyed by this: so filled with the fear of doing something wrong it seems she was paralyzed and could do nothing at all. I have felt I must find some sense of warmth and love and joy somewhere in that family. This time, at last, I found what I've been looking for.
>
> On my father's side, too, I know little about his parents' personalities except that his father was mean. Such sternness, lack of laughter and hearty pleasures in my forebears: does it matter? I cannot prove it is important to know where you come from to know who you are and then know where you can go; but I suspect it is. I think I have wondered if I was trapped in this mire, that the poison could get me, too, if it had everyone else.

M'Wese taught me how to look out for scorpions and scolded me if I didn't stand up straight or follow her expectations for good manners. I stayed outside a lot and played on the shady side of the house, where specks of green from roof shingles had been mingled by rainwater with grains of sand. The effect fascinated me. I made little villages there when I wasn't at the cemetery.

On occasion, M'Wese would take me to visit her one friend who had a child my age. Whether we got along well I don't know as what remains from those visits is the vision of their Palm Beach mansion on the ocean. The bathroom had a black lavatory and toilet. Even better was the approach: the road, deeply shaded by palms and live oaks, edged large lots with beautiful homes set far back. Shadowed by Spanish moss, they exuded a graciousness and timeless quality that set into me.

Some years later, my grandmother moved into a little studio in her backyard. She must have rented out the big house. The studio was where she was living in 1963, when my mother told me she was going to Miami to apologize to her sister Dorothy. I had never heard my mother apologize to anyone so this was momentous. What unfolded is the saddest story I know about my mother. Before I can tell it, I must explain more.

After we visited in West Palm Beach we went to Miami. Visits there were multilayered with complexities I did not always understand. My grandparents, aunts, and uncles had formed a family corporation long before I was born, which included the family orange grove worked by my mother's eccentric older brother, Carle; various parcels of Florida real estate; and two small hotels. The corporation was managed by Uncle Bedford, a banker. Handsome and with a history of competitive diving, he had a lot to do with how much us cousins swam. His son, Lansing, and I were close until his tragic death in 1995 in a wreck that also took the life of his wife and injured his children; his sister, Marilyn; and her husband. Marilyn wasn't born until I was seven years old, so I didn't get close to her until we were grown. Uncle Bedford was kind, responsible, and steady, a pillar in my life. He helped me a lot with my mother after I was grown. She adored him as did all of us.

The first hotel, the Marion, was built by my great-grandfather Henry Choice Price toward the end of his full and circuitous life. His last farming adventure, orange groves in Marion County, was wiped out by the Great Freeze of the mid-1890s. It is said that several of his father's formerly enslaved people came with him from Georgia to help establish the orange grove. After the freeze, undaunted, he headed to Miami to recoup. What happened to the formerly enslaved people, I do not know.

Miami was then a town of about two thousand, with mostly dirt roads. Great-grandfather Price bought a lot on one of the dirt roads one block from Biscayne Bay. By 1905, he had built a three-story Charleston-style house with double wooden verandas in front, thereby creating a home for himself and his second wife, plus having enough rooms to provide accommodations to the growing number of people arriving in Miami. His first wife, Lavinia Hickson Price, my great-grandmother, had died when her only child, my grandfather, was a toddler. Henry remarried within a few years. He and Lucy Banks added rooms as demand grew, so that by 1916 there were thirty or more. Soon after, the rooms were converted into small apartments, likely making it the first apartment building in Miami. Later, the family bought a small, Spanish-style hotel, the Therese, next to the Marion.

Mother and I always stayed in a room at the Therese. To the east was the bay, edged by a tropical park that is still there. To the west was a soda fountain where I bought frosty mugs of foaming root beer for five cents.

The center of town was several blocks to the south. I loved to walk there and explore the shops. Mostly, we visited relatives, which took us from Coral Gables to North Miami.

Aunt Dorothy lived in a modest Florida Craftsman bungalow on NE Seventy-Eighth Street, a long drive from the Therese. Going there was a happy time. Along with Aunt Beth, Aunt Dorothy was one of my saviors. Her plumpness felt good when she gave me one of her strong, warm hugs. She laughed a lot and was easygoing, warm, and friendly; plus, she had several grandchildren around my age.

Dorothy was the black sheep of the family. At eighteen she eloped. She never lived in a proper neighborhood in a proper sort of house, meaning one that met with M'Wese's approval. By 1925 she had four children. When I visited her youngest, Richard, in about 2008 for the first and only time after growing up, he told me this story. In 1935, my mother paid a visit to Dorothy's, staying for dinner. Dorothy's sixteen-year-old daughter and the rest of the family were enjoying a meal around their dining room table. My mother said something that prompted Helen to throw a glass of water in my mother's face. Richard could not remember what she said, but it must have been awful. This was not the only time my mother said something distasteful, though it was likely the only time a comment was met with water in her face.

This leads into that sad story about my mother. At some point when I was in elementary school, Mother had words with Dorothy. Later, Mother told me that she had criticized Dorothy's housekeeping and other aspects of her life. This would have been galling not only for its inappropriateness, but for the fact that my mother, who struggled with many issues in her life, was no role model. These criticisms ended their relationship, thus ending mine with that side of the family. So, during the rest of my growing up, I scarcely saw my sweet Aunt Dorothy or her children. Dorothy lived out her life in her not-proper welcoming home. I missed her so much.

By the planned apology in 1963, I was a wife and mother occupied with my own life. Nonetheless, I well remember when Mother told me she was going to Miami to make her apology. I was dazzled. She took off in early spring as I wished her success and a safe trip.

The drive took two days. She arrived in West Palm Beach to stay in M'Wese's backyard cottage until M'Wese returned. She was with Dorothy so they could visit Dorothy's newborn grandbaby nearby. Mother went to bed and was awakened at midnight by loud pounding on the door. Two policemen stood there. Dorothy and M'Wese had been hit head-on by a drunk driver that evening on their way to see the baby. Dorothy was killed, and M'Wese severely injured.

To this day, I cannot think of this without a swelling sorrow for my poor mother, for Dorothy, her life cut short, and her not knowing about the planned apology. And, for my grandmother, who lost her oldest daughter and never completely recovered from her injuries. The image of my mother at the door in the muggy Florida night, the policemen having delivered their grim message, with no one to comfort her when she was making one of the greatest efforts in her life, still fills me with anguish.

—

Our summer travels to Florida continued throughout my childhood and adolescence, the breach between my mother and her elder sister extinguishing those happy times but leaving other visits intact. Each summer on our way back to Birmingham, we stopped at Uncle Carle's orange grove. Even after I grew up, I continued returning to the grove as often as I could, taking my babies with me.

Carle was sent off to military school for a year when he was eighteen. The family thought it might straighten him out. When the experience didn't change his shadowy self, his father realized Carle was going to need a way of life suited to him. So, around 1920, my grandfather bought twenty acres near Fort Pierce, and the two of them planted baby orange trees in nineteen of the acres, leaving one corner wild. It grew into a magical place. It became the container for my uncle's life and one for me, as well.

In November 1980, I took my mother there for a visit. When I recently reread what I wrote in some travel notes, I was struck at the eternal quality, a certain timelessness that my uncle and the grove exuded. My eighty-year-old Uncle Carle had taken his usual long time to emerge from his weathered, moss-covered trailer in the palmetto thicket. While we waited, Mother and I picked Hamlins, which were almost ripe. Carle didn't even have crates for sitting, much less a cloth to spread on the ground. Thus, our visiting quarters were, as usual, the needle-covered thicket floor. There I sewed while we were talking, sitting on the ground with Mother and Carle soon tiring with nothing at their backs, then lying down—no pillows, looking toward the sky. At the end of our visit, I picked up a skeleton of a leaf, a perfect network of lacy veins. I remembered when, more than twenty years before, I picked up a similar leaf from the same spot. Time stood still.

Uncle Carle and the grove still dwell deeply with me. My bones are shellacked with the sunshine, the afternoon rains, the smells, and the green wispy enchantment of the place. The beauty and oddness snuggled their way in, setting up a tingling of sorts that is hard to describe. It was enhanced by the lush sensuality of the scattered hardwoods, the palmettos, the Spanish moss, and the orange trees. The fragrance of their flowers, white petals breathing, the beauty of their fruit were all massaged by the whispered songs from the Australian pines when a breeze blew.

The grove became my cathedral. Its walls were the majestic pines with their dark green segmented needles, its floor the sand carpeted by skeletons of leaves and fans of palmetto, its choir those pine-whispered songs, and its baptismal font the pool made by the powerful flow of the artesian well. Communion was the juice of a sweet orange plucked and squeezed straight into my mouth.

Knowing I loved to splash and swim in the sand-bottomed pool made by the pressure of the deep aquifer being allowed to surface, my uncle would open the large valve on the artesian well. The sulfur-smelling water would leap wildly into the scooped place it had previously created in the sand. Soon, I would be in a watery fairyland. Later, I would follow my uncle around the grove, fascinated by the irrigation ditches, the little shed in the middle of the grove for tools, and the rows and rows of trees.

When Mother and I first started visiting, Carle lived in a three-room rented shack at the edge of the twenty acres. He was a true hermit. He cut his own hair, went into town every few weeks for food, and wore his clothes until they were in shreds. He was slow in every way. It must have been a shock to him when, after some years, he had to move when the owner reclaimed the shack. Then, for his housing, he had a trailer set up on the wild acre. Later, he bought another trailer to house his growing collection of newspapers.

This collection was a result of years of subscriptions to the Fort Pierce paper and the *Miami Herald*. He claimed he was too busy to read them, so he saved them, saying, "I will read them when I retire." They had piled up in the shack when he lived there, floor to ceiling. Soon the rooms were full, except for narrow canyons among the piles to get from the bunk bed to the table in the middle room and then into the kitchen. For safety, more space remained around the kerosene stove. Finally, with no more space in the three rooms, the tiny bathroom was put out of use and filled with yet more papers. After that, he and visitors used the great outdoors to relieve themselves.

My uncle did keep up with news about the Everglades, which were very important to him. When the glades were going through a period of threat, he began a letter-writing campaign to newspapers about the necessity of saving the Everglades. The Fort Pierce paper even published an article about his efforts. He was very proud of that.

Carle was a small man with a quiet smile, gentle voice, and trim body. His eyes appeared muted even more than they might have under his gold-rimmed glasses. He had a musty smell about him as though a cloud of humus clung to him under his hand-cropped hair. He did very little cooking, but must have cooked chicken. Before he stopped letting us into his trailer, I remember a plate piled high with cleanly picked chicken bones. He did not even boil the eggs he took into the grove for his lunch. He would puncture both ends and suck out the two raw eggs he had every day. Somehow, he brought the intact shells back at the end of his day, and they, too, collected on another plate. Empty tin cans piled up outside.

That he didn't cook much led to one of the most unpleasant nights of my life, as we headed back to Birmingham. Mother was, as usual, late leaving West Palm Beach. Once we were at the grove, Carle took his usual hour to emerge from his shack. By this time, it was getting dark. Mother didn't want to drive in the dark, so we had to stay there.

The only food Carle could come up with for a supper was cornmeal, which he cooked in plain water. With just one chair inside because of the newspapers, I took my bowl of mush out to the front stoop. The dim light over the door was on, attracting myriads of tropical insects and mosquitoes. The mush was rancid. Insects fell into it. That first bite was all I took. I sat there for a while in abject misery, hungry, and stabbed by mosquitoes. Carle must have slept outside on the pine needles. The tiny bedroom was filled with newspapers floor to ceiling. Papers across from the bunk bed were supported by sticks from the piles to the wall. My mother was in the lower bunk and I in the upper, still hungry and itching everywhere. I barely slept, terrified I would be dead by morning from being smothered by newspapers if the sticks gave way.

The first time I stayed in the grove for several days was with a close friend the summer we were seventeen. My parents chanced traveling together, dropping Rosemary Downie and me off on their way to Miami. Outfitted with army and navy surplus gear, each with .22 rifles, we camped under an open tarp near his trailer. We soon shot two squirrels for a stew. My reasoning was the thought that if I was going to eat meat, I should be able to kill and prepare animals. As it turned out, the squirrel meat was too tough to eat, which ended that experiment. We stayed hungry that night. I kept eating meat.

After the awful newspaper pile night when I was ten years old, I had not expected more bad times there. However, Rosemary and I had a few frightening nights with creatures snuffling around our cots while we huddled under our blankets. Uncle Carle later told us they were armadillos. Rosemary remembers a neighbor's German shepherd guarded us after that. Carle let us borrow his car so we could go to the beach. Once we even got him to go with us, which seemed a minor miracle.

I think that over the days we were there, Uncle Carle became fond of Rosemary. Who could blame him, she was pretty and charming. When Rosemary married right after high school, he sent her a lovely gift. I think he really enjoyed our camping there. After this trip, I continued to visit him and the grove as often as I could.

Soon after my last time with Carle, a neighbor found him dead, slumped over the artesian well. The authorities estimated he had been dead for at least three days. It was February 1981. By chance, I have a small inheritance from him: the rattles from the rattlesnakes he had killed, his pocket watches that had quit working, and two peanut butter jars from the 1930s filled with buttons from worn-out shirts. They weren't a formal inheritance as he died without a will. It was simply that I happened to be at Aunt Beth's house soon after his death. They were part of the meager possessions his siblings had collected that no one wanted. I don't know whether my aunt and uncle ever found his stock certificates. The same neighbor who had found his body stopped by when his siblings were at the grove sorting things out. The neighbor thought they ought to know that Carle told him he had hidden his stock certificates among his newspapers.

—

Sometimes, coming back from Florida, Mother and I would take an easterly route so she could visit her first cousin in South Carolina. Christine and her husband had five children romping around their rural bungalow and enough love to circle their place a thousand times. I always looked forward to going there and experiencing their devoted family. Then we would visit the remnants of our pre–Revolutionary War ancestral home, Harmony Hall, in North Carolina. It is now restored and owned by the Bladen County Historical Society. Years ago, I got wrapped up in its history and preservation, and I am still involved with it. I suspect the history of this ancestral home of childhood mystery and pride is deeply stained.

## Chapter 7

# Harmony Hall, the Richardsons, and Turpentine

Harmony Hall has stood in Bladen County, North Carolina, for almost 250 years, remarkably, in one piece. Stories have been emanating from it, passed down in one way or another: overheard whispers slipping through loose boards, tales recorded in letters, bedtime stories told to children, notes in family Bibles, talk flowing among the generations through wartimes and peace and on to this very day. Like the sticky pitch from the plantation's long-leaf pines, the stories are hard to shake off.

Recently, one frequent visitor with inside privileges recounted, "The night before last, Monday night, around eleven thirty or midnight, I was sitting in the parlor reading a book with lantern light. I heard footsteps on the porch and turned to look. There were two men out there. I spoke with them. They had heard Harmony Hall was haunted. So, I gave them a midnight tour. One had a long red beard, the other hair down to his waist. I left them alone upstairs to look further but heard something suspicious so went to check. The drunk one kept repeating 'We don't mean no disrespect, man, we just wanted to check the place out.'" A few hours before these uninvited visitors arrived, this tough-looking storyteller had killed a six-foot-long Eastern rattlesnake on the property and cooked it for his dinner. Unlike some Harmony Hall stories, I know this one is true. I saw photographs of the snake from its entirety to fried pieces on a plate, getting this whole tale straight from the snake-eating man. All this happened the very same night, August 20, 2018, that Silent Sam, the Confederate monument at the University of North Carolina at Chapel Hill, was toppled by protestors.

Harmony Hall is the ancestral home of my mother's Richardson line, from which sprang stories of intrigue and heroism: a missing sword, land grants from the king of England, spying, faithful slaves, and war heroes.[1] I grew up hearing them, and they clung to me, too. My mother would take me occasionally to see the ancient house. Back then, it alternated between run-down and in ruins. It was always draped by my grandmother's and mother's obvious gratification from the still-standing ancestral home built before the Revolutionary War, but also their pride in our family line headed by forebear Amos Richardson. The Amos Richardson family story was told frequently, especially by my great-grandfather whose namesake I am. Blind the last seven years of his life, he dictated from memory yet another account of the lineage, carefully recorded in my grandmother's perfect rounded handwriting, not

*Figure 10.* Harmony Hall, near the Cape Fear River, Bladen County, North Carolina, 2017. Built by my fourth great-grandparents Colonel James Richardson (1734–1810) and Elizabeth Neal Purdy Richardson (c. 1727–1808), before the American Revolution. Photo by Gerry Dincher/Flickr. CC BY-SA 2.0.

long before he died in 1929. Should I be surprised, having gone this far in my quest, that I am discovering a dark side lurking beneath a pretty surface? The proud story of my childhood has more to it.

One Harmony Hall puzzle I have carried deeply for many years is a memory of my eccentric Uncle Carle of the orange grove telling me stories of how he played with war relics when he visited there as a child. I suddenly realized this couldn't be, since Harmony Hall was sold out of the Richardson line in 1874 and Carle wasn't born until 1901. Poring over family notes and letters, at last, on a cold day in the early spring of 2019, I found the answer. It was my great-grandfather William Marshall Richardson who had played with Revolutionary War relics when he visited Harmony Hall. His father, James Purdie Richardson (Purdie is also spelled Purdy in family records), had married Catherine Marshall from Anson County, North Carolina. Purdie and Catherine must have traveled from Anson County to Harmony Hall from time to time with their children to visit their grandparents.

Part of the dictation my grandmother took down from her then ninety-seven-year-old father was:

> Some other relics of the Colonel were preserved. These were a swallow-tailed coat of heavy blue cloth ornamented with bright-brass buttons, a brace of smooth bore pistols about a foot long and their housing, and his sword, scabbard and belt. . . . The relics above mentioned were kept in the attic of my grandfather's home [Harmony Hall] all of which were stolen during the Civil War by robbers, none recovered save the naked sword. With other grandsons we were sometimes allowed to play soldiers with these relics in the attic.

William Marshall Richardson must have given this account to his grandson, my Uncle Carle, who then told it to me, whereupon it got jumbled in my child's mind. The sword is another story.

Gathering all the fragments of the much-chronicled Harmony Hall has seemed like trying to weave together fragile pieces of lichen falling off its trees, elusive and almost impossible to hold together in a coherent strand. Contemplating all this, I grew excited thinking about this measurable person-to-person connection to Harmony Hall and the War for Independence: my uncle telling me the stories he had heard from his grandfather who played with Revolutionary War relics in the attic, and who knew his grandfather (my uncle's great-great-grandfather), who was the son of the shipwrecked man who had built the house. No wonder I have always loved going in that attic. Now, next time I go to Harmony Hall, I will climb those outside stairs to the attic and lay down the correct thinking in that long-empty space.

Growing up with the stories and occasional visits, I saw Harmony Hall as very much alive. Since it was said to be on the banks of the Cape Fear River, before I saw it for the first time, I always pictured it with a dramatic view. There is no such view. Even for someone standing on the second-floor porch, only land and forest are visible. Five or so years ago, I was finally able to walk from the house to the river. A path had been made for visitors. Prior to this, dense overgrown brush forbid such a walk. I was astonished to find the river at least a mile away. Recently, after several bad hurricanes hit North Carolina, the reason for this distance was obvious. The river flooded to within several hundred yards of Harmony Hall. It is a wonder that during the approximately one hundred years that Richardsons lived there, they did not all succumb to malaria or yellow fever.

—

Progenitor Amos Richardson and his descendants were a family meme that meant pride, power, patriotism, and American-style nobility. I did not have words for this as a child, but I could feel what was expected of me. Many records are available about Amos and his life in this country because he was, by my Aunt Beth's words in the genealogy book, "an attorney for Governor Winthrop, owner of vessels trading in the West Indies, owner of 5,000 acres near Stonington, and a merchant."

Amos Richardson was born about 1618 in England and died in 1683 in Stonington, Connecticut. He arrived in Boston around the age of twenty, already with the label "merchant tailor," perhaps taking such a daring trip because of fracturing political and religious conditions in England. His first record in America was as a witness on a 1639 deed, listed with Stephen Winthrop, the brother of Governor Winthrop of the Massachusetts Bay Colony. Amos must have been ambitious to have gotten himself in such circles at his tender age. Or perhaps he knew the Winthrops in England.

Amos continued close business and legal connections with the Winthrops and associates throughout his life. He served as an attorney for the colony, ran ships to the West Indies, and served in the General Assembly. He must have traded in human cargo, taking enslaved American Indians to the Indies and trading for Africans as well as molasses, cotton, tobacco, and salt. He fathered eight children and went on to amass thousands of acres of land.

When Amos arrived, slavery had been in place in the New World since 1502. By 1641, Governor Winthrop, a devout Puritan, helped the colony produce a code of laws making slavery legal that lasted 140 years. Though the Puritans sought religious freedom, it was just for themselves. They saw themselves as God's special people and their Bible as sanctioning human bondage.

Amos and Mary's fourth child, my seventh great-grandfather, was shot dead about 1695 in Connecticut going after a pirate. His wife's grandmother, my ninth, was convicted of witchcraft in Connecticut and probably hanged.[2] Subsequent generations followed who continued enslaving Africans and American Indians; marriages brought in new lines. This is how I learned that my own ancestors' labor and wealth from human chattel and West Indies trade helped found Yale and that similar practices helped in the founding of Harvard, Brown, and more, all by the time of colonial America. Many taught a racially charged theological and supposedly scientific curriculum that "proved" and demonstrated the justification for chattel slavery.

~

At last, I have arrived at the person I grew up hearing so much about: Colonel James Richardson, the builder of Harmony Hall, the great-great-grandson of Amos. Aunt Beth's genealogy book offered up these comments: "Served 1753–63 in the Provincial Army and war between France and England. Migrated to (or shipwrecked off) the coast of North Carolina. Settled 10 miles north of Elizabethtown on the east side of Cape Fear River. Called home Harmony Hall. Sons: Samuel and Amos." Nothing was recorded about what was grown on the plantation. I always assumed it was cotton, but it turns out that was not correct.

Being from these generations who ran ships between New England and the West Indies, James continued the practice until his shipwreck.[3] While waiting for his ship to be repaired, he explored the area and decided to stay. He soon built a small home. By 1768 he had married Elizabeth, a widow, across the river. She brought four children with her.

Oddly—at least it seems that way to me—with all the family records and wills, no mention of any crops or products from their land exists, except for the mention of the mill. History provided the answer. As a child, hearing stories about Colonel Richardson fighting in the Revolutionary War, I had no idea that he was one of the providers of the needed turpentine-containing barrels produced by the enslaved people at Harmony Hall.

There are still legends that the colonel had acquired a great deal of land, but the truth must be closer to the historical section of the nomination form that was submitted for Harmony Hall in 1968 to the National Register of Historic Places: "after the war on the tax list of 1784 . . . he was listed as the owner of 934 acres and six slaves." The house and porches are covered by a large gable roof with a full attic. The basement has loopholes, slanted openings for firing guns. The only stairs for the two-story dwelling are outside. Those stairs played a part in one story about Elizabeth.

My fourth great-grandmother, like the fiction about the amount of land James owned, is still the subject of untrue stories. One is that she lived in Jamaica on a plantation with nine hundred enslaved people and fled their uprising. She was almost certainly born in the United States. She did have a West Indies connection, however: her grandfather Henry Neale (Neale is also spelled Neal or Neel in family records) had a sugar plantation in Barbados. He was my fifth great-grandfather.

~

The sword story, passed down to descendants and thousands of visitors to Harmony Hall, happened because of James's service in the war. Upon his capture by the British, his sword was confiscated. Paroled, he went home. Wanting to rejoin his command and needing another sword, he made one, "with the help of his Negro blacksmith from a plowshare. The saber, long and heavy, could only be wielded by a strong man." My great-grandfather's notes continue: "He did not regard his parole as binding." I assume the blacksmith was an enslaved person. The sword was passed down to my great-grandfather William Marshall Richardson, who then gave it to his son James Purdie Richardson, a great-uncle whom I met once at age ten.

Here the sword begins a peripatetic journey to oblivion. More from my great-grandfather's notes: "Purdie Richardson needed a doctor's attention . . . instead of waiting until he could pay for a doctor's services, he went to Dr. Shaler Richardson in Jacksonville, the son of Dr. Clement Lanier Richardson . . . my brother. [Purdie] gave Shaler the sword instead of money."

For decades all my family knew about the sword was that it was missing. What I learned next happened because of Harmony Hall. In 2008, the then docent showed me a list of visitors who indicated they were descendants. The list included an Arnold Shaler Richardson Woolverton and an Elizabeth

Marshall Swearingen, both of whom I soon met. Arnold turned out to be the daughter of the Dr. Shaler Richardson who had received the sword. I recorded what she told me about it in my notes years ago:

> My father Shaler had the sword. It hung over the mantel. I remember it very well. It was very large. Any man who used it would have to have been over six feet or more. During the Depression, my father bought the sword from the person who owned it. I don't remember who that was but the person needed the money badly. My father died at age seventy-three. He had a son named Shaler Arnold, lived near Jacksonville. This Shaler died in a fall in 1964. I then had the sword and gave it to Shaler Jr., since as a male in the direct lineage, he thought he should have it. He was college age and there were people in and out of his apartment. The sword was stolen from him. He was not of an age to be responsible.

The discrepancy in these two stories can be attributed to the passage of time and the different generations.

So, there is the sad story of the sword. Arnold and I became good friends. She was about ten years older than I and a true blue blood. A slender woman, she held herself straight and as tall as she could given her short stature, emanating grace and elegance with ease and no sense of eliteness. Her manners were impeccable. We visited back and forth a number of times. The best was when we spent the night at Harmony Hall in 2009. Proud of her lineage, she supported Harmony Hall with monthly donations and had always wanted to stay there. Despite her age and gentility, she had no problem with the lack of running water and electricity or the need to use the forest when nature called. My younger son was also with us. It was almost surreal to have slept in a house that one's great-great-great-great-grandparents built before the American Revolution.

As for the story about Elizabeth Neal Purdy Richardson on the stairs: there is a strongly held local legend that Charles Cornwallis commandeered Harmony Hall during his march to Wilmington, North Carolina. Elizabeth was said to have crept up its exterior stairs and listened through cracks in the thin wooden walls as Cornwallis made plans with his staff in an upper bedroom. Supposedly, she dispatched the plantation overseer to warn General Greene. A few years ago, associates of Harmony Hall queried a state historian about this. The historian proclaimed that Cornwallis was never on that side of the Cape Fear River. Data show that Cornwallis was nearby, across the river. Some people have suggested that for extra safety Cornwallis and a few aides may have crossed the river to stay in Harmony Hall, leaving most of his men on the other side. Others have suggested that perhaps a woman connected to the Richardsons overheard something, wherever he was staying. Could there be something to the story for it to persist through all these generations?

These stories aside, I learned that the men and women in the Richardson line were enslavers. The men, if not serving others as ministers or physicians, were involved with law, politics, the state legislature, and wars. Quite a few descendants continue in these areas to this day. Eventually, an uncle of my great-grandfather, Edmund, was bequeathed Harmony Hall and one-third of the above-mentioned mill in his father's 1848 will. Edmund is cousin Liz Swearingen's great-grandfather. He, his family, and the enslaved people lived there through the Civil War; then, like so many others, they migrated to Texas. At that point, it passed out of Richardson hands.

Liz is the other cousin I connected with from the docent's list. We have become fast friends. One of my resources in my research is her gracious gift of letters, inherited from her aunt, that my great-grandfather had written to the Anson County Richardsons and Marshalls, our shared lineage. Another is the wealth of stories, some recounted below from her records, that she has generously shared. Our mutual interests led to a shared adventure in 2015, long before this book was even in my imagination.

~

The Richardsons probably connected with the Marshalls early in the nineteenth century. The Marshall progenitor, James Marshall, like Colonel Richardson, was a Revolutionary War soldier. Because Captain James Marshall and Colonel Richardson's son Samuel were both serving in the House of Commons in Raleigh in the early 1800s, it seems a good possibility that they became friends during their terms. Beginning in the 1820s, several marriages between Marshalls and Richardsons occurred, which account for Liz and me being doubly related.

Questions we had left us no choice but to travel to Anson County. Liz flew in from California. We found that Wadesboro, the county seat, had long passed its heyday. The tiny town center had a few stately trees and places of historical interest, sharply contrasting with the ugly shopping strip along its northern highway. Wadesboro also had a still-standing Marshall house. Several ancient cemeteries scattered around the county contained the remains of our shared ancestors. One had the graves of my great-great-grandmother Catherine Marshall and our shared Marshall progenitor. Finding that cemetery proved to be challenging.

After visiting the historical society and gazing at the Confederate soldier statue in front of the courthouse, modeled after another of our cousins, Liz and I visited the Marshall house. With no prior arrangements, we were delighted to be welcomed in by the owner and given a thorough tour of the graceful old home, still grandly perched on a gentle rise. We were possibly the first Marshalls to visit since 1907, when Liz's grandfather called on his mother's uncle who was living there. Her grandfather noted in a letter that he had talked with the "old slaves" who were still there and that it was one of the most moving experiences of his life. Unfortunately, he gave no details.

Back at our car, Liz and I studied directions to the Marshall cemetery and compared them to Google Maps. It was in the middle of the featureless northwestern part of the county, but for fields and fields of rolling land with stubbles of recently harvested soybeans or cotton edged by sparse roads. After much driving and frequent reexamination of maps we spotted a copse of trees in a large field. We were going to have to trespass.

Rounding the gate, we walked toward the spot of green with some trepidation. The sun was bright and plenty warm, the soil pale. Approaching, we began to see trees embracing a deep darkness surrounded by vines scrambling as though trying to provide a fence. Still, we were not sure. Our hearts beating faster, we looked for an opening into what seemed like a fairy tale where the castle is completely overgrown with briars. In the gloom, holding our breaths as our eyes adjusted, we began to see the tops of several ghostly stones. In a few more moments, I was standing before the tilted stone of my second great-grandmother whose Marshall family line was really the origin of my name. A weeping willow tree was engraved above her name.

Mrs. Catherine.
Consort of
Purdie Richardson
Died June 26, 1856
Aged 51 years.

My fourth great-grandfather (also Liz's fourth) Captain James Marshall had a much newer stone, one that gleamed brightly compared to the lichen-covered others. With later investigation, we found two women had applied to the government for a new stone in the 1930s, a benefit apparently available to veterans back to the American Revolution. About twenty graves were in that dark copse, most with familiar names, a few unmarked and forlorn, all still keeping company with cotton.

———

The Marshall/Richardson branches of the family, as with the McAlpins, had enslaved people for many generations, some preceding the Revolution. The branches of these lines are too numerous to list in detail. Virtually all now known to me were slaveholders. Married into the Marshalls and Richardsons were Lanier, Chamberlain, Washington, Jordan, Malone, Latimer, Edwards, Stanton, among others. I researched these with censuses, wills, histories, and more: sowers of dragon's teeth all. Some wills listed certain enslaved people by name. Those are in the dedication. Not surprisingly, my forebears had trouble "managing" their many enslaved people. I found several "runaway" and other legal notices pertaining to their human property, the earliest a 1709 ordering of whippings of three enslaved men and one woman. Heavy-hearted work, this research.

The Richardsons and Marshalls had some stories about their human chattel. One, in an 1853 journal article citing long-lived slaves, tells of Judy who died at Harmony Hall on October 15, 1853, at the age of 110: she was one of the first "settlers [*sic*] on the plantation where she died."[4] This suggests she was among Colonel James Richardson's enslaved people before the American Revolution and, as property, was passed down for three generations as Edmund was her owner in 1854.

Another story is about "Black" Simon, a contemporary of Samuel and Amos, the children of the builder of Harmony Hall. According to accounts by a descendant born in 1852, these three children played together and became good friends. The Richardsons admired Simon's intelligence and taught him to read and write. When Samuel grew up and became a minister, Simon followed in his footsteps. Simon was allowed to go about ministering to his "own people." He would be absent from Harmony Hall for six to eight weeks at a time, traveling by foot with a walking cane and valise strapped on his back. On one occasion he returned with an orphaned white boy he had found abandoned from a ship near Wilmington. This boy, John Martin, was raised by Colonel James. Simon lived so long he was also passed down to Edmund, who gave him a room adjoining the kitchen in his older years. According to family lore he was beloved by all. His wife was Judy mentioned

*Figure 11.* Shep Richardson, date unknown. Shep was born
into slavery at Harmony Hall, when my third great-uncle
Edmund Richardson lived there with his wife, my great-
grandfather's first cousin Sally Marshall. After the Civil War,
these Richardsons moved to Texas and took Shep with them.
He was about three years old at the time. Nothing is known
about his parents. Photo courtesy of my cousin Elizabeth
Swearingen, from the Swearingen-Richardson family papers.

above. When Simon died, "white and black were crying together when Simon's spirit took flight to the other world."[5]

Shep of Harmony Hall was born on the edge of slavery, presumably to
enslaved people owned by Edmund. At age three, Shep went with the Richardsons to Texas after the Civil War. He was a playmate of Edmund and Sally's youngest sons, James and John, as evidenced in letters that cousin Liz
found among her family's memorabilia. One from James described his favorite boyhood pleasure as "roasting peanuts and potatoes on long winter nights
. . . and enjoying the feast with our happy home circle" of father, mother,
brothers, and Shep. The most poignant, perhaps, was brother John's reminis-
cence in 1888: "I look back on the good old days at home spent in the field

with Shep and Jim as the happiest of my life." Shep and another child appear in the Texas 1870 census living close to the Richardsons with two African American adults of a different surname, perhaps parents of these children? In the 1880 census, Shep was listed as a servant living with the Richardsons. He was evidently dear to the family, as evidenced by the reminiscences and a tintype photograph of him kept with other family memorabilia through several generations, shared with me by Liz. It presents a somewhat haunting image of a young adolescent boy, dark skinned and with furrowed brow, with eyes gazing outward that appear to be asking questions.

And, finally, there are two unidentified photos that appear to be of the same mixed-race woman in fine clothes and accessories, likely taken fifteen or twenty years apart. One was in a trunk of my step-great-grandmother; the other was in my grandmother's trunk along with other family photographs from the late 1800s. I wish I could know the mystery of this handsome woman, sitting so erect, proudly looking slightly away from the camera. When thinking of all the enslaved people and these stories, I cannot help but notice that despite occasional alleged affection, I found no evidence that any of the enslaved were freed or manumitted except for a Peter from many generations before.

On the Marshall side, while I do not know of any stories about people they held in bondage, there is faint evidence that the Marshalls taught them to read and write or, at least, did not interfere when they somehow learned. An 1846 letter from Clement Marshall, brother of my great-great-grandmother Catherine, to his daughter Sally, states, "Your little brother and sisters talk a great deal about you, and also the servants. They are delighted whenever any of us receive a letter from you. Those who cannot read are very desirous to hear your letter read." At the age of fifteen, Sally was sent to the Salem Female Academy in Winston-Salem, North Carolina, founded by the Moravians, who believed in female education. Whether any of the Marshalls or the people they enslaved were ever punished for their literacy I do not know. Around 1830, North Carolina had passed a law forbidding teaching enslaved people to read and write except for the use of figures.[6]

The saga does not end here. The third marriage of great-grandfather William Marshall Richardson produced my grandmother and connections with yet more plantations and enslaved people. The spreading family crept across the South into Louisiana and up to Saint Louis, adding the production of sugar to that of cotton and turpentine.

I must say something here about researching and reporting the unsavory side of my ancestors and relatives. In my quest to comprehend, to fathom the maternal side of my past, it is the only way I know to try to understand who they were, how their lives were woven into their long history as enslavers, why my mother and her family had the attitudes they did, and how this might be playing out in myself. These ancestors were probably good people in the context of their culture. The complexities are vast.

If the dark side of the story of these admired ancestors had been passed down along with the accounts of survival and triumph, would it have made a difference? Would my life have been different? The lives of my mother, cousins, aunts, and uncles? Possibly. Perhaps the consciousness that we are all the same, that all human beings deserve freedom, respect, love, and kindness would have developed sooner. That could have changed things. For my mother, perhaps she would not have had views that caused her misdirected anguish and fear and resulted in her giving generously to racist causes.

I believe that as a society, we cannot have dialogue, we cannot move forward, if we do not know the full truth. Not knowing is insisting on staying in a state of purposeful ignorance that only hurts us.

*Part II*

# Coming of Age

## Chapter 8

# The Brooke Hill School for Girls and Ramsay High School

Toward the end of my fifth grade, I was called into a basement room at my elementary school. I had no idea why. After I did puzzles, spatial exercises, sentence completions, and such, my parents received a letter from the superintendent of schools. I had been chosen with some others to attend the public school for "gifted" students beginning the following term. The designated school happened to be a long bus ride to the western end of the valley. So, in the summer between the fifth and sixth grades, I learned I was, instead, being sent to a private school, the Brooke Hill School for Girls. How my parents found the money for tuition and got me accepted I do not know. I evidently passed the required testing and interview procedures. Perhaps, the tuition money was not as much of an issue as it seems to me now. My father did make an adequate or more than adequate middle-class salary in his supervisor role with the Social Security Administration. My parents must not have had any idea what a different world that school would be.

That summer, still ten years old and apprehensive about changing schools, I learned that anger could transform into power. In the process, I learned I had a temper. I was used to my neighborhood friends bullying me from time to time, a constant from the first grade on. One afternoon, one of my friends appeared in my yard to play. She provoked me so much, why I no longer remember, that I found myself pinning her to the ground, my knees holding her arms down while I lifted her head and pounded it into the grass. Somehow my mother heard a commotion, ran out, and pulled me off her. Good thing. Where my timid self fled to in those moments, I cannot fathom. The feeling of power and strength that had surged into my body became a gift. Even though I remained shy and often unsure of myself, I had met my core boldness and toughness. It stood by me well. From then on, no matter how unhappy I was, I knew I had a good chance of surviving.

—

Brooke Hill was a private college preparatory school attended by daughters of the most affluent, elite, and powerful families of the city.[1] The catalog explained, "the Brooke Hill School for Girls is distinguished by leadership of the brightest and best of Birmingham citizenry." I now know that the "brightest and best" had a lot to do with the exploitation of Black people. Diane McWhorter, a Brooke Hill graduate about twelve years younger than I, put this bluntly without cover of euphemism in her book *Carry Me Home: Birmingham, Alabama, the Climactic Battle of the Civil Rights Revolution.* The men of these families "were known statewide as Big Mules." This moniker for the city's powerful men appears in virtually all accounts of Birmingham's history. McWhorter suggests that the term was "a perhaps unconscious tribute to the most prized members of the largely black work force that excavated their fortunes in coal and iron." (This references the system of free convict labor discussed in chapter 2.) "'How many mules did we lose?' was their half-facetious response to a big mine explosion."[2] Had I known any of this when I started Brooke Hill, I doubt I would have understood. I did understand I had been plunged into a lily-white world of gentility, country clubs and their swimming pools, white gloves and hats, bridge parties, other parties, summer camps, sororities, and debutante balls, all tended to by Black servants.

By coincidence, my new school was in walking distance from my house so I simply continued the pattern of walking to and from school from the sixth through the eighth grades. For a short time, while in the fifth grade, I had a companion. A girl my age, another only child, had moved into a basement apartment just up my street. For whatever reason, though we got along well, we never became friends, possibly because her life took a different turn around then. I knew her as Patricia Neal. Now, she is now known as the author Fannie Flagg.

—

I began the sixth grade at Brooke Hill with eleven other girls. The rest of the school comprised seventy-eight girls from the seventh grade through high school and fourteen full- or part-time teachers. Fortunately, I already knew five of my classmates as they were neighbors. Although not over the mountain, my street, Milner Crescent, was just off Highland Avenue, a neighborhood with its own nice homes and important families. Brooke Hill, then in its third location, occupied a stately Craftsman house on a property that covered half of nearby Rhodes Circle. The house had been remodeled into classrooms, and a gymnasium/auditorium was added. The original library of the prior owners continued to serve that function, also doubling as a lunchroom and study hall, the walls of books and fireplace making for a cozy atmosphere. Classes were vigorous and stimulating. I'm sure they were better for me than I realized at the time.

The last names of much of the student body matched the names of some of the city's large businesses, steel mills, and attorneys, so it was easy to tell who was from which family and where their money came from. Most of them lived "over the mountain" in Mountain Brook. Soon, I was being invited into Mountain Brook homes. Being over the mountain meant, in part, that it was free from the steel mills' smog that settled along the valley floor. Mountain Brook had been laid out by prominent landscape architects including Frederick Law Olmsted. Houses were designed in English Tudor style, Italianate, French Norman farmhouse, and Federal Revival, among others. Roads were curved, trees were large and lush, and the homes were set among gracefully spreading lawns. It was beautiful then and still is.

Even though I didn't have the stylish clothes and penny loafers the other girls had, I nevertheless managed to make a few close friends, at least one each year. It was a given that I would not be in the popular crowd. It did not help that I had no skill in sports. It was agonizing to wait for the captains to choose the girls they wanted on their teams. I was always chosen last, which, at that point, was hardly being chosen.

Good grammar, good manners, and narrow feet must have helped to carry me along. Narrow feet were particularly important to my mother as she considered them a sign of aristocracy. For years, I had been forced to wear shoes that were too narrow as she thought they would keep my feet from becoming "peasant looking." That ended dramatically one day. I must have been eleven or twelve when I stepped out of the car into a searing pain, coursing white-hot up my legs and through my body. Such a wild scream reverberated in the air it took a moment to realize it was coming from me. I was unable to walk. This time, she was convinced I was not faking. The shoes had finally caused severe bursitis in my Achilles tendons, which troubled me until I was in my twenties. Much to my surprise, it came back about forty-five years later, toward the end of a long, strenuous trek in the Himalayas.

The friend I spent the most time with was Bobbie Lynne, a petite, slender brunette, and another only child. I often stayed overnight in her Mountain Brook home. Her father, in his easy chair reading a newspaper, spoke with us from time to time as we engaged in our pubescent activities. I knew he was a federal judge but nothing else. Now, I know that he, more than many, was aware of the increasing violence against African Americans. Bobbie and I didn't know that the escalation of bombings was paralleling our friendship.[3] Her father was ruling on many of the civil rights cases.[4] The year she and I became good friends, 1954, was the year of the landmark Supreme Court decision *Brown v. Board of Education of Topeka*, which declared segregated schools unconstitutional. The Alabama governor denounced school integration and threatened to close public schools. I have no memory of any of this. Until the 1960s, Judge Lynne's rulings were pro-segregation. He gradually began to change.

Bobbie's mother must have stayed home as most mothers did in those days. After I went to public high school, I didn't see Bobbie anymore. About six years ago, wondering what had become of her, I searched the internet and learned through an obituary for her father that she had died in 1988. She never married and had no children. Her death made me sad. I heard later that she had been "sickly." By the time Judge Lynne died, his wife was also gone. I expect after his change of heart, Bobbie and her mother had had to weather harassment, even possibly death threats, along with Judge Lynne.

My other good friend was Beth Greene. As with Bobbie, after the eighth grade, we lost contact. Brooke Hill records show she did not finish high school there. We did have an awkward meeting when I was nineteen and pregnant, waiting to see my obstetrician. Beth appeared in the waiting room, also apparently pregnant. She looked extremely embarrassed and barely acknowledged my presence. I was married; I don't know whether she was. In those days, girls from "good" families were expected to go straight from high school to college and certainly not get pregnant out of wedlock.

Most of my other classmates were friendly enough despite my not coming from a family like theirs. At the time, I did not realize the girls were being groomed for a life in Birmingham society. I was surprised at being included in their country clubs' events: luncheons, bridge playing, and pool parties. Even in my preteen years, watching the giggling girls trying to act grown-up summoning the tuxedoed African American waiters made me extremely uncomfortable. The waiters stood ramrod straight around the edge of the plush rooms, waiting to spot a wiggling finger or waving hand.

On the eighth-grade prophecy page of Brooke Hill's annual, the *Brooklet*, mine stated: "Marcia E. Herman in *Who's Who* because of her famous spend-the-night parties." There was only one party, and it seemed a miracle that it happened. My mother must have realized I needed to do something to pay back all the invitations I had gotten over my years at Brooke Hill. So, a spend-the-night party was arranged at a time when there were no roomers. I don't know how many girls came out of the twenty-five in our class that year. Plenty did, bringing bedrolls, pillows, hair curlers, lipsticks, and all the other accoutrements needed when you're thirteen years old. Bedding was spread over three bedrooms. We played 45s on a little record player. What we ate I do not know. Some of the girls stayed up all night talking and laughing. I couldn't muster the ability to do that and fell asleep around four in the morning.

Before we went upstairs to bed down, some boys arrived, mostly older brothers of the girls. Where my parents were is a mystery as I do not remember seeing them. They must have walked through from time to time, but maybe they were more discreet than they should have been. The boys got rowdy, and I got uncomfortable. They finally left before anything terrible happened. I still remember the name of the most obstreperous: Drayton Nabers. He went on to finish college at Princeton and law school at Yale, and became the chief justice of the Alabama Supreme Court. I hope he straightened out. As for me, the prophecy prediction turned out to be partly true: I unexpectedly went on to be in various *Who's Who* listings numerous times but not for parties.

I was thirteen the entire eighth grade, not turning fourteen until two weeks into high school. A lot happened that year. I read *Gone with the Wind* in three days despite my mother's disapproval. It wasn't the contents; she didn't like my idleness. I was captivated by the romanticism and don't remember anything about the racial issues and the Civil War. I started my period in January while dust-mopping the living room floor. My mother had me fitted with braces because she thought my mouth had lost its "natural beauty." That summer, during our annual stay with my grandmother, I learned to sew using her chain-stitch treadle machine. After I'd worked hard to attach a gathered skirt to a bodice, a thread came loose and got caught in something. The entire waist unraveled, and the skirt fell off. Upset, I nonetheless understood the lesson. That paled compared to the worst thing that year. My beloved little Dingy got sick and died. My mother would not take her to the vet, despite my desperate pleas. I thought my heart would break. It was my first experience with deep loss and grief. Papa buried her under the peach tree aside the porch terrace. The gift Dingy gave me remains, as does my sorrow. The fury at my mother has barely attenuated.

My time at Brooke Hill ended with the dual graduations of the eighth graders and the high school seniors. Dressed in white, wearing our first pair of high heels, we marched down the aisle to "Pomp and Circumstance." We were feeling quite grown-up, and emotions were high. Hearing that familiar tune still brings me feelings of angst and sentiment. Afterward, we went to a classmate's house for a party. I didn't realize this was going to be the last time for almost two years that I would even slightly fit in with a group.

—

Writing this has helped me realize that when I got to Brooke Hill, a dark gloaming was wrapping its way around me. By high school it seemed complete. On reflection, I realize a vital aspect was missing: the sustaining underpinning of connectedness to nature fostered by my father. During the Brooke Hill years, Papa and I camped a few times at the nearby Cahaba River, but mostly I was too busy navigating puberty, a new school, and an unfamiliar social system. I had lost my "groove." I was rarely exposed to those sudden patches of yellow-throated primroses that thrilled my spirit, my beloved daisies swaying in the breeze, or other glorious sights waiting to bathe me in awe.

My parents did provide me with advantages. Along the years, I was given lessons in piano, tap dancing, ballet, and art. I was a Brownie and, then, a Girl Scout. I collected stamps and learned from that. Additionally, the lessons and skills I learned from other adults in my life and at the camps I attended at ages nine, eleven, and twelve gave me the feeling that I could *do* things. My parents were careful to take me on trips to expose me to the world. Between the sixth and seventh grades, we went to New Orleans with my beloved Aunt Mary and Uncle Harvey. West of New Orleans, we visited New Iberia Parish, where my grandmother had grown up. We saw the huge plantation house Bayside-on-the-Têche, built by M'Wese's great-uncle. We never went overseas, but when I was fifteen, we drove to Mexico accompanied by the one friend my mother had from her New York days. Betty was quite misshapen from scoliosis and childhood polio. Her sweet presence likely helped prevent some of my parents' terrible fights and gave me a lesson in grace. Other trips included New York City and Montgomery, Alabama.

Going to summer camp was important. I stayed about two weeks each time. I loved the ceremonies, songs and s'mores around campfires, the mess hall with good food and happy chatter, and the gross fun of peering into the latrines with a flashlight to watch the maggots wiggling when I had latrine duty. But not all was good.

Camp Winnataska was where I had the most humiliating experience of my twelve years. I was in early puberty and desperately wanted what, in those days, we called a "training bra." All the other girls had them. My mother refused to get me any. I was so dreading not having the shape of a bra that would show through my T-shirts and cover my budding breasts that I made one using scraps from an old sheet, sewing the pieces together by hand and adding snaps for fastening. One evening, a cabinmate found it after we had all gotten into our pajamas. Their comments and laughter burned me with such shame and embarrassment the embers still turn orange when I think of it. Nonetheless, my love for the camp with its tumbling creek and mountains remained.[5] The director was a kind man who knew a great deal about nature. I looked forward to when he would take us into the fields and forest to teach us about succession growth, the way the sunshine sanitizes objects, and so much more. The camp paid homage to the American Indians with prayers to the four directions and spirits, another loved lesson.

———

At home, there were still roomers much of the time. Were it not for the strange men tramping across our living room, reaching into their pockets for the weekly rent, there would have been no other people in our house. I have flitting memories of an actual assault by one of the roomers when I was around the age of ten. I believe whatever memories formed, they are suppressed, and it is just as well to leave them that way. After that, I learned how to avoid the roomers. Socially, my parents made one or two attempts to have my father's office friends over. These were unhappy affairs and did not continue. Thus, I grew up with virtually no family social life.

Several roomers have remained in my memory. One was a medical student. When I cleaned his room, I would sit on the edge of the bed with his anatomy textbook. Another was the only female who ever stayed with us, a sixteen-year-old cello player from New York City whose mother had rented a room with us for her summer with the Birmingham Symphony. At least, I thought that was the story. Looking Virginia Rubottom up recently, I glimpsed an archived article I could not further access that hinted she had run away. As an adult, she became a renowned pianist. She stayed in bedroom no. 5 and practiced diligently. The sound entranced me. My mother would go through her wastebasket and remove the exceptionally long letters Virginia received from her mother. Mother would read and annotate them. They are likely among her papers that I have yet to clean out.

The story of another roomer is ghastly. A thin young man, he left for work as a display creator for department store windows every morning, returning every evening. Because he had the room with an outside entrance, we never saw much of him. My mother sent me down periodically to clean his small quarters. The last time I went, we had not seen him for several days, but then, it was easy to miss him. When I opened the closet to dust the floor, there were several mason jars I had not noticed before. I picked one up. It was heavy, full of a thick, reddish-black liquid covered by green mold. I knew how mold looked from spoiled food in our refrigerator. The jars were full of blood. We never saw the young man again. I suppose my parents notified the police. The influence of these three roomers fertilized my growing interest in medicine and music. In my adulthood, I spent years in laboratory work and medicine, and I took up the cello in my sixties.

The high school in my district was small, with only four hundred students. A long brick building perched partway up Red Mountain, four stories with many windows, it was served by several wide staircases. In my first two years at Ramsay, 1955 to 1957, I disappeared into wretchedness largely caused by my actual disappearance from any social groups or friends.[6] Changing schools caused me to lose my Brooke Hill friends. The few at Ramsay from my childhood were being rushed for sororities and belonged to social groups I was not invited to participate in. I had no close friends, and no boy asked me for a date. I was sad and depressed and had trouble sleeping. My parents had their fights. My precious little dog was dead. Dyed-to-match sweater and skirt sets were the in-thing to wear. I did not have any. Only some of my clothes were fashionable, which added to my troubles. I can still picture the elite girls with their matching cashmeres and straight skirts. Their gold two-part sorority pins, connected by a tiny gold chain, were pinned on their pointed breasts, shaped by conical bras that were fashionable at the time. The little chains swayed when they walked. Not only did I not have such a pin, I didn't have bosom enough to shape. I did manage to keep up with my schoolwork, consistently being an A and B student, as I had always been.

To make matters worse, there was a second episode of tooth pulling and painful braces during my freshman year. My mother was not satisfied when my first orthodontic work ended. She thought I should look prettier. Part of the treatment this time was to play the trumpet (to press my teeth back) and to tape my lips together each night when I went to bed.

Envying the clothes of the other girls motivated me to teach myself more sewing. Pretty soon, I was making most of my clothes, which enabled me to have fashions more to my liking (but still no dyed-to-match outfits). I had to fight to get my mother to pay for bobby socks. She despised them, thinking they looked trashy. She finally gave in, but my punishment was that I was not allowed to put them in the washing machine. Trying to hand scrub the inevitable red stains from Birmingham clay made my hands raw and red, but I persisted. Soon, I developed the idea to persuade my parents to give me a set allowance, fifteen dollars a month, to cover all my expenses, including cloth, patterns, clothing I couldn't make, school lunches, supplies, books, and personal items. That way, I didn't have to beg anymore. I still had to handwash my bobby socks.

In the angst and self-doubt during the better part of my first two high school years, I read to bounce myself off the characters in books since this wasn't happening with real people. My parents must have noticed my quietness and constant reading. Mother surprised me with two purchases, the first during this period; the second, a bit later when things were getting better. Surprise is too mild a word. I still feel amazement that she did these two things.

She noticed the deep grooves at the base of my left thumb from having to use right-handed scissors to cut cloth. I had told her about the pain. Soon, we were in Loveman's Department Store, where she bought me expensive Wiss left-handed dressmaking shears. I still have those shears. In fact, I used them the other day to cut cloth to make a cello bib. The second surprise was a dress for an event my first boyfriend had invited me to. I wasn't up to making elaborate dresses so again we went shopping. I became enamored with a graceful full-skirted dress with a snug bodice. The cloth was taffeta-like with a white background and clusters of purple grapes all over it. It was expensive.

—

Toward the end of my sophomore year, I burst through the shadows in which I had been swimming, into a sunshine that grew ever brighter. Maybe my mother's unexpected gift of the shears was a factor. Maybe it helped that I was jumping into real turbulent waters between my freshman and sophomore years, during my second summer on the little Maine island with my cousins. It gave me a boost. The swirling waters began to calm. By the next year, much to my surprise, I got asked on a date by a student at the exclusive boys' boarding school Birmingham University School, known as BUS. I must have met him at the dances Brooke Hill gave for the eighth graders.

Allen really liked me, in fact, we thought we were in love, but we did recognize that since we had never been in love before, we couldn't be sure. After all, adults labeled such things as crushes or puppy love. We talked of marriage. Long phone calls weren't allowed at BUS, so we wrote copious letters even though he wasn't far away except during vacations. He was from Annapolis, Maryland, where his father taught at the Naval Academy. He left for college in my senior year, coming back for a visit during Christmas vacation. Things had changed.

Two girls, having just moved to Birmingham, enrolled in my class late in my sophomore year. I could tell they were not going to be in the cliques that I had been excluded from, so I saw my opportunity to befriend them. They both became fast friends, and their families godsends. Rosemary's parents bought a house on a steep hill off Highland Avenue close to mine but not on the best street. My mother disapproved. Rosemary's diminutive, redheaded mother had a tinkling laugh and lighthearted demeanor. Her tall, handsome Canadian father was quiet, sweet, and friendly. The Downies were the most nonjudgmental people I have ever known. Jill's parents were of German background; it showed in their behavior. They bought a Craftsman home I had passed many times as a child walking to elementary school. Jill's parents, Mr. and Mrs. Moerlins, welcomed me warmly, as had Rosemary's. I soon became part of both families. The Moerlinses' mild gruffness and certain forcefulness were no impediment. Both Jill and Rosemary had siblings. My life turned around. Then began a furious tumble of events that enriched my life and gave me a handful of sometimes painful and sometimes exhilarating teachings.

The exact order of events is not important. I decided to investigate religions. Christianity had not sat well with me, but I felt it deserved a further look. I attended services at several denominations including Methodist, Presbyterian, and Episcopalian.[7] At the last, I liked the rituals and the easygoing quality, but I could not embrace the words of the prayer book. Somehow, I ended up with a small group of Baha'i adults who met just up the street from my elementary school. That experience taught me that the world of religion and spirituality was much broader than what I had been exposed to and led to a negative high school experience.

The influence of the Baha'is showed in an essay my class was required to write on our religious beliefs. Yes, that topic could be required in a public school back then. With my now being an A student more frequently than a B student along with my appropriate involvement in extracurricular activities, I was scheduled to be inducted into the National Honor Society. I was gratified because my father would be proud. Next thing I knew, after the teacher read my essay and gave me a good grade, I was taken off the list for induction. I learned that the essay's content, which included thoughts about reincarnation, meant I was not an appropriate candidate. I would be a bad influence. This rejection helped cement my already growing feeling of alienation and radicalization. That I had begun to dress in more of a beatnik style didn't help.

By then, I had fallen in with the small oddball group of "intellectuals." We read a lot. Our discussions were intense. Somewhere in all this I came down with a mystery disease and missed several weeks of school. I finally got better, then relapsed the summer between my junior and senior year while being a camp counselor in Mississippi. I ended up hospitalized, subjected to repeated and suffocating clouds of rubbing alcohol fumes since no one seemed to know what to do but to try to get my fever down. My parents had to come get me. When I was well enough, never having gotten a diagnosis, I got myself to the medical library at the University of South Alabama Medical School, where I pored over textbooks until I figured out what I had had: infectious mononucleosis. True, I had been kissing my boyfriend. He had been sick. I was months getting my strength back. My mother thought that I was being lazy and that the doctor was in cahoots with me to excuse my laziness. She wanted more work out of me. For weeks at school, I had to sit on the top stair to rest if I had to change floors for classes. There were no elevators. Over time I got completely well from the mononucleosis, but I will never forget how profound fatigue feels.

One benefit of getting introduced to the medical school was that I developed a relationship with a woman who prepared cadavers for the incoming medical students. I would go when I could to watch her work and study real anatomy. I thought I had habituated to the ghastly setting: a room reeking of formaldehyde, full of embalmed bodies on gurneys, some covered, some not, their blood vessels filled with substances that made arteries red and veins blue. The whole effect was surreal. I learned my habituation was only partial one afternoon when I paid one of my visits and was taken aback by her cup of coffee and sandwich an inch from the shoulder of the cadaver she worked on.

Cadavers or not, having been a victim of the "kissing disease," I still needed to learn more about sex. There was no sex education in schools. Girls were taught at home that they should keep themselves "pure" for marriage and that it was their fault if boys got too aggressive. My mother told me sex was dirty and unpleasant and above all else I was to remain a virgin until marriage at the proper age, which she declared was twenty-eight years old.

Naturally, I was curious and set out to learn more. I had read enough of the Bible to know there was quite a bit of sex in it, so I read it again cover to cover. I also began skipping lunch periods and study halls at Ramsay to walk to the nearby library branch and read about reproduction and sex, including Freud. His books were in the reference section, so I couldn't check them out. In time, I read them all, becoming quite enamored with his teachings. After I grew up, wiser and knowing more, I reversed my opinion about Freud. As for sex, not surprisingly, despite my mother, Freud, and the Bible, I didn't wait until I was twenty-eight.

~

One day, early in my junior year while changing classes, I spotted a thin, serious-looking boy almost a head taller than the crowd around him. I was smitten. I don't think he saw me that day, nor for weeks after that. I made inquiries. Scott played the trombone in the school band. He was two years behind me but made up one full year in summer school, motivated by his dislike of school. Despite the considerable distance to his house from Ramsay, he usually walked home, lugging his instrument. I started following him at a discreet pace, our routes conveniently being similar. Eventually, he noticed me. His being shy with tight pecuniary habits proved an asset to my efforts. My timidity fit with his. So much walking quietly together eventually led to sharing halting conversation. The next time my first boyfriend, Allen, came to visit, I broke up with him, though it made me sad. We had learned a lot from each other.

By then, Scott was in the oddball crowd as well, and I was sneaking into his room at his house, where we read Schopenhauer, Nietzsche, Kant, Goethe, and even Marx and Engels while we talked and listened to classical music. I had not grown up with classical music, and I fell in love with it as I fell more in love with him. Scott began to take German lessons from a couple who, fleeing from the Nazis, had come to the United States. Like Scott's parents, they attended the Unitarian Church. Frederick Kraus, a dentist and a physician from Prague, became a leader in the Civil Rights Movement, but we were not to know that until later. Frederick had a long face framed with large ears highlighted by frequent smiles. He was never without a little notebook in his pocket where he chronicled happenings in his life. He was devoted to science, literature, classical music, nature, and, especially, human rights. His wife, Anny, was from Vienna. She was short and a bit stout, which gave her a sturdiness that supported the warmth and love everyone felt from her. Her

*Figure 12.* Our dear friends and mentors Frederick and Anny Kraus, taken some years after Scott and I had left Birmingham. Courtesy of their daughter, Ingrid W. Kraus.

kind face was framed by soft brown curls. How fortunate we were to become their surrogate children and to learn so much from this wise, kind couple.[8]

Anny gave the German lessons. Scott encouraged me to join him. His motivation was to have help paying for the lessons. Mine was to get more time with him. We got a lot of that, since the walk from Ramsay to their house was two and a half miles each way, up and over Red Mountain. Anny always greeted us with a plate of warm chocolate chip cookies. She stroked our cheeks and called us "Hazilein" (Little Rabbit) or "Schatzilein" (Little Darling). Our mothers had never done things like that. The Krauses were dear to us for as long as they lived. We visited as often as we could after we married and moved away. Their daughter, Ingrid, four years younger than I, who then seemed a child to us, remains one of my dearest friends.

Scott's home life and my home life could not have been more different. Scott's home was like a sweaty summertime about to blink out. Mine was a gray, threatening wintertime. Scott's parents were abusive and neglectful toward their five children. My mother was overly involved with my life. His fun-loving parents left much of the child-rearing to their maid, Willie Mae White, and to Scott, who was five years older than the next child. We learned later that his father was gay, though we had suspected it for a long time. The dynamics interjected into Scott's home plus the parties his parents gave added to the tarnished glitter covering the unhappy children.

Scott's mother had a real talent for decorating so their home was attractive. Modern, bright colors and spacious. My home was cold in comparison, with no parties, no social life, no alcohol, not even a television until my junior year. The furniture and decor in my home, while solid middle class, comprised a mishmash of antiques that had come with the house, plus random pieces of new and used furniture bought as needed.

Imagine my reaction to witnessing one of Scott's parents' parties. Liquor was flowing, cigarettes glowing, and music playing supporting wild dancing as it disintegrated into a striptease game. I was holding my breath, peeking from around a corner at the clothes coming off, the men and women finally getting down to their underwear. I was watching one couple in particular. It was the woman's turn to remove a garment. I was scarcely breathing. She was down to her bra and underpants. Preparing for shock and embarrassment when her bra came off, I let out a breath when, out of her bra, she pulled a falsie. That gave her three more items to remove, whereas her partner had only one and thus would have been naked had he continued playing. To my simultaneous relief and disappointment, he quit. Another time, sneaking out of Scott's room one morning, through a partly open door to his parents' bedroom, I saw his parents and a male friend in their king-size bed. Ted was their closest friend, an obstetrician-gynecologist from New Orleans. I hadn't known how close. I'm not sure I knew the phrase ménage à trois then. One thing all this did was to prepare me for households quite different from what I was used to, which turned out to be a good thing.

—

My dear friend Jill Moerlins and James Howard had become a couple. James was already a friend of Scott's and part of our crowd. He lived in easy walking distance from Scott's. Soon, the four of us were spending a good bit of time together, especially at James's house as it was the most welcoming. It was another large Craftsman, this one perched on Cliff Road, a curving street along Red Mountain. The house hung off the mountainside in a cluster of trees and an air of mystery and promise. Two items defined the interior. One was a long sword that belonged to James's father and that had been in his family for generations. The other was a larger-than-life oil painting of James's plump, stark-naked Cherokee mother. James died in 2018, and since then, I have learned the painting has gone missing.

James's father was different from other fathers I knew. A distinguished-looking Harvard graduate, he had brought his family to Birmingham to be the first director of the Birmingham Museum of Art. During World War II, he had become the second deputy chief of the Monuments, Fine Arts, and Archives program to preserve the cultural heritage of Europe. Because of this, James had grown up partly in Europe during dangerous, intense years. The household had a cosmopolitan air, liberal and, if anything, too laissez-faire, all overseen by his friendly mother with copper-colored skin and coal-black hair. James became an artist.

~

At my house, rancor permeated the air. At least, during my last two years of high school there were few to no roomers. My mother was getting more controlling, I suppose in reaction to my becoming more independent. My father was spending evenings in his office on hobbies to keep himself out of her way. To further my independence, I needed money. I got a job in a bookstore in downtown Birmingham. One side of Birmingham Book and Magazine sold textbooks for the public high schools. I worked there several hours most every day after school. The owner became another of my adult saviors. One day, when I arrived, she told me my mother had come in and demanded that she fire me. This kind, strong woman refused. I know I told her how grateful I was and thanked her. I wish I had done more. I have always regretted that after I grew up, I didn't look for her again and thank her with my adult self. Now I no longer remember her name.

My mother and I had constant clashes. I was usually in an explosive state. Her trying to get me fired was the last straw. I remember coming home that evening, finding her in her bedroom, confronting her about it, and yelling in response to whatever she said, "Go to hell." I left. Rosemary's parents were already on my growing list of helping adults. They took me in. I insisted on paying for room and board, but they wouldn't let me pay much. Rosemary's mother reacted as my bookstore employer had when my mother arrived threatening the police if they continued to allow me to stay there. Gertrude said, "She stays here." That was that. I did have the opportunity to thank Rosemary's parents many times. I stayed with them the better part of my last semester of high school. What a joy it was to be part of their happy family. My poor father. I don't remember whether he and I ever talked about this. That must have been a very sad time for him.

I fell into a demanding pattern of activities: going to school, studying, hanging out with Scott and sometimes Jill and James, taking the bus after school to work at the bookstore, and returning by bus to the Downies' house. My job paid seventy-five cents an hour. I don't remember whether I realized that requiring students to purchase their textbooks was a strategy to keep Black children, already in inferior schools, from their educational rights. I certainly realized this after a Black woman came in to buy a textbook for her child. The memory of this event is another racial injustice seared in my mind before I even knew much about what was going on.

The pleasant but somber-looking woman came to the counter. She was slightly plump and dressed plainly. I no longer remember other details of her appearance or the subject of the textbook. I found what she wanted and laid it on the counter. I told her the price. With a trembling hand, she began to reach through the top of her blouse into her bosom. I had seen this in movies but never in real life. She extracted a small bundle tied in a white handkerchief. She could barely untie the knot. Finally, she laid open the handkerchief. In the middle was a silver dollar burnished with age. She picked it up and passed it over to me, quivering as it was in her hand. I held out my hand to take it. The silver coin burned sorrow and shame into my palm. Then, then, I knew white privilege, though not by those words.

After she left, I quietly put one of my own paper dollars in the cash drawer and put the silver dollar in my purse. Over the years, I would take it out of its keeping place, feel it, pregnant with lessons as it was, look at it, turn it over in my hand, and let it speak to me lest I forget. Sadly, somewhere in the latter half of the sixty-plus years that have passed since that book purchase, the silver dollar has gone missing. I still think of that precious coin and the despairing dark-skinned mother quite often. And I still hope to find that precious coin.

The book episode happened about five years after the *Brown v. Board of Education* ruling by the US Supreme Court, which declared state-sanctioned segregation of public schools a violation of the Fourteenth Amendment. I vaguely knew about it, but, because it had had no effect on Birmingham schools, it wasn't real.

In a few more weeks, having accomplished the college essay and application ordeal, I managed to graduate. The last thing I remember about being at Ramsay High School was the principal calling the entire student body into the auditorium for an announcement. It scared me. I thought perhaps another war had started. He spit into the microphone, "Don't you worry, we will never let this school be integrated." A war had started. It had already been going on. I just hadn't seen it.

Within another year, I was beginning to learn about the unspeakable violence against African Americans in Birmingham that had been going on since I had moved there as a young child. The first bombing of an African American home was in 1947, when I was attending the first grade. The bombings continued, escalating, all through my years at Brooke Hill and high school. Other atrocities were happening. Researching for this book, I kept learning more and asking myself how I could have not known about this as it was occurring. So, in the spring of 2019, I asked a few close friends from those days and queried others via email who had been known as part of the brightest cohort in my Ramsay class. I picked four atrocities that occurred while we were attending high school together.

1956    Nat King Cole was attacked by the Ku Klux Klan at the Birmingham Civic Auditorium.

1957    Ku Klux Klan members kidnapped, tortured, and castrated a Black man named Judge Edward Aaron.

1957    Rev. Fred Shuttlesworth was beaten at Phillips High School trying to enroll his children.

1958    Fifty-four sticks of dynamite were placed behind a Jewish synagogue, Temple Beth-El. They failed to go off after being doused by rain. I knew that synagogue as I walked past it on Highland Avenue every day on my way to high school.

I also sent this group a copy of a photograph that had been in the newspaper of boys our age at another high school holding a racist banner.

Two friends who lived in liberal households and read newspapers reported they were aware of the violence. Several, like myself, were unaware that these hideous acts were going on. Of the ten classmates I polled via email, two emails bounced back and seven people never replied. The one reply wrote, "I just recall not understanding why black people, who were the kindest to me as a child, were treated so poorly, made to drink from separate fountains, and called the N word." Her final thought, after I expressed my surprise to her that no one else had responded, was, "Many people our age don't want to acknowledge that racism is alive and well." She pointed out their silence was my answer.

*Chapter 9*

# College and Marriage, 1960

In June 2019, I was on the campus of St. John's College, Annapolis, Maryland, fighting back tears as I had some years before. I needed to visit the alumni office. It was a perfect early summer day, cool and clear. My previous visit, about five years earlier, had shown me a grief I had not known was so deep. Grief that I had not been able to attend St. John's more than one year. Then, I had parked near my old dormitory. It looked the same after nearly a half century. I walked over to the huge sycamore I used to sit beneath, leaning on its sculptured trunk, studying ancient Greek. Resting my eyes, I would gaze into the upper trunks with their beautiful taupe bark patterns. I was waiting to meet my daughter, who by then was living in Annapolis. When she found me weeping, I explained my realization; her understanding soothed me.

This time, taking in just about the whole small campus with one turn of the head, I asked myself, what does it feel like, this campus, this college? What *did* it feel like? How did it feel going there out of the depths of smog, soot, racial violence, Jim Crow, general backwardness, and an unhappy family life? A capital campaign was going on, marked by flags hanging along the walkways with a logo and the phrase "Freeing Minds." My mind had surely been freed and set off on a journey. My body was freer as well.

Standing there, those fifty-seven years later, I found myself searching for an image that would represent what it was like when I had first arrived, about to turn eighteen years old. What came was a quartz crystal: the symbol for what it felt like as I settled in those many years ago. Quartz comprises four oxygen atoms surrounding a silicon atom, which forms $SiO_4$. Its earliest known name, κρύσταλλος (kristallos), was recorded by the Greek Theophrastus circa 300 BCE. (Though he is not read at St. John's, many other early Greek scholars are a core part of the program.) Quartz crystals are either left-handed or right-handed, mirror images of each other. Quartz polarizes light passing through, bending the ray either left or right depending on the handedness of the crystal. Quartz is eternal and has abundant uses and colors. It is beautiful. A single crystal can be large enough to see by the naked eye. A central core with oxygen, which gives us life. Yes, I thought, that is how I felt entering the rhythm of the semester. St. John's was inclusive, and differences were accepted, even encouraged.

~

Marking the campus center is the Georgian-style McDowell Hall, in existence since 1694, paid for with thousands of pounds of donated tobacco grown by enslaved people.[1] I didn't know this back then. It is likely that they helped erect the hall, though I cannot find any relevant records. The first classes in McDowell as St. John's College began in 1789. Many scholarly and musical events, dances, and welcomes were and are held there for visitors, students and faculty, and, way back, persons such as Generals Lafayette and Washington. McDowell Hall has been in constant use as a school for 326 years, interrupted only by outbreaks of occasional fires and the hall's service as a Union hospital during the Civil War.

I attended many seminars in its classrooms and drank many cups of tea over intense discussions with classmates and tutors in the basement coffee shop. Its walls still feel the same, exuding intelligence, solidity, and the urging of scholarly examination while wrapping the habitué in a warp of history. I didn't know when I attended that I was benefiting from the forced labor of captive Black people.

Somehow, I had discovered the school and gotten myself admitted, my father and me prevailing over my mother, who was opposed to my going there. He delivered me and my paraphernalia to the campus in September 1959. Rules for students were liberal by the standards of the day, but the sexes were still in separate dorms. We women had a house mother, a faculty member named Eva T. H. Brann. She still teaches there, which makes me feel young every time I see her name.

My room looked out on the sycamore tree. My roommate was a niece of Vladimir Nabokov of *Lolita* fame. Whether it was her having descended, in part, from prominent Russian nobility with a sense of privilege, or something else, we clashed deeply. It must have been irreconcilable because she was moved to another room. Thus, we each had a single room, unheard of for freshman. I gloried in having my own space. I decorated by turning a Chianti bottle into an aquarium. Having added one guppy, I was surprised one day to see a dozen tiny guppies swimming in the bottle perched on my desk. With no equipment that allowed a rescue, I would stare at the mother and babies and contemplate existentialism. I positioned my portable typewriter, books, and notebooks carefully on the desk and kept detailed lists of what I needed to do every day. It did not take long before I was typing the required essays. The dining hall was across a small square. The food was good. That did not stop me, about halfway through the semester, from fasting for three days. I took in nothing but water just to see what it was like.

With scarcely more than four hundred students in the entire college, classes were small and all students took the same classes. The teaching was intensely Socratic. For our seminars, we sat around a large table and were addressed by our titles and last names. The professors were called tutors. We addressed them by Mr., Miss, or Mrs. There was no professorial hierarchy. We read and discussed real books, not textbooks digesting ideas for us. Works by Sophocles, Plato, Aristotle, Homer, and others made up a large part of seminars in the freshman year.[2] For anatomy, we read William Harvey's *Concerning the Motion of the Heart and Blood* and had a cat to dissect to help us discern the errors in Harvey's 1628 description. For mathematics, we read Ptolemy and Euclid, fortunately in English translation. We studied ancient Greek and soon were making translations. In physics, my favorite exercise was calculating the logarithmic spiral. This showed exactly how it was that the slide rules we depended on for certain mathematical calculations worked.

Classes in music theory provided some relief from the intellectual tenseness. I was thrilled with all this. The music tutor was Viktor Zuckerkandl, who, with his background in conducting, as well as teaching at both the New School in New York and Wellesley, came to St. John's in 1948. Zuckerkandl taught us theory and emphasized music's contribution to the mysticism of human lives. Stimulated by my former roommate, who was an accomplished pianist, I had taken to practicing scales and what simple music I could find in the school's practice rooms. One day Mr. Zuckerkandl passed by and accidentally gave me a great compliment. He knocked on the door thinking I was my former roommate.

All this stimulated my desire for lessons. I found a teacher in town and paid for lessons by ironing and mending for her. At the end of the second semester, I played Beethoven's "Für Elise" in the recital. Aunt Mary and Uncle Harvey came down from Lancaster County along with their daughter and her husband for the event. That was the last year I had formal piano lessons.

For fun, occasionally several of us would pile in someone's car and drive the thirty-five miles to Plum Point, Maryland, known as a source of petrified shark teeth. For social justice efforts, we would drive the seventy-five miles to Fort Detrick, Maryland, the US biological weapons and research center, with signs to protest the government's efforts to weaponize ticks and insects.

I have never since been in an environment that was as exciting and stimulating, albeit demanding, where I learned critical thinking, and where the pedagogy was authentic. I had found my lodestone.

Scott and I wrote many letters to each other that year. He was in his last year of high school and working at the Avondale branch of the Birmingham Public Library, learning to repair books. He saved all the money he could. Some he used for train tickets to Washington, DC, where we would meet, wander the Smithsonian, attend free concerts, and prowl through used bookstores. Impressed by St. John's, he applied for the next fall and was awarded a work-study scholarship. His parents promised to provide financial support for expenses that he would not be able to cover. Through all this, our relationship, sealed by love and desire, was fed by common needs, traumas, and interests. We knew we wanted to stay together. By the end of May, I had completed my final paper on *Antigone*, and suffered through the oral don rags. I packed my bags, said goodbye to friends, and headed back to Birmingham.

An unmarried couple living together in 1960 was not done, especially when the pair were seventeen and eighteen years old. To parental horror, Scott and I managed to do it anyway. Our friend James had a half sister, Towanda, who was looking for someone to take a summer sublet of her apartment, the top floor of a bungalow. The house at 3830 Glenwood Avenue was amid areas familiar to us. Somewhere along the way we were told that Bull Connor lived down the street. We knew who he was, so it was concerning to think he might be a neighbor. Now, writing this, I have not been able to confirm that this was correct. True or not, at the time we thought it was, and that bad enough. We arranged a look at the sublet.

Towanda was not home. We had no idea where she was. We checked out the sparsely furnished rooms, stopping at a locked door. We heard scrabbling noises, then child-sounding yips and chirps. Soon convinced a child was locked inside, and not knowing where Towanda was, we broke the lock open. We beheld two wild and filthy naked girls staring numbly at us. The shock of that scene is still etched on our minds. We estimated they were about two and three years old. The room was bare except for feces smeared on their bodies, the floors, and the walls. They spoke to each other in an unintelligible language.

At least Scott had some experience with children. I had none. I had never babysat, never changed a diaper, nothing. Instinct took over, and I swept the children up and put them into a warm bath. He looked for something to put on them. We clothed each one in T-shirts he had found. These were the days, at least as far as we knew, before social service agencies. All we knew was to take them to James's parents.

We left them there and never knew what happened to them until 2019, when I learned a little more.

Earlier that year, I was in New Orleans doing research for this book. Having found that James's youngest son lived there, I arranged a meeting. Seth was still grieving the death of his father a year earlier. He had so much of his father in him it was uncanny: his serious look, his dark hair and slightly shaded skin, his angular facial bones, and many of his mannerisms. After sharing some memories about James before Seth was born and hearing from Seth about himself, I got around to asking him about his Aunt Towanda's two children. He told me of an episode when both children were badly burned about a year after our horrifying experience. Again, they had been left alone. Seth had not heard of Scott's and my event with the children, but he was not surprised. Recently, he had tracked down one of the girls. Not unexpectedly, she is completely estranged from her mother. He never could find the other one.

We did rent the apartment, which in retrospect seems either remarkable or stupid. In addition to abandoned children, the apartment was filled with fleas. Many bug bombs later, we made it habitable. Scott found a job in a popular bookstore, Smith and Hardwick, owned by Virginia and Anna Praytor, two spinster ladies, as unmarried women were then called. I found a job in a sandwich shop in the heart of downtown not far from major department stores like Loveman's and Pizitz. They were targeted a few years later in desegregation efforts. We both biked to our jobs.

At the sandwich shop I snuck food to eat when the manager wasn't looking. The rules were that employees were to pay almost full price for anything we ate. My salary was twenty-five dollars a week plus tips. Given that most customers were sales ladies from the department stores coming in for coffee or lunch break, tips were not a lucrative source of income. I remember all the work required to serve tables of four people each ordering coffee: handling so many dishes, offering refills, bringing cream, and keeping sugar bowls filled. Coffee was five cents per cup. The tips weren't much for all that effort.

Our lives developed a rhythm with us working, attending the Unitarian

Church, and trying to save money. Scott introduced me to an older couple he had befriended, Gene and Bettie Crutcher. Bettie was a nurse. They were an unusual-looking couple, especially at that time. Bettie towered over her husband by half a foot. Both were big-boned and strong looking and appeared honed by hard work.

Gene, at the post office at the time, was there when I met him. He leaned out of his window and strained to peer down my shirt before I realized what was happening, then making a sexist remark that caused me to be wary of him for the rest of his life. Bettie and Gene became instrumental in what came to be called the Movement, the civil rights struggle in Birmingham, through the 1962 opening of their liberal bookstore Gene Crutcher Books, set in Five Points. The Crutchers were friends and an important factor in our lives for many years, Gene's sexual improprieties or not. Many years later, most of their six children let it be known that he had sexually abused them, with Bettie's complicity.

Our parents, not surprisingly, continued to be disgruntled with our living arrangement. Scott's parents, hardly icons of morality, were nonetheless distressed that we presented a bad example for their four younger children. To us, that was laughable. My parents, though not approving, became accepting enough to come over for dinner once or twice. Money was a constant worry. We became concerned about the effect of income tax on our small salaries. With some investigation we realized our taxes would be lower if we were married. Another factor pushing us toward marriage was the arrival of the census taker. The awkwardness of giving information about ourselves as an unmarried couple was unpleasant. With further pressure from Scott's parents, we decided to get married before we left for Scott to matriculate at St. John's College, even though I knew I would have to drop out. That was my punishment for getting married. My mother no longer agreed to provide my support and tuition. For reasons unknown to me, my father could not or did not overrule this.

~

Scott and I cobbled together a small wedding. His parents had to sign a permission form since he was still a minor. We picked my birthday, September 17, for the occasion. I was turning nineteen. In those days, marriage license applications required being tested for "venereal diseases." We had our blood drawn somewhere downtown. Scott started feeling faint so he lay down in the back of our Volkswagen panel delivery truck while I drove us back to the Crutchers' house. My dear father had loaned us $900 to buy this used vehicle. He never would cash the checks we gave him to repay him. We were living in the bus after we had to move out of our sublet in August. The Crutchers let us park in front of their house and use their bathroom. We made a bed in the back of the bus with dog mattresses we found. We joked about those dog mattresses for years.

The Unitarian Church was the obvious place for our last-minute event. We had to arrange for using the church and meet with the minister, Rev. Alfred Hobart. Reverend Hobart was later to become a major figure in the Movement. Concerned about our very young ages, he counseled us accordingly. Finally, he said, "I guess you know what you are doing or you would not be here." He agreed to perform the ceremony that Saturday. Rosemary's parents could not accept having a wedding without a reception so they arranged to bring punch and other fixings to my parents' house after the ceremony. Rosemary, already married, could not be there as she lived in another state. I wore a slim dress that I made of voile. The color of butterscotch, it was overlaid with a leafy pattern of autumn colors. We got to the church early. Someone already there pointed out that we had no flowers. I dashed to the edge of the parking lot and picked some leafy branches for a few of the vases the church kept on hand.

Our four parents attended, along with the Downie family and a few of our friends. Reverend Hobart read words we had written influenced by Kahlil Gibran's poems. We were surely too unconventional to have the traditional script. We failed to save a copy of our vows and Reverend Hobart was never able to find his so we have no record of what we actually wrote. Having little money meant we had no rings to exchange. My mother had engraved wedding announcements made to send to her Christmas card list, which must have been painful for her given her disapproval of my early marriage.

There are four snapshots of the event. In one, at my parents' house, Scott and I are standing behind the cake and punch bowl. I am holding Rosemary's three-year-old sister in my arms, and the three youngest of Scott's siblings are standing in front of us. Scott looks handsome and older than he was with his glasses and nice suit. Another photo shows two of my closest friends, Jill and Valerie, sitting on our porch with Rosemary's grandmother. Even Jill and Valerie are long gone. Valerie committed suicide not long after. Jill, after divorcing her first husband, married James Howard. Seth told me that James, who was also married once before Jill, went on to have five more wives after Jill died from cancer in 1983.

Scott had to return to the bookstore that very afternoon to help with a special event. The store, a two-story jumble of thousands of books in seeming disarray, was a perfect setting. *To Kill a Mockingbird* had recently been released, and Harper Lee was making the rounds doing readings. Scott came back with the book signed by her. She wrote,

> To Mr. and Mrs. Scott Giddens:
> May I be one of the first
> to wish you all the happiness in the world.
> Harper Lee
> September 17, 1960

It still seems surprising to me that Scott had to pay for the book. It was already a fourth printing and was priced at $3.95. I couldn't attend the event as I needed to pack for our departure to Annapolis the next day. We spent our wedding night at my parents' house on Milner Crescent.

~

In Annapolis, with the help of a rental agency it took only a few days to find an affordable, furnished, one-room efficiency close to the campus. Married student housing did not exist. Scott started classes and his work-study requirement, which was in the college library basement repairing books, using skills he had previously acquired. He remembers his supervisor, Mrs. Fletcher, as being a kind woman. I must have taken my sewing machine with us because, with a Vogue pattern, I made a sophisticated dress to wear while looking for employment. I searched newspaper ads and ended up in Baltimore, learning what that phrase "pounding the pavement" meant.

Aiming for medically related work, I finally found a job in October as a laboratory technician at the Church Home and Hospital, a multistory brick building with a cupola on top. Affiliated with the Episcopal Church, it was a few blocks south of the Johns Hopkins Hospital and not at all the latter's caliber. However, it had its claims to fame: Union troops were treated there, and later Edgar Allan Poe met his death in 1849 within its walls. Each morning and evening I drove past blocks and blocks of run-down rowhouses and endless bars on corners during my commute. Even then, the hospital was suffering from the effects of suburban flight. The patients were overwhelmingly poor. I despised the commute but was excited to be doing something in medicine.

According to standards of the time, I had to wear a white uniform, white stockings, and white shoes because we went on the floors in the morning to draw blood from the patients who needed the tests we performed. I carried out all the blood sugars and BUNs (blood urea nitrogen, which evaluate kidney function) and performed bleeding and clotting times. A laboratory then was still a world of glass test tubes, pipettes, racks of glassware, Bunsen burners, and bottles of chemicals and reagents. All the tests were performed by hand. Glass syringes and reusable needles were used for blood drawing. The older technicians taught me the art of phlebotomy, first on an orange, and then on themselves. My first real patient for a blood draw caused terror when I entered her room. She must have weighed at least three hundred pounds. She announced she had just had her thirteenth child. I am fairly sure I had to get help.

Scott went to his classes, studied Greek, and worked on other assignments. In the evenings I worked on translating sections of the Bible and some writings of Aristotle from Greek for the challenge. We reveled in the intellectual atmosphere. We had time to walk around the quaint environs, browse the bookstores, and attend the college's Friday evening lectures in the arts and sciences, punctuated occasionally by concerts. One weekend we saw an old pump organ with a for sale sign in an automobile showroom. For some crazy reason, we felt we had to have it. We wrote a check for the full price, thirty-five dollars, on a piece of newspaper. At the time, one could write a check on anything. We were told the organ was from a theater back in the silent movie days. It still worked, and I played it occasionally. Now no longer working, it sits in a log cabin on the grounds of the house where Scott lives just outside of Chapel Hill. The log cabin is on old maps as having been a "colored school." Another time, we bought a beautiful old rolling pin from a table of ancient tools set up on the sidewalk near the Annapolis Harbor, with its yachts and glistening water.

Later that fall, things got complicated. A slightly bigger apartment became available upstairs. During the move, Scott got in a disagreement with the dean. The move was good as the new efficiency was a bit bigger, and had a window opening onto the roof. That allowed us to buy day-old bread and chicken backs, which we hung outside to keep frozen. By then, it had become clear that Scott's parents were never going to send us any money. Our pooled money from his work-study and my job was not enough to live on much less pay tuition. None of this seemed to affect our ardor, though perhaps it made us a bit careless. By mid-November, I was pregnant. We struggled along, me driving through occasional blizzards to get to work and Scott trudging through deep snow to classes. Winter was so cold. We went back to Birmingham for Christmas. Returning to our tiny apartment, we didn't last long. Not enough money and a baby on the way, Scott withdrew from St. John's, I resigned from my job, and we returned to Birmingham. It was January 1961.

Birmingham was feeling pressure from the increasing civil rights activities and retaliation from the Klan. Nineteen sixty had seen the Greensboro, North Carolina, sit-ins at the Woolworth's lunch counter. Martin Luther King Jr. had been sentenced to four months in prison for another sit-in. John F. Kennedy had been elected the thirty-fifth president, but not with our help. We were still too young to vote. And in Birmingham, Reverend Shuttlesworth was becoming more active. The bus boycotts had happened. The number of racially motivated unsolved bombings was increasing. We had no choice but to return to Birmingham anyway. We needed our friends and community.

# Part III

# "Bombingham"

## Chapter 10

# Back to Birmingham, 1961

Scott and I made the long trip back to Birmingham in our Volkswagen delivery truck with our two most precious possessions—the pump organ and the antique rolling pin, its patina reflecting the warmth of many pies—along with whatever else would fit. Route 11, no interstate then, wended its way through valleys between and aside various mountain chains including the Shenandoah and the Blue Ridge, on into Alabama between Sand Mountain and Lookout Mountain. The route followed a colonial trail that went from Canada to New Orleans. In Virginia it is known as the Lee Highway, named after Robert E. Lee, whom I have learned in research for this book was a very distant cousin.

The ride was long and pretty enough, but our worries about where we would stay and how we would support ourselves distracted us. I was two months pregnant, and we had no jobs and no family that would take us in. We would not have wanted to stay with either family anyway. My mother, already unhappy that I was married, was especially distressed that I was pregnant. If my father was dismayed, he kept it to himself. All this must have caused him deep anguish, which saddens me to think of. As for Scott's parents, the little attention they gave to his four younger siblings used up whatever parental interest they might have had toward their oldest son and me. They never did blossom into grandparenthood. They required our soon-to-be offspring to call them by their first names. As time went on, it was painfully obvious to our growing children that their paternal grandparents hardly knew their names or even their ages.

We were unprepared for what was happening racially in Birmingham and the state. We still did not know the depth or extent of the depravity perpetrated on African Americans, actions that reached back to before the city was founded. This would come later. Our immediate need was to look after ourselves and our coming child. Gertrude and Laird Downie, who had kindly taken me in several years earlier, came to our rescue again.

The Downies housed and fed us while we looked for an apartment to rent. Gertrude's joy in my being pregnant still resonates with me. Being barely nineteen, pregnant when no one else thought I should be, without any experience or support network, was unsettling. Her approval took away my apprehension. It was the greatest gift I could have then. She had four children, the last one born less than four years earlier; thus, her advice was timely and experienced. A practical woman, she prodded me to make some maternity clothes. She knew better than I how soon I would need some.

By April, we had found a place in a working-class neighborhood in Avondale, not far from our familiar Southside. A three-room cottage behind a larger house, it had a little peaked roof over the front door. To the left was a concrete-block garage where we stored what would not fit in the tiny dwelling. We also found jobs. Scott returned to Smith and Hardwick Bookstore, staying almost two years. He also did a stint at Alverson-Draughon Business College to learn bookkeeping and typing. He tells me he still uses these skills.

As we were trying to turn our place into a home, we were confronted by the ugly background of Alabama, burning buses and the furious mobs of segregationist white people. On Mother's Day, the Greyhound bus carrying the Freedom Riders, an integrated group testing the recent Supreme Court ruling prohibiting segregation of interstate buses, arrived in Anniston only to be attacked by a mob with chains, pipes, and bats. The bus was firebombed. The passengers were beaten by Klansmen as they barely escaped alive from the burning bus. A second bus arrived in Anniston an hour later. Its passengers were also severely beaten. Authorities stood by, allowing this to happen. The police were "home with their mothers."

Meanwhile, in Montgomery more than one thousand Black citizens and civil rights leaders gathered in the First Baptist Church to support the Freedom Riders. A mob of white people surrounded the church and vandalized cars. As they grew more violent, they attacked Black homes with guns and firebombs. The governor declared martial law and called in the National Guard. President Kennedy sent in US marshals. During this same time, the president expressed an interest in sending men to the moon. It was surreal.

~

I now know more of what was happening around this time. In the process of researching this period, I again consulted Diane McWhorter's 2001 book

*Carry Me Home.* The sheer quantity of details and complexities in this well-written and thorough book makes it hard for me to parse out subjects of interest. Persistence is required. Over my life in Birmingham so much went on to terrify African Americans, to expand Jim Crow, and to quash civil rights efforts that I never knew about. I discovered that McWhorter had reissued her book in paperback in 2012 with a new afterword. I ordered this edition to read the new material. In it, she added material about the complicity, contrivance, and cooperation between the *Birmingham News*—via then editor Vincent Townsend and his "boy," the reporter Tom Lankford—and the local government and the police force. Lankford was also public safety commissioner Bull Connor's "boy." Of course, Townsend and his shenanigans were only one small piece of a huge story.

McWhorter obtained the new information from talking with Tom Lankford, who, in the heyday of all the unrest, had been given free rein and expense money by Townsend and the paper's then owners, the Newhouse family. Part of Lankford's job involved acting as spy for and coconspirator with the Birmingham police in an effort to put a stop to the union and civil rights movements. In the end, it is hard to know what to think about Lankford as he also did things that helped the other side. McWhorter called him "mischievous."[1]

One of the previously unknown events Lankford shared with McWhorter was the shocking information that Vincent Townsend was privy to an order from Bull Connor to have Rev. Fred Shuttlesworth, a major Black civil rights leader, assassinated and did nothing to stop it. The assassination was planned around the time the Freedom Riders were coming through. By good luck, the assassin chickened out, and the killing did not take place. This was not the first attempt against Shuttlesworth. On Christmas 1956 the Klan exploded sixteen sticks of dynamite under his bedroom window. In 1957, when he and his wife tried to enroll their children in Phillips High School in downtown Birmingham, he was beaten with chains, bats, and brass knuckles, and his wife was stabbed. His story is long and inspiring.

Suddenly, as I was reading this new material, my body filled with cold chills. Certainly, the depraved activities were part of the reason. Mostly, it was that with this reading I connected the name Townsend with a childhood playmate, Mickey Townsend, who lived up the street from my house. Could it be? I Googled and was relieved when Vincent Townsend's obituary did not include a Mickey in the family. Then, another link showed up. There it was. Mickey was the complicit editor's son. I was stunned to think I had played with his son and was in Vincent Townsend's house from time to time. What might I have heard there? What was I exposed to? This small discovery, and the sudden chills, now cause me a bit of reflection. We humans must be as half-blind creatures stumbling through life having little knowledge of where we really are and with what and by whom we are touched. Those unbeckoned whispers are so faint. What if we knew more as we wound our way through our life's trajectory?

Even after I grew up, I had had no idea that the senior Townsend was, in McWhorter's words, "the phenomenon . . . and the city's powerbroker, in the sense that power was wielded actively rather than as resistance to change. He had unchallenged rule." The *News* also owned the most powerful television and radio outlets in the state.[2] My little friend Mickey became Vincent Townsend Jr. He joined the paper as his father's right-hand man straight out of college and soon took over as editor.

―

After we'd spent a few months living in our small house, some of our things were stolen from the garage, including the trunk filled with clothes I had made in high school. I remember one of my favorite dresses with a sad fondness, a silk print with a royal blue background topped with thickly scattered small green roses. I loved that dress with its bolero, formfitting bodice, and graceful full skirt and was proud of making it. The loss of it and my other high school clothes somehow marked the transition from childhood to adulthood. An associated event happened at the Unitarian Church when I volunteered to help with coffee after the services. I still remember the moment it hit me that I was being related to as an adult and not an adolescent. It seemed incongruous, but it got my attention and helped me behave accordingly.

The job I found was with an independent testing laboratory, Medical Laboratory Associates, in Five Points. My earnings, according to the Social Security personal earnings and benefit estimate statement for 1961, totaled $2,127 for the entire period I worked there. My experience in Baltimore had enabled me to find this lab position. In those days, training alone was enough to qualify a person for many aspects of laboratory work.

This was my first real job as an adult in Birmingham, so it was no surprise that it was the first place I experienced threats and discrimination because of racial issues. My responsibility was to perform the protein-bound iodine test, PBI for short, used then to assess thyroid function. Because solvents were used and contamination of the testing space by iodine from other sources was an issue, I was put in a small room designated just for PBIs. As it so often seemed in my life, I was once again isolated. Only during coffee breaks and lunch could I participate in the banter and gossip of the other technicians. I have no idea what I may have missed out on.

It was there that I learned to drink coffee. Good coffee has since become a lifelong pleasure. The laboratory had strictly set morning and afternoon fifteen-minute "coffee breaks." Augmenting the coffee were delicious pecan sticky buns made by a nearby bakery. It became my job to buy the buns daily from a shared fund. I liked being able to get outdoors and move my legs, a welcome break from sitting alone on a stool much of the time. The other technicians, not surprisingly, were all white and older than I. They were nice to me, especially as my pregnancy progressed, even giving me a baby shower.

~

My pregnancy was proceeding without problems. Somehow, Scott and I managed to pay for prenatal care from one of the top obstetric practices in Birmingham. The obstetrician must have had a low opinion of me as he counseled me to not drink vanilla flavoring or eat clay. Rampant prejudice against women, lower social classes, and gay people kept racism company. Social classes were sharply divided, and people dressed accordingly. Intellectualism was detested. The good ole boy system was in charge, white people only, of course. Newspapers could not be believed. Slowly, the ugliness of all this wrapped itself around us, ever tightening.

Childbirth protocol required women in labor to have their pubic hair shaved, and their arms and legs strapped down on the gurney upon entrance to and in the delivery room. A three-day stay after a normal birth was expected. Husbands were not allowed in the delivery room. Laboring women were generally given total anesthesia for the birth. There were few alternatives available, and one had to learn about them from word of mouth.

With Bettie Crutcher's help, I found a "natural childbirth" book and read it avidly. I did not want anesthesia. There was little I could do about the other restrictions. In the end, there was nothing I was able to do about any of them. Nitrous oxide was forced on me when my baby was starting to crown, and I had already been through the worst. As though having my arms and legs strapped down was not enough, my glasses had been removed. Being so nearsighted and not able to see added to the forced helplessness and to my fury. The indignity, the subjugation of women (they don't know what is good for themselves), and the assault on my personhood made me wild with rage.

My obstetrician yielded for my next two births. No strapping down, no anesthesia, and I kept my glasses on. Keeping my pubic hair was just too much for him, so I had to give in on that.

Not having health insurance, Scott and I did our due diligence. We visited St. Vincent's Hospital, a Catholic facility close to us. All his siblings had been born there. We were told to bring $200 (roughly $1,680 in 2019) for me to be admitted. It took several months for us to make that much. Unable to resist my increasingly smoldering defiance, I asked what would happen if I arrived in labor without the money. I was told I would not be admitted. Pressing further, I said, "So, I would have to deliver in the grass in front of the hospital?" "Yes," was the reply by the wimpled nun in her black habit.

In early August 1961, I went into labor. We arrived with our money. The birth went well, except for the forced anesthesia and no eyeglasses. Our beautiful eight-and-a-half-pound baby boy met the world in a bright delivery room without his father present. I was bursting with pride and love and wonder. In those days there was no rooming in. I longed to have Greg in my arms, but that was not allowed. At least they did bring him to me every four hours on the clock for breastfeeding as they did for the bottle-fed babies. The nurses found breastfeeding to be peculiar and a nuisance. There was no such thing as a lactation consultant, and no nurses offered help. Fortunately, Greg and I seemed to know what to do. On day two, I wandered down the hall and saw my name on the list for enemas if I had not had an "appropriate" bowel movement by the following day. Horrified, I managed to get myself discharged with baby in arms without further torment to my body.

Those first few weeks with our baby seemed to be infused with a diaphanous magnetism. I was drawn with such force to his sweet-smelling, wiggly body, all arms and legs, and his tiny mouth that drank from my breasts so eagerly. I filled with awe. Each day, Scott and I could see him getting stronger. Soon he was holding up his head. Such joy. I did have a moment of despair when I was still weak from childbirth. Scott was at work. A full half-gallon glass bottle of milk slipped from my hand as I removed it from the refrigerator to pour a drink. Splinters of glass exploded and floated in pools of milk as they sought corners and low places. I was barefooted. For a moment, I felt I could not cope. Now, when I picture that scene, it predicted the pooling and spreading of racism in Birmingham, the shards of glass, the burning crosses, the beatings, the dogs, the bombs; things that were coming that we did not yet know and that brought such deep anguish to the city and many of its people.

The few weeks after Greg was born that I was given off by Medical Laboratory Associates went by quickly. I barely had enough time to hire someone to look after our precious baby. In those days there were no daycare centers for babies, and no one in the family to care for him. It would not be the only time we, with what we now recognize as white privilege, hired Black women to look after our children. In the one photograph we have of Louise Haskins, she is holding Greg as she looks at the camera. Her face is young, her skin dark, her body slender. I cannot find her in my search of the 1940 census, the latest publicly available. She may not have lived in Birmingham at that time. It was hard to leave our baby, but we needed my income even though Louise's weekly salary of twenty-five dollars plus the required Social Security took half of it. It was very unusual to pay Social Security back then for a home worker. Back to work I went.

~

Medical Laboratory Associates was on the first floor of a brick building on the east side of Twentieth Street South. The main part was a large room filled with lab apparatuses and machines tended by bustling, white-coated technicians. Among its curiosities were the containers of frogs atop a counter backstop. In those days the African clawed frog, *Xenopus laevis*, was used for pregnancy tests. The first morning urine of the woman (hopeful or despairing as each case may have been) was injected under the skin of the frog. If she was pregnant, five to twelve hours later the frog would lay eggs. My little room was off one end of the main lab. I could hear the technicians' excitement when a frog responded to the hormones in the gravid urine so I would come out to join in peering at the poor frog and its doomed eggs. Kitty-corner from my room was the supervisor's room. I was soon to be called in on two occasions for questions and discipline.

I wore my waist-length hair alternating between braided down my back and wrapped up in a bun. I did not use makeup. Hence, my daily appearance vacillated between the beatnik look and the missionary look. In the missionary mode, I must have looked quite severe. It was for the long braid that I was first called in. The supervisor did not want a beatnik look in his laboratory and suggested I cut my hair. After that, I kept it in a bun. I was used to getting called out about my appearance from my high school days. One example was being made fun of for wearing sandals during my senior year.

Not long after the hair reprimand, I was called to the supervisor's office again. Standing with my hands behind my back, my hair tucked in the bun,

I waited with fear and dread. This time, he told me I would be fired if I did not conform to the procedure for calling patients for their blood draw. As it had been at Church Home and Hospital, technicians were required to draw blood on the patients needing tests in their domain. A large waiting room at the entrance of the laboratory was for white patients, and a small, windowless room nearby was for "colored" patients. We were to address the white patients by their titles: Mr., Mrs., or Miss. The Black patients were to be called by their first name. I had refused to do this from the beginning, calling all patients by their title of respect. Obviously, at some point the supervisor found out. Since I refused to change the way I addressed people, I started looking for another job. My time at Medical Laboratory Associates lasted from February 1961 to March 1962.

Throughout my life, people have asked me what compelled me into civil rights actions and protests. I have always answered the same way. My father taught me to be kind and fair and stand in truth. I rebelled from the status quo starting with the Dick and Jane readers in the first grade. Why? Their message was not fair. Over and over, I experienced things happening that were not fair or right, to me and to others. I rebelled against the system that took my glasses away, making me unable to see as I labored to bear my first child. That did not happen again. I could not be comfortable addressing the Black patients whose blood I was to draw by their first names. Refusing to do that became my first bold act truly outside my own needs. In between all this was the influence of Frederick and Anny Kraus, which began when I was in high school, and later that of the Unitarian Church. The Krauses had escaped the Nazis. They knew persecution. They fought for the tyrannized and oppressed. They acted on their beliefs and what was right. How could I not?

—

I had heard that the Medical Center, part of what was now called the University of Alabama at Birmingham (UAB), was starting to integrate certain areas. I must have learned this at the Unitarian Church. Many church members were liberals associated with the growing health-care complex, the medical and dental schools, and Hillman Hospital, where I used to hang out with the cadavers. Dr. Joseph Volker had come to Birmingham in 1948 from Tufts College to head the new dental program at UAB.[3] He also started the Unitarian Church in Birmingham and had been Scott's Sunday school teacher. In 1962, he became director of the entire Medical Center and was in charge of desegregating the medical school. Having ties with Dr. Volker was another lifesaver.

As McWhorter put it in *Carry Me Home*, "a new kind of carpetbagger—with moral rather than financial motives—descended on Birmingham . . . , a true rival to steel."[4] The Medical Center, where Scott and I were both soon to work, had grown to occupy over sixty blocks in downtown Birmingham. Dr. Volker had been able to convince nonindustry leaders that the Medical Center would be good for Birmingham. Little did we know how much our work, friendships, and even the place where we lived would be entwined with these "carpetbaggers" and affected by the increasing blossoming of the Civil Rights Movement. By now, Birmingham was beginning to be known as "Bombingham." Between 1947 and 1958 there had been at least twenty-three bombings against African Americans. For reasons unknown, the years from 1959 through 1961 were quiet. That respite was soon to end.

*Chapter 11*

# Birmingham, 1962

The year 1962 began with yet greater draconian actions to avoid integration of public spaces. Birmingham's parks were closed. Bull Connor ordered the golf course holes and swimming pools to be filled with concrete. Bombings of Birmingham's African American homes, churches, and other buildings resumed after a gap of three and a half years. Scott and I finally had more access to news. Thus, the ever-increasing racial violence was no longer mostly invisible, at least, to the degree events were being reported. The next year, after another move took us partway up Red Mountain, we could even hear the Klan's dynamite detonating. The sound of the explosions traveled down the valley and echoed off the mountainside. The first four bombings this year occurred the same month we moved to a slightly bigger place.

We were beginning a pattern of looking for better living quarters every time we began to make a little more money. This next move took us back to Southside, so we were, once again, close to downtown, work, friends, the Unitarian Church, and such family as we had. Our new place was just two blocks from Lakeview Elementary School of my childhood. I must have walked by this new dwelling thousands of times. Scott and I were fortunate that Louise Haskins continued with us, eventually taking care of Greg in three different places during our peripatetic Birmingham years.

We were now in a remodeled brick carriage house. Set farther back from the street than the other houses, with a row of windows across it, a brick patio, and a huge tree in front, it had a certain charm. Though small, it seemed bigger because it had two stories. It provided our growing baby boy with a little yard for play. We even got a cat to round out our family. As soon as Greg learned to walk, he loved to chase the poor thing, which soon learned to hide under the beds. All was well until large quantities of roaches started falling from the ceiling onto our dinner plates. So, nine months later, we found ourselves moving again. My parents were pleased that we were close by. Papa always found something to help with when he visited. Mother, true to herself, often found things to criticize. We did not let her know that we were about to become more involved in civil rights activities. What she imagined was bad enough from her point of view. There must have been some nice moments with her. Sadly, if there were, I do not remember.

I continued working at Medical Laboratory Associates while looking for laboratory work at UAB. Our Unitarian contacts there were invaluable. I was thrilled to soon be offered a position as a medical technician in the Department of Endocrinology and Metabolism. Scott continued at Smith and Hardwick Bookstore for another year.

On March 12, 1962, just after we moved again, Scott and I were featured along with an older couple on the front page of the society section of the *Birmingham News*. It was accompanied by a large picture of us. We viewed it with some hilarity, being that we were obviously not society people. Later, we were to learn about the newspaper's dark side. The article stated, "The bride may take the groom, but not always his last name. Ever since Mr. Caveman dragged the little woman off (kicking and screaming) to his cavern for keeps, families have been known by their common nomenclature." Now, as I record this quote, the language and social construct it represents seem appalling. At least some things have changed for the better.

The article went on, "'It seemed only right,' says a local laboratory technician of her desire to hold onto her last name. 'That was MY name,' she adds. So, she, Marcia Herman, and her hubby, Scott Giddens, became Mr. and Mrs. Herman-Giddens." I wonder whether being featured in the paper (comedic or not) made me feel a little more important and grown-up as I entered the medical research world at the tender age of twenty.

This same month, I began my new position as part of a sophisticated research laboratory in academic medicine. The main laboratory room comprised black counters covered with complex analytic machinery. A technician stationed in a smaller adjacent room soon became a friend. Marjorie Walz, less than two years older than I, already had an undergraduate degree in chemistry. She was tall, slender with hay-colored hair, and single, a state she remained in for the rest of her life. Another technician in the main lab was an African American woman named Etherine Pearson. She too was slender as most people were in those days and had a sweet nature, working with quiet competence and never making ripples.

Etherine's presence revealed an obscuring fabric that had surrounded my childhood in a way I had not fully perceived: I had grown up in a scabrous apartheid world. I felt the fabric as a thick opaque cloud now moving away from a glowing moon it had darkened. The exposed piercing of moonlight began to reveal what had been hidden from me, from all of us designated as "white." I had never had the experience of having an African American colleague or friend. I had never even been in the same room with an African American who was not a servant or a janitor. I had had no way to know their joys and loves and sorrows, their skills and talents, their sufferings and longings and anger, and all that makes us human, except for the glimpse into their terrible poverty I had when I was ten years old and, again, when I worked at the bookstore downtown.

In reflecting on this now, I grieve for the Black people in the cruel Jim Crow system I grew up in and their vicious suffering, still with us. My inchoate thoughts swirl. What did the white adults who went before me take from me, rob from all of us, with their hate-filled apartheid system? Culture, knowledge, experience, friendships, broadened boundaries. Freedom. No one, no matter their skin color, was free in Birmingham's violently enforced apartheid. The scope of what was stolen from the Black people had definition, and I did not know it. I had not known it. And I was stolen from as well, as were we all.

Neither Marjorie nor I ever knew Etherine's background for medical laboratory work. I am sure we were not comfortable asking. That I was working alongside a Black technician was extraordinary. In 1962 it was still against the law in Birmingham for Black and white people to be in the same room unless the former were staff waiting on the white people. The university, with its research and grants overlapping with the local Veterans Administration, a federal agency, must have been protected from local ordinances and state law.

The Klan, in cahoots with the police, continued exploding dynamite at homes and churches and burning crosses. African Americans had to cope with terrorism while carrying out their daily lives, as they had for centuries. White people helping with civil rights were now afraid, too. All of us, every day. I wonder now whether I thought about how much courage it must have taken Etherine just to come to work every day. She, Marjorie, and I became friends, but our friendship could never go outside the lab. Etherine was a member of the Sixteenth Street Baptist Church, which would be bombed in 1963, a church now known around the world for what hate and bigotry can do. She must have known I was a Unitarian. She asked Marjorie once whether she would like to visit her church. Marjorie recently told me she would have but for fear of violence against Etherine and herself, as well as retribution against the church.

My supervisor, Ludwig Kornel, MD, was a refugee from Poland. I would like to think that may have given him some understanding of what ethnic and racial hate can do. His supervisor, S. Richardson Hill Jr., MD, became the dean of the medical school in 1962. I knew, though Dr. Hill didn't, that he and I were distant cousins through our Marshall-Richardson-Lanier-Hill line in Anson County, North Carolina. At the same time, Dr. Volker, Scott's former Sunday school teacher, was promoted to second vice president for health affairs.

I was part of a research team of technicians and physicians. We accompanied the physicians on their daily rounds, visiting patients in their rooms and hearing specifics of their cases. We all attended conferences. Under the direction of the endocrinologists, we technicians carried out experimental protocols using electrophoresis and chromatography that sought effective and economical ways to extract corticosteroids and other hormones involved in human well-being or disease. I learned to perform various endocrine analyses including 17-ketosteroids, 17-hydroxycorticosteroids, pregnanediols, and triols, and buccal smears for chromosome analysis.

Eventually, my defiant side reared again when I was assigned a certain procedure with laboratory mice. I no longer remember the details, but I know I thought it involved too much cruelty, so I refused to carry it out. My refusal was evidently tolerated as I kept my job. There I was, with my still not fully appreciated white privilege (unnamed at the time), willing to risk refusal of an assignment. It is doubtful that Etherine would have felt able to take such a chance. I did not escape unscathed, however. My punishment came from the mice themselves, ungrateful creatures they turned out to be. I contracted a rodent-borne virus, lymphocytic choriomeningitis, and spent days in bed in a darkened room barely able to move, with my head hurting more than I knew was possible. Painkillers didn't touch it except when they put me to sleep. Finally, I recovered and went back to work. In the beginning, all the research activities and patient rounds and conferences were heady stuff, but after a while it became more routine.

—

Easter came that year on April 22. I had been working in my new position for a month or so. Scott continued at Smith and Hardwick Bookstore. We fell into new routines, leaving our now nine-month-old boy with Louise every day during the week. Sundays we took him to church. I officially became a member of the church that Sunday, along with a man named Larry Fiquette. I only know this because before Larry died, a decade ago, he found the Easter bulletin and mailed it to me with a tender note. He and his wife, Sidney, were to become some of our closest friends after I joined the church. Larry was a newspaper man.

The church was barely over Red Mountain, on a sharply curved road leading to the Birmingham Zoo. It was modern, a clean-lined A-frame with a wing on the left. The many windows filled the sanctuary with light, but we were all aware that so much glass increased the danger should a bombing occur. The church gave Scott and me a goal and a home. Later, it provided a refuge as Birmingham became ever uglier and more dangerous.

Defying Birmingham's segregation laws, the minister, Reverend Hobart, was inviting pulpit exchanges among himself and Black ministers by holding forums for African Americans and hosting integrated performances of dance and music. He oversaw classes to prepare white and African American children for integration of the public schools. Two of the children killed the next year in the infamous church bombing were participating.

Not surprisingly, bomb threats to the church became more frequent. This year, 1962, the FBI, though far from trustworthy, did help save the church from being destroyed by the Eastview Klan Klavern 13, the same one responsible for the violence against the Freedom Riders. Klavern 13 was a particularly vicious group, too violent even for some of the other Klan groups.

During all this, two white women and one Black woman who had somehow become friends decided to start a women's club so Black and white women could get to know each other. This was courageous because of the law forbidding the two races to be in the same room socially. In addition, there was the increasing overlay of violence. Starting with ten women, the club eventually grew to twenty-four. I was honored to be asked to join. Most of the white women were from the Unitarian Church, with a smattering of Jewish women from nearby temples. The Black women were from the leading echelons of the African American community. The founders named the group the Friendship and Action Committee.

We met once a month in various members' homes and occasionally in a more public building, usually a church. Some meetings were at night and some in the daytime. The latter were especially risky since it would be easier to see us going into the meeting place. Scott and I even had a gathering in our home after we bought a house in 1963. By the time the Friendship and Action Committee began, I was becoming good friends with two church women who had also joined the committee, Sidney Fiquette and Helen Knox, both with small children. I probably missed quite a few meetings until March 1963, when I started working part-time.

Typical of me, my memories are often of odd little things rather than major events. Until my second child was born, in early 1964, I would take toddler Greg with me to the daytime meetings. I probably stopped attending after Marcus was born because it would have been too difficult and disruptive to take two small children and we could not afford babysitters. The African American women lived in the "Dynamite Hill" section of Birmingham, once a white neighborhood, now a target of the Klan and their dynamite. It was about five miles from where we lived to the northwest. Most of the homes were brick ranches with long sloping lawns. One exception, a large Queen Anne with the appealing address of 1 North Eleventh Court, was the home of Sallye and Frank Davis, prominent leaders in the African American community.

Sallye and Frank are remembered not only for their good works but for their oldest child, Angela Davis, a scholar and controversial civil rights activist who has grown to international fame. Her siblings, two brothers and a sister, also went on to notoriety. As our meetings continued, Sallye and some of the other Black women noticed that Greg was somewhat lacking in clothes. They began to give me hand-me-downs that their own children had outgrown. That was probably a first gifting in that direction in Birmingham. The clothes were a big help given our limited budget. Thrift shops were not common in those days. Both of us received rather meager salaries.

Another memory from the Davis home was a splendid New Year's party. I wore my nicest outfit and dress shoes. Soon it was time to help ourselves to a buffet-style spread on their large dining room table. It was classic fare for the South: black-eyed peas, collard greens, cornbread, and more. I was fond of all that. We stood around eating and chatting. My efforts to appear suave and sophisticated slipped away like butter in a hot skillet when my fork clunked against something hard in the greens. A tooth peeked through the collards! It looked like a human tooth. With my racing heart, and trying to cover my alarm, I soon realized it was from a pork jowl. Obviously, pork jowls were a new experience for me. To this day, I serve black-eyed peas and greens on New Year's Day and always remember the Davises.

There were some class issues in our group, described by Ed Harris in his 2004 book *Miracle in Birmingham*. His wife, Sandra, another friend, also belonged to the committee. Ed wrote, "The white women were mainly young middle class Unitarian and Jewish, the black women were certainly part of the 'upper class' of Birmingham, 'well to do.' The black women were older, in general, and might shop in Atlanta or New York for their clothes. They were stylishly dressed for the meetings. They were somewhat more formal. The white women did not 'dress up' for the daytime meetings. One of the black women was quoted as saying after some discussions at a meeting, 'I wanted to integrate, but I didn't want to integrate down.'"[1]

No one had air-conditioning in the early 1960s. Nonetheless, another steamy, mildewy summer did not slow down our friends Gene and Bettie Crutcher as they began working toward opening their bookstore at 2008 Magnolia Avenue in Five Points. The address no longer exists. Back then, Five Points had a large working fountain where its five streets converged, which gave the area a stately look. The flat-roofed one-story building was smallish but had a handy basement. The lecherous and leering Gene, also known for his photography and love of books, was sixteen years older than I and eighteen years older than Scott, as was Bettie. That gave them some parental authority. They had helped us many times over the years so Scott willingly pitched in to help them set up the bookstore.

Opening that August, Gene Crutcher Books was in business from 1962 to 1973. The bookstore was a haven for hippies, intellectuals, political activists, and misfits, and a welcome respite for anyone with liberal tendencies. Gene liked all sorts of people. He also liked to argue with customers regardless of their beliefs. He provided books and printed material not found anywhere else in Alabama, even if he did not agree with the contents. He had *The Communist Manifesto* and the communist *Daily Worker*, as well as the journal of the white supremacist National States' Rights Party. Gene and Bettie also offered books and magazines they did like that lacked a source in Alabama or were hard to find. These included the *New York Times*, the *Village Voice*, *Southern Exposure*, Beat poetry, and more. The store was compared to City Lights in San Francisco, especially after Allen Ginsberg visited and left graffiti on the store's bathroom wall. To this day my sons remember seeing issues of *Playboy* scattered on the dusty floor. They were too young for titillation, but they noticed that these were not your ordinary fare.

Scott and I hung out there a lot when we had time. By then, I knew not to lean over the counter when Gene was on the other side. With the store's mise-en-scène seasoned with more than a bit of danger, a lot of intellectualism, interesting people, publications not otherwise seen, and Gene puckering his lips and pontificating, it was the place to be if you were one of "those." Gene specialized in paperbacks, which were the up-and-coming thing, albeit disapproved of by the owners of the bookstore where Scott worked. In the early days of the store, Scott assisted Bettie with bookkeeping and, when he had time, pitched in as a salesclerk and all-around helper, all volunteer, of course.

Gene and Bettie had six children: Annie, Beth, Kay, Bill, David, and Sara. So, when threats started coming into the bookstore and their home, the plume of hate and efforts to intimidate had a large human target. Their children were older than ours, with the youngest almost overlapping. Annie recently shared some of her fifty-five-year-old memories of the harassment. She said,

> We did have threats, many and varied ones. There was a cross burned on the roof of the bookstore. Once I was in a car with several kids from [the Unitarian youth group], including a Black friend, when we were pulled over by a vigilante with a gun in Mountain Brook. We were harassed and terrorized, but otherwise escaped unharmed. We had phone calls, ugly mean ones. I answered one that was threatening me specifically in reaction to a [William] Saroyan play I was in out at Tuxedo Junction, *Hello Out There!*, under the direction of Lenny Ravich.[2] The other teenager was a young Black guy and there was a photo in the *Birmingham News*, so . . .

By the time the bookstore closed, Scott and I had been gone from Birmingham a half dozen years. Times were changing, and more choices in publication were available. Bettie had learned that she had the autosomal dominant form of polycystic kidney disease, and it was beginning to affect her. Children have a fifty-fifty chance of inheriting the disease from a parent. Tragically, these odds more than played out, with four of their six children later manifesting the disease. Kay, Bill, and Sara have been gone a long time now. David had a kidney transplant and is still living in the family home on Sixteenth Avenue South. So, with Bettie increasingly unable to help with bookkeeping and times changing in Birmingham, the store shut down.

The summer heat was abating as it usually did by my September 17 birthday. I turned twenty-one and went to register to vote as soon as I could. At that time, everyone had to go to the courthouse downtown to register. The strategy was to make registering hard for everyone, especially African Americans. This was still three years before the 1965 Voting Rights Act. We all knew by then that few Black people were registered because Jim Crow laws and practices were highly effective in ensuring that few could pass the complicated procedures. Still, I hadn't expected trouble for myself. After all, I was white and middle class.

My plain clothes, long hair, and lack of makeup must have betrayed me again. I don't remember much about the day except standing in a long line and finally reaching a clerk in the correct window. The clerk looked me over and, after a frown flashed on his face, asked me to recite from memory a certain paragraph from the Constitution. Of course, I could not, so I had no choice but to leave without being registered. The day I was successful has faded from memory. I must have dressed up, styled my hair, and worn makeup. I have never been good at memorizing. For several years at least, Scott and I each paid the annual $1.50 poll tax so we could vote. In today's money, that was about $25 for the two of us, certainly a hardship for low-income people. The poll tax was finally outlawed for state elections by the Supreme Court in 1966.

My voter registration experience was a mild form of what routinely happened to African Americans. Randall Jimerson, the oldest son of Rev. Norman C. Jimerson, recounted an example in his book *Shattered Glass in Birmingham.* Reverend Jimerson and his wife had been recruited from Virginia so Jim could serve on the Alabama Council on Human Relations.[3] Randall recorded his mother's experience of registering to vote in 1962. After standing in a line of Black and white people and finally reaching the clerk, Mrs. Jimerson, who was white, was told she had to take a citizenship test. The clerk then asked her the name of the first president of the United States. She provided it and was then declared as registered. As she left, she overheard a Black person being asked to explain an obscure passage in the Constitution, then being told she failed and, therefore, could not register.[4]

Eleven days after my birthday, Martin Luther King Jr. came to Birmingham to speak at a Southern Christian Leadership Conference convention. The event seemed unusually quiet, possibly in part because public interest and reporters were focused on Oxford, Mississippi. On the fourth day, as King was speaking to the three-hundred-person audience, a large white man went onstage from the audience and began to punch King in the mouth. King turned the other cheek and called for the man—a storm trooper in the American Nazi Party—not to be attacked. The kind treatment did not sway the man. He punched King again four months later in Chicago. Meanwhile, at the University of Mississippi, a deadly riot was occurring when the first Black student enrolled. More than three thousand federal soldiers were brought in to restore order.

~

Sit-ins (actual or attempted) by African Americans had been going on in Birmingham at least since the 1960 Greensboro, North Carolina, sit-in at the Woolworth's lunch counter. The volatile situation in Birmingham called for an additional strategy. Somehow, it was decided to try having groups of white people order meals at restaurants and counters with the plan of their remaining quietly eating after African Americans showed up asking for service. Scott's mother and I volunteered for this at Loveman's, a major department store in downtown Birmingham.

Loveman's had a mezzanine where I had often had refreshments when shopping as a teenager. My familiarity made it a suitable place for Barbara and me for our sit-in. We dressed as though for church, normal at that time for shopping. Sitting at a table where we could look over the railing and see the first floor of the store, we ordered our food and drink and began slowly eating. As time went on, our anxiety built when no African Americans showed up. We waited, and waited more, peeking at our watches, glancing over the railing, and trying to look like ordinary shoppers. Worried that the demonstrators might have met with some obstacle, even violence, we waited still longer.

Finally, to buy more time, with us having long finished our food, Barbara pulled out a cigarette for herself and offered me one. That was the only smoke of my life. The most I had ever done was a puff or two as an experiment. I copied the way Barbara held her cigarette and tapped her ashes. Of course, I was not inhaling. The experience was one of the longest and tensest waits of my life. Finally, we left. We never did know what happened. Scott had a similar experience at a lunch counter in Five Points. He waited and waited; the Black demonstrators never arrived. With all the moles and spies that Bull Connor and the FBI had, they may have learned about these whites-first sit-ins and somehow done something to stop them. We will never know.

—

By October, driven out by the roaches in our rented carriage house, we had found another place. This time, it was a third-floor apartment on South Twenty-Sixth Street just across from the Highland Avenue park where I played so often as a child. Scott and I always moved our belongings ourselves in our Volkswagen panel delivery truck, sometimes with the help of a friend or two. It wasn't too hard as we had very little furniture. We used orange crates for side tables, toy boxes, and anything else they would substitute for. Crates were wooden in those days, and one could simply collect them from a grocery store. Our books were on board-and-concrete-block shelves. Even from the beginning, we had many books. The rest of our furniture was a motley assortment of other people's discards.

The apartment was one bedroom with a small screened porch, along with a windowless interior room for Greg's bedroom; $37.50 a month. We put Greg's favorite plaything, a plastic horse on springs attached to a metal frame, in his little room along with his crib. I still remember our chasing him, and him squealing with delight, as he sped there to run away on his hobbyhorse.

Later that month, in late October, one of those events that sears itself in memory occurred. The Cuban Missile Crisis had begun on October 15, when US intelligence discovered signs of medium-range missiles being built by the Russians on sites in Cuba. Of course, Scott and I didn't know about negotiations taking place or exactly what was going on. We did know that on into the negotiations, President Kennedy demanded that the missiles and sites be dismantled, thus bringing tension between Russia and the United States to new heights.

As these tense days played out, Scott and I went to work as usual. My colleague and friend Marjorie kept a radio in her workroom. One late October afternoon, I was standing at the counter in the laboratory working on a test when she came in to tell Etherine and me that Chairman Khrushchev had sent a letter to Kennedy even further escalating the crisis. We were on the brink of a nuclear war. There was real fear that the red button could be pushed. Terror spiked through me, and I could hardly breathe. All I wanted was to be with my precious baby if we were about to be blown up. Helpless and panicked, I was miles from Greg and Scott. As one might expect, Scott and I each left work as soon as we could. We had not even been able to talk to each other. With great relief, we arrived home and huddled down, the three of us together, tensely listening to the news.

The crisis eased, and life went on. Christmas came. We could not afford a Christmas tree, so I found a nicely shaped tree branch that we set up in a flowerpot, hanging homemade decorations on it. My parents came for dinner.

~

I don't remember what we gave Greg that year.

## Chapter 12

# Birmingham Explodes, 1963

Though starting to wane, steel was still king in Birmingham. The night view of the blast furnaces from Red Mountain presaged the year of 1963 in Birmingham. With each pouring of molten iron from the steel mills' giant containers the city seemed to transmogrify into the bowels of hell. Hell's firmament glowed a fiery orange. Streaks of sparks belched across the sky so bright it hurt to look at them, and anyone watching knew the heat was deadly. Indeed, the city was a special inferno that year.

The year began with a new governor and a January 18 reminder in the *Birmingham News* that "Birmingham voters whose poll taxes are unpaid will not be able to cast ballots in the March 5 Mayor-Council election." Four days before the reminder, George Wallace was sworn in as the new governor. In his inaugural address, he pledged, "segregation now, segregation tomorrow, segregation forever." After all, his campaign speechwriter was Asa Carter, known for starting a local Ku Klux Klan Klavern.[1]

That same month Papa invited me to go with him to Miami. He had a horse race betting scheme, his only vice. Even that wasn't a true vice since he was careful, always betting small amounts yet making enough money to cover his trips. Working on his scheme and gardening were the only activities he undertook for his own pleasure. In Miami, the sunny days and familiar territory of my childhood were a happy respite from my normal obligations, dreary cold, and racial tensions.

Back home, Scott and I were in the thick of things. Between our friends and contacts at the church and our time at the Crutchers' bookstore, we knew much more about what was going on. Members of the church were being threatened, along with the church itself. Scott and I figured we were too young and of too little influence to be targets. Late winter saw the formation of efforts to oust Bull Connor from power if for no other reason than economics and the parks, which many wanted open. An election, lawsuits, and strategies ensued. Finally, the Alabama Supreme Court ruled that the new mayor-council system was valid. Bull Connor was legally out but refused to step down.

Sometime in early March, Scott and I moved yet again. We had found a much larger apartment for little more rent than we had been paying. This one was the entire top floor of a large Craftsman-style 1920s house on the upper end of the street I had grown up on. There were plenty of windows, and Greg had a proper bedroom. Our landlady was an elderly woman who never bothered us except for one incident, the morning she left the house with the stove still lit. A burning stench drove me to invade her living quarters, whereupon I found a fire around the stove and an astonishing level of dishevelment despite her cultured appearance as a fine southern lady. I summoned the fire department; the house was saved, and so were we, thankfully.

With us barely settled in, Scott was offered a position as a computer operator for the Department of Epidemiology in the School of Dentistry for $400 a month, almost twice as much as I was making. Dr. Volker recommended Scott to John Dunbar, a young star in dental research who needed help with the school's new computer. With Joe Volker the head of the Medical Center, his recommendation had clout.

These were the early days of computers, and no one at the dental school knew anything about them. Scott's supervisor was another epidemiologist. Scott was given a stack of manuals and a small windowless room in which to study them. He told me, "By the time I got out of the room in a few months, I knew more about that computer than anyone in the state." I have no doubt this was true. Scott had a natural affinity for computers and programming and was later recruited by a textile company and from there to Duke University Medical Center, where he worked for many years, teaching and excelling in his field. As for epidemiologists, Scott and I became good friends with another one from UAB. He was responsible for teaching me to like alcohol: he arrived after the birth of my second child with a bottle of sherry, announcing, "Every nursing mother needs a sip of sherry in the evening."

The computer Scott shared a room with was an IBM 1620. Fifty-seven years later, Scott tells it this way: "The 1620 was about the size of a small sports car. I was the 'computer operator' and then, 'programmer.' It used punch cards and was solid-state (no vacuum tubes) which was leading technology at the time. The second computer, in 1964, was the IBM 7040, which was much more powerful and took up most of a big room. The floor in the room was raised so the cabling could be underneath. The 7040 had large tape drives and all-in-all looked very impressive. It was the Medical Center research computer. By then, I was the 'systems programmer,' and, finally, 'systems analyst' for that computer." With all his computer contact, we had piles and piles of discarded punch cards around the house. They lasted us for years, providing a steady source for grocery lists, jogging records, general notes, children's games, and all sorts of other things.

———

Just before moving to Milner Crescent, we let Louise Haskins go. She had become preoccupied and was not caring for Greg properly. The final incident was when Greg developed a fever of 105° and she did not notify us. We never did learn what difficulties she might have had. It was late winter and bitter cold ensued, resulting in hospitals so full our pediatrician could not get a bed despite Greg's severe pneumonia. It was a frightening time. We took him to the doctor every day, heavily bundled against the single-digit weather. Every day he was thinner and weaker. Finally, he turned the corner, but his appetite did not recover for years. Throughout his childhood he was rail thin. I no longer remember who looked after him when I returned to work, but eventually my friend Sidney began to do so.

Scott and I carried on with our work and family life as civil rights groups increased the intensity of efforts to desegregate Birmingham. The Southern Christian Leadership Conference invited Dr. Martin Luther King Jr. and Rev. Ralph Abernathy to come to Birmingham to assist. The fiery and fearless local Rev. Fred Shuttlesworth began leading thousands of African Americans in marches and boycotts. This movement became known as the Birmingham Campaign. Bull Connor, still in power despite being voted out, refused to issue parade permits. On April 16, King, Abernathy, and Shuttlesworth were jailed. The world knows the eloquent and moving letter King wrote from his cell, "Letter from Birmingham Jail."

The local newspapers persisted in keeping demonstration reporting on back pages if they had it at all; for the rest of the country it was front-page news. Hundreds of reporters and TV cameras were in town. For thirty-eight days, Birmingham had two city governments. Finally, the legally elected government filed suit to force Connor out. He managed to remain by posting an appeal. During this time, civil rights leaders, especially James Bevel, were training schoolchildren for a "children's crusade." On May 2, the children left the Sixteenth Street Baptist Church in groups to walk to the mayor's office to speak with him about the city's segregation. The first day of this protest, hundreds of children were arrested. On the second day Bull Connor, illegally holding the title commissioner of public safety, gave an order that quickly flew around the world, soon followed by descriptions of the events punctuated with horrific photographs: children were sprayed with hard streams of water from fire hoses, hit with batons, and threatened with snarling German shepherd police dogs. Hundreds more were added to those already in jail. The final number of adults and children arrested was more than 1,500. With the jails full, children were put in wire cages at the state fairgrounds.

Many years later, I found out that the father of another childhood friend also worked for the *Birmingham News*. He was present during these horrific events, standing with a colleague near Bull Connor. They both said to Connor, "This is not right." A high school classmate recently told me that our mutual friend's father returned to his family that evening crying. Later, he wrote an editorial about the wrongness and horror of the event. His reward was Connor bugging a business he owned and telling him, "I am going to run you out of town." Fortunately, Connor did not succeed. My friend died in 2019. I never had a chance to speak with her about this.

When Scott and I learned about the fire hoses and dogs we and our tight-knit community filled with horror and shame, fear, and impuissant rage. We had no way of knowing the extent to which negotiations were being conducted or long-range plans made for the protests. Later we learned that the federal government had already been involved with these events, along with scores of white and Black leaders.

A few days later, on the evening of May 5, Joan Baez, Pete Seeger, and others arrived to perform at Miles, a Black college in west Birmingham. Scott and I rode there with our dear friends the Krauses. We were part of the crowd of hundreds of Black people and a scattering of white folks. Earlier this day, later called "Miracle Sunday," African Americans by the thousands had protested downtown. Bull Conner ordered the firemen to use their hoses. This time the firemen refused.

Back at Miles, Scott and I flowed into the auditorium, carried along with the crowd. I remember thinking about what could happen if the auditorium were bombed. After some songs, Joan Baez asked the audience to stand, hold hands, and join her in singing "We Shall Overcome." With tears streaming down my face and holding tight to the older Black woman to my right, I felt so filled with hope and sorrow I thought I would burst.

In our sadness and despair, perhaps even that night, Scott and I shared a tenderness with each other that biology, always in the background, stirred. I soon found a new life was conceived. Nine months later, almost to the day, I gave birth to my second child. Early in this pregnancy, I began to not feel well. I sent my supervisors a memo suggested by my doctor: "I am requesting permission to begin working part-time, . . . beginning June 1, 1963 . . . ill health and a run-down condition. My family situation also requires that I spend more time at home." Two days later I received a very cordial note from Dr. Hill granting my request.

Lest there be an impression that Scott and I were always in bliss, we did have our share of marital fights. He had a shorter temper than mine, and I had qualities that were aggravating. This year, we had one of our worst fights. The reason has long fled. I grabbed Greg and a few clothes, and headed south out of Birmingham. Greg and I stayed the night in some drab motel. I was mortified in the morning to find, after an all-night rain, the highway had flooded. I had to call in to work since I couldn't get back to town. By evening we were home.

On into the summer, one morning when I went into Greg's room to get him out of his crib, he was awake and standing, holding on to the railing as usual. His left leg was swollen to twice its usual size. His room was at the back of the house and three stories high, so I assumed a bee or wasp had entered an open window and stung him. He seemed unaffected other than the swelling. I searched for a sting site, but all I could find were two small puncture marks about a quarter of an inch apart on the outside of his left foot. It must have been a weekend because Scott and I took him to the home of a friend whose father was a physician. There were no urgent care centers then. He took one look at Greg and said, "He has been bitten by a pygmy rattlesnake." It turned out he was familiar with these, having suffered a few himself while gardening. We had been in the backyard the evening before. Since Greg was handling the bite well, he said there was nothing we needed to do. Those fang marks were Greg's "show and tell" at nursery school and kindergarten for several years. How sad he was when they finally faded away.

We had another puncture that summer, this time in our finances and what tranquility we had. We had saved enough money to purchase a Volkswagen bus: brand new, a shiny Wedgwood blue. Our old panel delivery truck had finally broken down beyond repair. Scott and I proudly drove it home and parked it in front of our place. We went upstairs to our apartment. Moments later we heard a terrible crash. Rushing to a front window, we saw a sedan had crashed into the back of our new vehicle, and a shaken teenage boy was climbing out of his car. The police declared our bus totaled since the engine had been demolished. We did not have insurance yet. The boy was fifteen and had stolen his mother's car keys for a joyride. His family had no insurance either and did not offer us any compensation, so, with the help of an attorney from church, we sued. We had our day in court but never got much from those people. It was quite a setback. We bought another bus right away using the totaled one as a trade in. Scott worked many overtime hours to make the money for it.

—

Now that I was working part-time, I spent more time with two other mothers from our church, Sidney and Helen. Sidney's husband, Larry Fiquette, was a newspaperman, then at the *Birmingham News*. Helen's, Victor Knox, was an insurance salesman. Sidney died in 1993, and Helen in 2017. We stayed lifelong friends. By the time of Sidney's death, I had already experienced the loss of a close high school friend, Jill Moerlins, in 1983 from cancer.

Sidney had two little boys, and Helen three. As the months passed, our children became friends, paralleling the development of our friendships. Sidney and Larry lived in a bungalow on a street that frequently showed up in my Birmingham years, Twenty-Eighth Street, which led down to my elementary school. Since Sidney and I lived close by, we visited often. Helen and Victor lived in a modern house in a thicket of trees eight miles over the mountain so it was harder to see Helen. Both were "housewives," as women who stayed home with their children were called. Sidney had worked as an art teacher but lost her job after attempting to attend the segregated Alabama state fair in a mixed group.[2]

Sidney was the proverbial artist: always noticing things, waving her hands, trying unusual and interesting activities, and disliking structure. She was also more than slightly wild, I was to learn later. Her slenderness matched an angular face and strong chin that punctuated her personality. The Fiquettes left Birmingham in 1965. Helen and her family remained for the time being. In early 1966, soon after Scott and I left Birmingham, Sidney wrote to me, "Maybe we can take a wild trip next summer. I still haven't heard from Helen, really don't know what the devil with her." Another time, she wrote, "I want to break from solid to atmospheric—push through until at least I know that I'm going there. It means tossing out all manner of Teutonic traditions—one red, yellow, blue and going to magenta, cyan, and yellow." *There* was where she always wanted to be and couldn't quite define. When I think about her life cut short from leukemia diagnosed only two weeks before her death, I still ache with sadness.

Helen, with her olive skin, certain facial features, and straight dark hair, looked part American Indian but was not. Her shortness, tinged with a hint of plumpness, gave her a certain sturdiness. Helen was zealous and thoughtful, prone to analyzing with an intense earnestness anything and everything that crossed her path. She stayed on her issues like a hummingbird partaking of nectar among red flowers. Her husband at the time, with his conservative-sounding insurance career, could not have been too staid being married to Helen. Like Sidney, Helen turned out to have a wild side, which exploded into civil rights activities progressing into the hippie movement. It was not good for her children. Whether this emerging wildness affected her marriage, I don't know. It is possible that her husband's affair with a prominent dancer came earlier. I was prissy compared to them. We called ourselves the Three Musketeers. I was the youngest, Sidney six years older, and Helen eleven. Both being Birmingham natives, they could never be called outside agitators.

We three spent countless hours together sipping bad coffee and discussing how to raise our children as we watched them play. Dr. Spock's *Baby and Child Care* was our authority. Our inclinations were to follow the patterns our children naturally expressed rather than impose strict schedules. We were gentle, did not believe in hitting, and loved them with an inexorable passion. Spock, known for his phrase "you know more than you think you do," supported our approach.

We gave our children opportunities for art, games, block-building, observation, dance and music, and anything else we could think of to enrich their development. We gave them space to play freely outside. We took them to see things. It was a precious time and circumstance that is, no doubt, less common today. Meeting as often as we could, we savored the richness of being together and guiding our children. We wanted them to grow up to be fair and kind, as well as to be smart.

―

The frightening backdrop of our outside world pushed Scott and me together to protect and provide a normal life for our son. The demonstrations went on week after week, with the African Americans continuing to promote nonviolence and the Klan continuing to bomb. From March 1 until September 12, eight bombings occurred. All were directed against African American places, except for Loveman's Department Store. A church was destroyed, and the Black-owned Gaston Motel, a site of civil rights activities, was damaged. The rest of the targets were homes. The home of Martin Luther King Jr.'s brother, A. D. King, was destroyed. The home of Arthur Shores, a prominent African American attorney, was targeted twice. One bombing killed the family dog; the second, while repairs from the first bombing were underway, injured his wife.

One of the bombings I particularly remember hearing was in August. I was home, several months pregnant, resting. I heard an explosion. I sat in anguish, finally gathering myself together to turn on the radio.

Nationwide momentum was building for a huge March on Washington in August. Helen, Sidney, and I wanted to go, but we knew we couldn't. A quarter of a million people, mostly African American, marched and heard Martin Luther King Jr.'s historic speech, "I Have a Dream." The backlash from the Ku Klux Klan intensified.

Two weeks later, on Sunday morning, September 15, nineteen sticks of dynamite placed by four Ku Klux Klan members exploded at the Black Sixteenth Street Baptist Church in downtown Birmingham. The world soon knew that four young girls dressed in their Sunday best to sing in the choir had been killed: Addie Mae Collins, Denise McNair, Cynthia Wesley, and Carole Robertson. Others were injured. Two young Black boys, Johnny Robinson and Virgil Ware, were shot dead later that day because of their skin color, Johnny by a police officer, Virgil by a white teenager. The officer was never charged; the teenager and his friend, both Eagle Scouts, were minimally sentenced. Justice was eventually served for the three still-living bombers—Bobby Frank Cherry, Thomas Blanton, and Robert Chambliss, all Ku Klux Klan members—after thirty-nine years of intense efforts by the police and FBI. Herman Cash died in 1994 without being charged.

Birmingham was an inferno. We, along with the world, raged and grieved. Some of our church elders went to visit the families who lost their daughters. I no longer remember how Scott and I coped in the days following. I managed to go to work the next day. Etherine Pearson, my coworker at the lab, was a member of the church. She had arrived ten minutes before the dynamite exploded. What courage and fear propelled her to come to work the next day? Marjorie and I soon realized Etherine was still in shock. We must have encouraged her to go home. We weren't doing so well ourselves.

The funerals for the two dead boys took place quietly. Carole Robertson's family chose to have hers separately. It took place on that Tuesday, the day I turned twenty-two. I was four months pregnant. The remaining three girls had their joint funeral Wednesday at the Sixth Avenue Baptist Church, also a site of civil rights activities. On the corner of Sixth Avenue South and Sixteenth Street, it was familiar. The church was an impressive three-story building of the yellow brick so often seen in Birmingham. A large stained-glass window was on one side. The main entrance was reached by climbing a dozen wide steps, which I soon did.

I asked Scott's mother to go with me. We became part of the mass of people trying to park and get into the church. Tense and frightened, we watched white men in suits, clearly FBI agents, circling parked cars and noting license plate numbers, my mother-in-law's included. No one we knew, Black or white, viewed the FBI as friends. Arriving early, we found seats in the sanctuary, becoming part of the handful of white people in attendance. Martin Luther King Jr. gave the eulogy. In my trembling fear and fog of grief, I remember none of the eulogy. I know that thousands of people attended, most having to stand outside.

Appallingly, that was not the last bombing of the year. Ten days later two more occurred, exploding shrapnel over wide areas. Remarkably, no one was hurt. In October, brave Black employees at the university's Medical and Dental Basic Science Building formally requested that the cafeteria be desegregated. It was finally accomplished in April 1965.

—

Life does go on. October was always a welcome month in Birmingham. Heat and humidity dissipated with the changing axis of the earth, and it was easier to feel some vigor in everyday activities. One day, taking a walk with Greg up the nearby street crawling along the side of Red Mountain, I saw a house with a sign, "For Sale by Owner." Scott and I made the daring decision to buy it, undaunted as we were by our lack of money or its being fifty-six steps up to the front door from the street, and twenty-five down from the alley to the back door. The alley, narrowly carved in the side of the mountain, offered the only parking spot. The steep bank between the alley and the house was terraced into two levels supported by five-foot-high stone walls. The front of the house, steeply sloping to the street, was terraced as well.

The owners, the Zumbados, fortunately for us, were generous people. They wanted $12,000 for the house with a $500 down payment. All we could spare was $250. They lent us the other $250, and we took over their mortgage. We paid off the $250 loan as we could. The wood frame house was a bungalow adapted to the challenging setting. It had a full basement, a main floor with three bedrooms, one bath, and a partially finished second floor. Just below the front, somehow a concrete-floored patio had been built, providing the only level area on the entire lot for children to play and adults to enjoy being outside. Three crepe myrtle trees were evenly spaced in holes left in the concrete. It was edged with sturdy iron rails. On a rare clear day, the view below of the city creeping and winding across the valley was spectacular. In the winter, when pollution was bad, I used to marvel that the world appeared to end just past the patio. One could not even see the houses on the other side of the street.

So, in early November, at ages twenty and barely twenty-two, we had moved yet again to our first purchased house, 1429 Twenty-Eighth Street South. Before we had finished placing our meager furniture, setting up our kitchen, and hanging pictures, another date most people will never forget shattered us, this time throwing a dark and frightening veil over the nation. I was on my way from work to pick up Greg. I had the radio on and heard the horrific news that President Kennedy had been assassinated in Dallas earlier that day. Having just arrived at Sidney's, I sat in the car listening in disbelief, finally staggering into the house weeping. The next several days are a blur. Scott and I were paralyzed, sickened, and frightened. Our poor little son, just a few months over two, had to fend for himself while we listened to accounts of the shooting and then the funeral over and over. Later, we learned that many of Birmingham's white adults and schoolchildren had cheered and laughed when they heard the news.

We did not know it then, but moving into this house was our last move before we left Birmingham. I don't know what we did that Christmas. I was very pregnant, and times were sobering.

—

Fear hung over us and the city like the smog from the steel mills.

*Chapter 13*

# Birmingham, Tuskegee Institute, and Project CAUSE, 1964

The glistening snow that ushered in January must have had a chastening effect on the city. The year turned out to be almost bomb-free and relatively quiet. In Birmingham, snow only stayed white the first day. After that it was gray and then black. Although it sounds silly now, I didn't know that fallen snow stayed white until we moved to a less polluted city in 1966. In these winter afternoons when I was home from work, Greg and I would make a snowman or two, and I would watch him trying to clear some of our steps with a spade just his size. My size was ever bigger. My belly had gotten so large and uncomfortable my last month of pregnancy that when I walked, I had to hold my hands under my abdomen to support the little creature that was soon to be Marcus. Otherwise, it was too uncomfortable. Given that, I was anxious for the birth to arrive.

That finally happened in early February. Scott and I did not need to arrive at St. Vincent's Hospital with $200. We had health insurance from our jobs. This time, with the same obstetrician, I was able to keep my glasses on, not be strapped down, and have no anesthesia. Marcus was almost nine pounds two ounces. Thankfully, the birth went smoothly . . . until . . . he got stuck. I pushed and pushed and was almost in despair and full-blown panic when he finally moved into the world.

With two children to care for and no financially reasonable childcare options, I left my job at the Medical Center. Except for summer activities in 1964 and 1965, I did not work for pay again until October 1968, when I took a position in the Department of Botany at the University of North Carolina at Chapel Hill.

Greg adapted to being a big brother without any seeming problems.

*Figure 13.* Me with baby Marcus and big brother Greg, hanging diapers on the neighbors' clotheslines, late 1964.

Fortunately, he was out of diapers. Our new house had a washing machine in the basement but no dryer. The neighbor on our left had clotheslines and was kind enough to let us use them. One of my favorite photographs is of me hanging up a long row of diapers on a bright late autumn day, with Marcus holding on to my leg and Greg watching. I am wearing an apron, my hair is parted in the middle and pulled back, the diapers are flapping in the breeze. I am glorying in the marvel of my precious children.

Scott had been recruited away from UAB to work for Ingalls Iron Works by the former manager of the Medical Center's computer center. This man's wife, a dental student, got involved with the replacement manager. Things were messy, and Scott was glad to leave the intrigue. That he received a larger salary didn't hurt. This Ingalls building was not too far from our home. From the fancy oak-paneled entrance and upper management suites Scott had seen, he was looking forward to a nicer office. No such luck. His assigned space was dark and windowless.

There, Scott wrote complex payroll programs in assembler language, a type of programming that is close to machine language in form and content. It is useful for control of programming down to byte and bit levels. This was needed because Ingalls's crews worked for varying amounts of times in many states, creating many income tax deductions to consider. Scott's skills increased greatly with this experience.

Ingalls lost Scott within eight months or so as he was recruited back to the Medical Center. This time he was in the Department of Cardiology, with another increase in pay. He was now a senior systems analyst working on the department's new, real-time DEC PDP-7 data acquisition computer. We were finally beginning to relax some about money.

Springtime arrived in a haze of pink and white exploding bloom. Dogwoods, azaleas, and other botanicals flowered in perfusion. April was the peak month. It also brought the only bombing that year. "Dynamite Hill" was again targeted. A Mr. Crowell was bombed for socializing with white people. The damage must have been severe as the Maulls' house across the street was also damaged. A third neighbor was also targeted, but that dynamite was found before it exploded.

The Maulls' two sons were knocked out of bed, and the windows of their daughter Carolyn's bedroom were blown out. Carolyn attended the Sixteenth Street Baptist Church and had been good friends with the four girls killed in the 1963 bombing. Fourteen years old, she was acting as church secretary that Sunday, so she heard the phone warning from the Klan. The bomb went off before she could tell anyone. She had marched in the Children's Crusade. Now Carolyn McKinstry, she saw her life shaped by these events. She wrote in her memoir *While the World Watched*, "We were terrorized our whole existence growing up. Bombing was so routine back then."[1] I have recently had the pleasure of getting to know her and to share some of our experiences.

I was finding out fast how hard it was to be a full-time mother with small children. Helen and Sidney would have been further along in this realization since I had just stopped working. By now, we three had a total of seven children. Our devotion to them did not keep us from wanting a life in an intellectual environment where we could participate in meaningful adult activities. We were *The Feminine Mystique*. Betty Friedan's book had been published the year before. We each read it voraciously. It seemed to be about us. We were supposed to be fulfilled by our marriages, housework, and children. We embodied the definition of the American woman, the "housewife-mother." We spent hours intensely discussing the ideas in the book as we looked after our children, mending clothing as we talked.

As I read this book and Simone de Beauvoir's *The Second Sex*, my high school love affair with Sigmund Freud crashed. Feminism was being given form in us as we three read and talked and formed our analyses of the so-called feminine nature. Friedan stated that the experts had declared, "'Normal' femininity is achieved, however, only insofar as the woman finally renounces all active goals of her own, all her own 'originality,' to identify and fulfill herself through the activities and goals of her husband, or son."[2] Women who wanted careers outside their home were accused of "penis envy." We knew we were not the "normal" feminine ideal.

Now, it is recognized that Betty Friedan was disingenuous in describing herself as a housewife. She had a career outside the home as well as household and childcare help. Her world was her own social class and race. I am not sure we recognized the book's shortcomings at the time. We did recognize that there were parallels between women's struggles and African Americans' struggles, and that no matter how hard our situation seemed, it was nothing compared to Black people's, especially Black women's. Our privilege washed around us, coating us like vermeil. Sometimes, we discussed our efforts to comprehend the double burden of being a woman and African American and knew that we really could not.

So, we kept washing and changing diapers, cleaning house, buying groceries, washing clothes, exposing our children to learning opportunities, serving dinner to our husbands, enjoying sex, and having more babies. Even as we did, we kept struggling to understand ourselves, our roles in society, our roles as mothers, and our growing dissatisfaction while wondering what to do about it. With a whispered fury we barely recognized, we fussed, finagled, fought, and fumed, and in the end, we kept on forming our dreams.

—

The Cold War was still in its heyday. As children, we had practiced crouching under desks and gathering in school basements in the event of a nuclear bomb. We heard rumors about backyard bomb shelters. In Washington, the House Committee on Un-American Activities had stoked the fires of communism's threat. Fear of communists followed me into adulthood as it became intertwined with right-wing organizations. My mother ate from and fed those fires. She belonged to the John Birch Society and admired aspects of the Klan. As part of her paranoia, she worried that Scott had become Fidel Castro's right-hand man, his operative within the United States.

Castro had become prime minister of the Republic of Cuba in 1959. Because of the tight budget Scott and I had, during winters Scott wore his father's heavy World War II coat. Between that and his beard, his appearance resembled Castro's, and my mother was convinced of their association. She could not be dissuaded. While it made us alternately sad and amused, it was flattering. Such a young man had such a responsible position on top of fatherhood and working full-time! We were subjected to many lectures about our evil ways. Occasionally, we lost it and argued with her. Sometimes, a book would go missing and turn up later with her annotations in the margins. She had found wording that proved to her that we were, indeed, communists. For the record, we were not.

Meanwhile, Lyndon B. Johnson, president after Kennedy's assassination, was exploring his own role on the world stage. He presented his Great Society vision in his State of the Union address on January 4. When I was listening to it, I had no idea I would be caught up in two of the programs he presented: the War on Poverty and Project CAUSE (Counselor Advisor University Summer Education Program). The War on Poverty was probably the most ambitious social program since those to ameliorate the Great Depression.[3]

The federal government didn't waste any time. Soon I saw an ad in the *Birmingham News* about a free program to train people to counsel "disadvantaged youth." Persons interested in taking a qualifying examination were to register at the Birmingham Employment Security Office. I called Sidney and Helen and read them the ad. None of us had any special job training, and this might be our way into the bigger world.

At the specified time we showed up, sat in the large room with many desks and other people, and took the examination. We had no expectations, but it was something for us in our angst to try. A month later, all three of us received a letter saying we were being offered a place in the program Project CAUSE, to be held at Tuskegee Institute, Tuskegee, Alabama, from July 20 to September 11. Helen, Sidney, and I had made the three top scores in the Birmingham office. What had started as a joke and been seemingly unthinkable, happened. With our husbands' support and approval, we prepared to attend Tuskegee Institute as part of a group that included the first white people to attend the school.

Our scramble began. We had to find childcare, which meant hiring African American women. We got in supplies and food and did the best we could to prepare for an eight-week absence. Scott remembers that the helper we hired, Annie Harrington, sometimes stayed overnight when he had late work or meetings. Like me, Helen also had a baby, though hers was a little older than mine and already weaned. Marcus was five and a half months old when we three mothers left for Tuskegee. I was breastfeeding and was hopeful that I could use a breast pump between weekend visits with Scott and the children to keep up my milk supply. The so-called pump was a crude plastic device that looked like a toy bugle. The flare end was placed over the outer part of the breast, and a suction bulb squeezed, which hurt. It hardly worked.

All my life after that summer, looking back on leaving my beautiful, chubby, breastfed baby, I have felt shame and guilt. That I was breastfeeding certainly added an extra dimension to leaving Marcus. From this distance, I can see that my situation demonstrated the bind women were in as described by Betty Friedan. Men, obviously, couldn't have the breastfeeding issue. It is doubtful, even so, that they would have felt tormented with guilt by going off for eight weeks to a training program.

Feminist issues or not, it is remarkable that all three of our husbands were so supportive and willing to take on the childcare and household management in addition to their jobs. We were deeply grateful, and I still feel that. On the weekends, Scott would drive down with Greg and Marcus. The visits were bittersweet, seeing my children and then having them leave so soon. My milk soon dried up so Marcus was weaned. My craving and pleasure in the intellectual stimulation and experiences I was having compensated somewhat for my guilt and sadness. This is painful to admit, but there it is: the waters of dilemma mothers of young children swam in, given the middle-class social mores at the time.

———

There is a backstory that requires explanation before I can write about my experience at Tuskegee Institute. I knew I would need to conduct a good bit of research to fill out my Project CAUSE experience after the passing of fifty-five years. My records comprised a few cards with schedules and grades, my final community report and case study, some glossy photographs, and a yellowing booklet about us trainees, titled, "As They See Themselves and Wish to Be Seen." We had been asked to write a statement for it that included the place where we were born and educated, marital status, occupation, travels, religious affiliation, and more. We dutifully complied in a variety of styles.

This program was the first antipoverty government effort to train Black and white civilians together. Everything that had happened led me to believe that Project CAUSE was, to use the colloquial expression, a big deal. Plus, the year 1964 was in the throes of a dying Jim Crow with a potential for increased violence.

The program began with our getting fingerprinted, taking the Minnesota Multiphasic Personality Inventory, and taking an IQ test. This multisite national program would seem to necessitate an archive given the importance of this social experiment and training and the number of documents generated. A photographer took many photographs. I assumed it would be easy to find all I needed online to fill in the blanks in my memory.

I was wrong. My initial searches yielded nothing. Two requests to Tuskegee University Archives yielded a single paragraph. This absence of information led to my filing a Freedom of Information Act request the summer of 2018 with the US Department of Labor, the federal department that had directed Project CAUSE. It reported that it had nothing. I requested a second look. Still nothing.

Finally, I filed a request with the FBI. Because the FBI had been involved with racial issues in Alabama for years and because data like fingerprints and personality tests would likely be of interest to it, surely it would have records. On September 6, 2018, I received a letter, "'Project CAUSE,' FOIPA Request No.: 141-5388-000." Nothing.

Eventually, I found a handful of obscure references for the 1964 Project CAUSE in government manuals. Twenty thousand had applied, and two thousand had been selected. About seventeen hundred counselor aides entered the field. Other mentions included that a training had been conducted in the "skid row" section of Denver and that programs were held in forty-seven locations around the country.[4] There were only a couple of photographs, and the Tuskegee program was not mentioned.

For more information, I tried contacting fellow trainees using the booklet "As They See Themselves" for names. I finally reached someone. In his mideighties, the trainee remembered only that he had attended. I gave up.

Scott, knowing I couldn't find much, did more, discovering the only significant find: Tulane University listed "Final report of Project CAUSE, July 20–September 11, 1964," as a holding at its Amistad Research Center.

The author was Bonita H. Valien, the publisher "Tuskegee, Ala.: College of Education, Tuskegee Institute, 1964."

—

So, off I went to New Orleans in March 2019. It was only the second time I had been to New Orleans since Hurricane Katrina. My arrival just a few days after Mardi Gras was greeted by thousands of Mardi Gras beads decorating everything from gutters to fences and trees. I took the St. Charles trolley to Tulane, enjoying the clickety-clack of the wheels and the late spring flowers, their colors vying for attention with the Mardi Gras beads. The air was sparkling, and the emerging grasses were emerald green. It was a beautiful day in that remarkable city. The Amistad Research Center was on the edge of the campus. The main room, with its wood trim and book-lined walls, was the classic research space. The staff knew I was coming and pulled the files quickly. The only substantive document was the succinct report by Bonita Valien, the project director. A mimeographed booklet, it was only fifty pages. While thrilled to access it, I was disappointed there were no photographs or ancillary records. I read through it and, with permission, took photographs of pages that were informative.

In the process of my explaining my interest in this report, the head archivist asked about my papers and photographs. We worked out a plan that as soon as I finished with my materials, I would donate them to Tulane's Project CAUSE files. It delights me that the few items I've held on to for fifty-five years will be valued and cared for in this wonderful center.

The Valien report stated she and her staff were responsible for developing the programs for all two thousand trainees around the country. Tuskegee Institute was the central site. Curious about Bonita Valien, I learned she was an African American sociologist of importance. She studied under W. E. B. Du Bois and earned a PhD in sociology at the University of Wisconsin. Joining the faculty at Fisk University, she soon married Preston Valien, an associate of Dr. Charles S. Johnson, Fisk University's first president. She died in 2011 after a productive life.[5] If there are more records on Project CAUSE anywhere, it appears that they have either evanesced into the Alabama blue sky or been hidden. If the latter sounds paranoid, read on.

—

It is early November 2019 as I write. This ancillary research has continued longer than I expected. Chilly weather is settling itself, brought in by western breezes. I watch the swaying tree branches outside my office windows. With each tiny zephyr, swirls of yellow and brown leaves sashay to the ground. I cannot get my mind off knowing that my first great-grandchild was born three days ago across the world and in the opposite hemisphere in another breeze. His father, my oldest grandson, told me about holding his newborn in an open window the day before. A warm spring breeze tickled his cheek, and he startled a bit. The very first the little one felt, gentle yet stimulating. So different from the breezes developing from my research and the feelings they engender in me. My mind jumps from this precious new life to what an unexpected thread of research related to Project CAUSE is suggesting. It is a cold draft. I will likely never know the truth.

Now that I was about to donate my Project CAUSE materials, I again contacted the archivist at the Amistad Research Center. She mentioned the close association between the Valiens and the sociologist Dr. Johnson when they were at Fisk. I looked him up and learned that his first major study on the South was on venereal disease in Macon County. This was the first chill. I had not anticipated all these years later that I would find myself caught in the corroding chain of the study of syphilitic citizens in Macon County. The study rattled through there for decades: through the community, Tuskegee Institute, the hospital, and the then all-Black Veterans Administration Hospital. Finally, like a coiling, spitting viper, it encircled the now infamous syphilis study, biting its subjects and their families all the way to the final survivor, a control subject, who died in 2004. The last widow receiving settlement benefits died in January 2009. Was Project CAUSE touched by this viperous chain?

Since 1972, when the *Washington Star* broke the silence, I had been aware of the shocking "Tuskegee Study of Untreated Syphilis in the Negro Male." That year, a whistleblower, Peter Buxtun, as a last attempt to direct attention to what he had learned years before, sent his concerns to a reporter at that newspaper.[6] After decades of proclaiming the study as valid and worth any harm caused to the subjects, the Centers for Disease Control and the US Public Health Service were finally going to be investigated for their forty-plus-year "experiment." The study of the sequelae of late-stage disease followed approximately four hundred untreated and uninformed syphilitic Black men in Macon County and two hundred disease-free men as the control group. Ill effects were documented in life and even death, for those who were autopsied. In 1981, *Bad Blood: The Tuskegee Syphilis Experiment—A Tragedy of Race and Medicine* by James H. Jones was published.[7] I read it at the time, not thinking of any possible connection with my days at Tuskegee.

Another chill. Syphilis control was a serious issue before the discovery of penicillin. Earlier treatment employed mercury and arsenic and was difficult, dangerous, and often ineffective. Around 1930, Macon County became a demonstration and study site partly supported by the Rosenwald Fund.[8] The fund's medical director wanted a sociological analysis of the African Americans participating in the project. He hired Dr. Charles Johnson, a close colleague of Dr. Bonita Valien and her husband.[9]

Consider this: thirty-plus years later, Dr. Valien was in the county directing Project CAUSE. Questions arose in my mind. Did she know about the Tuskegee Syphilis Experiment? How much? If she knew, how were our program and fieldwork affected by what she knew? One thing was clear. We trainees knew nothing about the syphilis study going on while we were there. We were in the midst of it and were even sent to the participating hospital if we got sick. The shuffling, dark-skinned men we may have seen making their way down the hall could have been experimental subjects, suffering from untreated late syphilis.

In pursuit of my questions, I queried the archivists at the center. The reply came:

> The Preston & Bonita Valien Project CAUSE papers contains a 10-page list of patients in the Tuskegee Syphilis Experiment.[10]
>
> The correspondence in the folder pertains to a conference being held at Tuskegee Institute in 1952. . . . Preston Valien received an invitation to attend and contribute "sociological facts on the patients." Also included in the folder is a conference program (16 pages). Stanley H. Schuman, who led the clinical investigation, is listed as in attendance, but I don't see his name attached to any sessions.

Looking Dr. Schuman up, I learned that he authored or coauthored several papers in the 1950s on the Tuskegee Syphilis Experiment.[11] After penicillin was available, untreated infected men were still being sent home to their wives and children.

My backstory was darkened: an invisible sepulchral density lay over my time at Tuskegee Institute. Bonita H. Valien had to have known that the experiment on untreated syphilitic men was going on at the same time she was directing Project CAUSE, and furthermore, she had access to the list of the subjects if not her own list.

The list would have likely been relevant to planning our field trips.

~

Tuskegee, in Macon County, was a good three-hour drive from Birmingham in 1964. July 20, the day Helen, Sidney, and I were to be there, was a Saturday, which made it convenient for Scott to drive me down as we only had one car. Neither one of us had ever seen the institute campus before. We piled the children and luggage in the car and headed off. By the time we got there, the mountains had disappeared into a plain, and we rolled into the Black Belt, so known for its rich dark soil as well as the large Black population who still cropped cotton mostly as sharecroppers. Cotton plants in midgrowth dominated the landscape.

The campus comprised a number of large red-brick buildings, mostly Greek Revival style, with some influenced by the Federal style. There were a few older buildings clearly stemming from the Victorian period. Macon County, then, as now, had a population of around twenty thousand to twenty-five thousand people, approximately 80–85 percent African American. As of 2018, 30 percent were designated as poverty level or below. In 1964, it was likely a good bit higher. There we were at a town named after an American Indian tribe from East Central Alabama, the long-gone Muscogee, the land now echoing the residue of slavery and plantations.

We found my dorm, and I steeled myself to leave my children, especially my nursing baby. I cannot imagine Scott's thoughts as he drove home now fully responsible for his work, the house, and two little ones for eight weeks. I don't remember whether I had a roommate. My room was plain, even stark. The only thing I know I did in that room was sitting from time to time on the edge of my single bed trying to pump milk from my breasts. That pale blue sweet milk went untasted until finally there was none. The sorrow still lies deep in my bones.

During orientation we found that our fellow students comprised eleven women in addition to Sidney, Helen, and me, and twenty-nine men. A handful were African Americans. We ranged in age from twenty-one to fifty-one, with me the second youngest. Several men had served in the Korean War. Except for two women, the rest of us were from southern states. The faculty divided us into two groups for field studies and group discussions. Helen and I ended up together. I don't think any of us realized we would be taking personality and intelligence tests and required to keep daily diaries that would be scrutinized. Or how packed the schedule would be.

Classroom days usually went from eight o'clock in the morning to eight in the evening. Lectures were intermingled with hours of discussion. We had an hour off for lunch and an hour and a half for dinner and free time. Evenings comprised an hour of "daily reconnaissance." Sometimes, instead, we had longer lectures with an "integrated seminar" in the late afternoon, an hour and a half off for dinner, then two hours of small-group discussions followed by the daily reconnaissance. When that was the schedule, it made for a thirteen-hour day. We had classes in sociology, economics, counseling, and employment service techniques, plus fieldwork.

The sudden influx of white students onto the Black campus was clearly taken into consideration by the planners. According to Dr. Valien's report, this "added an element of the program which had to be considered and understood." She continued, "A few of the white trainees said they did not know . . . Tuskegee was a predominantly Negro institution. Those who had this knowledge are not necessarily exempt from fears and concerns as to what to expect. Local pressures sometimes reinforced these fears as is illustrated by a response by then Gov. Faubus to an article about applicants to Project CAUSE which appeared on the front page of an Arkansas newspaper." Faubus advised the applicants accepted to Black institutions to decline their appointments. He also let it be known that he might reevaluate state participation in the program.

Certainly, the avoidance of possible racial issues, whether from minor clashes or actual violence, was paramount. I doubt I will ever know whether FBI agents or US marshals were a presence during the program. Surely, there must have been a fear of possible Klan activities. Dr. Valien's report wrote, "Use of individual diaries is an effective means for daily evaluation of the progress of the student and to assess problems and student attitudes about the program and Project CAUSE." The diaries were used as an integral part of the program. These diaries, "which were confidential and read only by the director [Dr. Valien] permitted the trainee to ventilate their feelings in a constructive manner. . . . It is a strong belief that these daily accounts provided a source of therapy for the trainees, kept staff on their toes, and gave advanced warning of serious problems which might have been allowed to develop."

An episode did occur with Sidney that demonstrated the degree of the fear and tension that was only natural in 1964, with young white people on the campus for the first time, especially when something touched on sexual matters. The dean called Sidney into his office. He chastised her for not wearing a slip, making clear that it was a provocative act and that he expected her to wear a slip from that point on. A common manner of dressing for women during hot, humid summer days prior to air-conditioning was to wear loose dresses. Without a slip, with a low-angled sun, the silhouette of one's legs could easily be seen. Most women knew this and did wear slips. Not rebel Sidney, but acquiesce she did. What the dean and faculty evidently did not find out was that there were some sexual encounters between the white trainees and Black trainees or students, slips or no slips.

My mother must have caused a minor incident, as well, but I never heard exactly what happened. One day at lunch, I had just gone through the food line. Looking for a seat, I heard her voice behind me. It is a wonder I did not faint. There she was standing in the dining hall in the midst of staring students. She had to see for herself what was going on and what a Black college looked like. After she found the campus, how she ever located me I can only imagine as she would have had to ask any number of people. She had a knack for barging into places without proper protocol, so, I assume, a bit of a ruckus had to have ensued.

———

We trainees soon fell into classroom routines and later into the fieldwork. Despite having little spare time, most of us managed to have some pleasant occasions. I enjoyed visiting the George Washington Carver Museum and marveling at his inventions, the best-known peanut butter, enjoyed the world over today.[12] Looking forward to the library, I was shocked that students were not allowed access to the stacks. Instead, request cards had to be laboriously filled out after searching the card catalog for the wanted books or topics. My library plans came to a halt.

Sidney, Helen, and I made friends with some of the students who had cars, so we took occasional short road trips. We never risked having a racially mixed group. One of the white male students, married at that, had developed a crush on me, and his behavior became a nuisance during one of these excursions. That was the closest I came to any sexual encounter. That didn't mean that I didn't notice that there were times that sex hung in the air like steam after a hot summer storm. One memorable evening several us were invited to a musical event at a Black fraternal organization, perhaps the Elks. We filed in, Black and white, skittish as electrified cats, and sat around tables in near darkness. The air floated with eroticism like a heavy perfume. Loud music with a hip-moving rhythm was playing. The throbbing bass and charged rhythm pulsated through me, dragging sex with it.

Mostly, we went to class, did our work, wrote in our diaries, participated in the discussions, and made every effort to be good students. We were learning a skill that might lead to a job. Furthermore, we were getting a stipend. I made more per month for those two months than I had ever made before in that amount of time. College credit was another perk, and it ended up being helpful to my patched-together undergraduate work after we left Alabama.

Dr. Valien's report from the Amistad Research Center supplied course details that I had not understood at the time. The full scope of the intentions of the program remains mysterious. I thought our goal was to learn about community evaluation and counseling. She stated, "Of secondary emphasis was the counseling aspects of the program." She went on to explain that the training emphasized the culture of lower socioeconomic groups and their strengths and cognitive styles. The fieldwork was designed to ensure exposure to poverty that provided insights into the attitudes, hopes, and aspirations of poverty-stricken youth. The campus interviewing experience added to this, as well as providing an experience for the interviewee. The program took care to ensure that the trainees did not view themselves as fully qualified counselors.

The fieldwork was spirit crushing. I had seen poverty from a distance, with the desperate sagging shacks that had never seen a coat of paint piercing the cotton fields on the annual Florida drives with Mother. Part of my agony was feeling like a voyeur inserting myself into the wretched lives of people I did not know and whom I could not help. Poverty up close was looking at yellowed, peeling newspaper pasted on the inside walls of a two-room leaky shanty in a desperate attempt to keep winter winds at bay. A dirt floor. A swept yard. An old woman saying it was easier to see the snakes that way. Sometimes, not even a well or a privy. Sometimes hunger gnawing. Ragged clothing. Dirty, runny-nosed children.

It seemed nothing had changed since the mid-1930s, when Walker Evans recorded such scenes, albeit of white people, in *Let Us Now Praise Famous Men*.[13] Here we were thirty years later. Thirty years! The program provided me and, presumably, the other students with a few photographs of ourselves with our group leaders, making visits to the mostly Black families. The sampling of white households we visited in our program were sprinkled around like a few grains of salt on top of pepper. The photographs I have look like copies from Evans's book. I still wonder what happened to all the others that the project's photographer took.

*Figure 14.* Project CAUSE field trip, August 1964. *Left to right:*
Helen Knox; unknown child; Marcia Herman-Giddens (me); trip
leader, name unknown; child's father, name unknown.

A happier exposure was my interaction with the seventeen-year-old African
American girl to whom I had been assigned for my counseling project. The
case study I wrote begins, "Barbara, her mother, and her brother live in a
neat looking concrete and brick house a short way back from a dirt road that
leads from Rosenwald Heights to Tuskegee."[14] Given our fieldwork experiences, this family appeared almost middle class. My report describes their
tidy home as having polished oak floors, an encyclopedia set, a home medical
guide, two televisions, a sewing machine, and nice appliances in the kitchen.

Barbara and I spent a good bit of time together. She was an attractive
young woman, tall and slender, who looked older than she was. I ate at least
one meal with the family. On one occasion, using a borrowed car, I took her
and her family to church, which I also attended. Barbara came to the campus
with me for the required formal interview.

It was unclear to me how the family was coping as well as it was after the shocking news Barbara shared with me early on. Her father, a well-thought-of minister in the community, had disappeared six months earlier after dropping her off at a friend's house. A month later his body was found in a field not far away. The family was told his body was too badly decomposed to ascertain the cause of death.

Now, revisiting all this and what I learned about the Tuskegee Syphilis Experiment, I must consider that he could have been one of the syphilitic subjects. Barbara told me that he had had a spell of temporary blindness caused by a "nervous disease" shortly before his death. "Nervous disease" is consistent with late syphilis. If he had been in the study, the authorities would have known and may not have wanted to investigate his death. If he had been white, I expect there would have been a forensic examination, whatever the state of decomposition. I wish I knew the family's last name as I now have the names of the study subjects. Even though I did not know about the syphilis experiment in 1964, it is interesting that I wrote in my report: "I feel that there are some significant underlying issues regarding her father's death and that further exploration would possibly bring out more conflicts than I am equipped to handle."

During the last visit with Barbara, she stated that our experience together had been a rich one for her. It was her first biracial relationship, and she said it helped her not believe all the "gross things people say about white people," such as, "they think we're all dirty and no good, and, even if they try to pretend they like us they really don't." She was considering college. I hope she made it. My time with Barbara and her family was a rich experience for me, as well.

The church services I went to during the eight weeks in Tuskegee were deeply emotional experiences. The dynamic services, with their adulatory singing, fiery praise, back-and-forth response with the preacher, ebb and flow, clapping, shouting, and swaying were not anything I had ever experienced in white churches. At first it seemed shocking, but soon my feeling that the congregants were indeed filled by divine Spirit quelled any hesitations I had. An electric enchantment soon slipped into my heart, and the staid services I had experienced as a child hung flat and spiritless in too-quiet, colorless sanctuaries.

The Tuskegee program ended on September 10 with a banquet. I was happy to be going home, back to my babies and my husband. I knew I was going home a different person.

Fifty-five years later, in the reading room of the Amistad Research Center in New Orleans, reading Bonita Valien's report, I found a poem of mine that I had forgotten having written until I saw it. Muffled memories stumbled their way back into my mind, and I remembered, pen in hand, writing the poem as part of our required evening diary. Above it, Valien had written that after the fieldwork the trainees' fears were lessening. "Subsequent diary entries concern themselves with interesting and rewarding accounts and discoveries which the trainees began to make with reference to themselves and their own situations." She meant realizing their racial bias. My untitled poem was below.

gray rain
gray shack rumbles with the thunder
the light bulb sputters
white eyes

a tiny hand
reaches for the breast
the white eyes looked down
and the little one is moved

the warm smell wraps itself
around me
I want to hold these people to me

smooth warm rain on the grass
and
cold fear
his dignity rose over me
their fear stabbed me
my blood ran out to them
my white face sears my being

—

By the time I got settled back into my home with my precious children in my arms again, it was mid-September and the weather was cooling off. I turned twenty-three still being accused by my mother of being a communist. My time at Tuskegee now added to her earlier decision about Scott being Castro's right-hand man and cemented her beliefs. Sadness would creep around me, prodding and poking at my inability to convince her that we were not communists. It worried her deeply. And she harped at us about it frequently.

Later that autumn one of those things happened that stays, in this case, literally a knife in one's memory. I had made it a point not to leave my children alone with my mother. However, one afternoon I urgently had to be somewhere. The reason is lost to me and to Scott. Having no other options, I asked Mother if she could come. She willingly did so. I got home as quickly as I could and found her in the bathroom with ten-month-old Marcus propped against the tub, diaperless. She was sitting beside him with a butcher knife. Panic and terror wrapped me. Hardly breathing, I struggled to sound calm as I approached to take Marcus away. As quietly and steadily as possible, I asked, "What is happening?" She replied, "Marcus had a stool and this seemed the best way to clean it off his bottom."

~

There were potential dangers from our own actions, as well. One of our first experiences in having Black people stay with us involved Miles College. One of the professors was a white man from the Northeast. His wife was African American. They stayed with us whenever she came to visit him. It was risky for us and even more so for them. In addition, Miles would have fired him if the administration had known he was married to a Black woman. It was just too perilous for a Black school. Or, for anybody in Birmingham. It was bad enough that the husband had been arrested several times for being in the school where he taught.

Fortunately for Scott and me, the year ended safely and peacefully. We were getting used to the new minister at the Unitarian Church, Rev. Larry McGinty. I was becoming better at playing the alto recorder. Scott was already good at the soprano. We started going to a recorder group, taking turns at hosting it. Papa would babysit when needed. It was such fun to play medieval music with friends, enjoy comradery and delicious refreshments every few weeks, and, for a while, forget the cloud of scabrous racial struggles overshadowing our city.

## Chapter 14

# Tuskegee Again and the Concerned White Citizens March, 1965

The sweet fragrance of orange blossoms must have mingled its way into Birmingham's smoggy, cold January days. Uncle Carle had not met my children, and even though Greg was only three years old I wanted him to experience the magic of the citrus grove. The thought of warmth and the tropical setting I knew from my many visits made the appeal irresistible. The orange trees would be blossoming, while mature fruit still dangled, which was always a marvel to see. So, I bundled the children into our Volkswagen bus and headed south. In those days, there were no seat belts or even car seats. Children were basically loose in the car. We did not know to be afraid.

We stopped in McIntosh, Florida, for the night with my mother's first cousin Eloise McCrae. As a child I had always loved visiting this family, with Eloise's five children romping around a real country house. That is where I learned to milk a cow. The air was warm already. The next day we arrived at the orange grove, about ten miles from Fort Pierce. My first cousin Toby, son of Aunt Beth (who had created the genealogy books), was there on a short college break. A photo shows Toby, me, and the children sitting on the leaves in the one wild acre of the grove, where Carle had his trailer. Carle is sitting on an orange crate lacing a shoe. Palmettos are leaning over in the background. It was February 1.

The old three-room cabin Carle used to live in was vacant, and the owner was letting us use it. We must have managed with sleeping and cooking needs because we stayed a little over a week. Another photo is of Greg on the same step I had sat on so miserably at age ten, with the mosquitoes falling into my rancid corn mush dinner. February 3 was Marcus's birthday. Uncle Carle had never been to a birthday party for a one-year-old. We took Carle to the beach with us to watch Marcus enjoy his first ocean experience.

Greg loved the avenue of Australian pines that bordered the rows of orange trees as much as I did. I can still see my little boy, so happy, running down the sandy road under the arch their branches formed, their dark green needles softly swishing in the breeze. It pleases me still to think of how much Uncle Carle enjoyed the children, his gentle ways harmonizing with their innocent joyful pleasure in their new experience.

⁓

Back home, our lives trembled between our struggle to make a good life for our children and our involvement with civil rights. None of it was on a grand scale, Scott and I just did what little we could do. Whether it was the ongoing tension and fear pervading the civil rights community or just things that would have happened anyway, there were some unravelings throughout the year that touched our life. Some caused a smattering of disagreements; mostly, we were on the same page. By late February, there was the usual swelling force of buds: daffodils everywhere, bright yellow forsythia, spots of pink from quince and azaleas. The occasional days of warmth expanded our feelings, whether they were filled with angst or joy.

The beauty was marred by the February 21 assassination of Malcolm X, followed in five days by a killing closer to home. Jimmie Lee Jackson was an African American civil rights activist in Marion, Alabama. He was beaten, then shot by state troopers as he was participating in a peaceful march supporting voting rights. He died on February 26. Voting rights activities were already increasing, but his death galvanized supporters and helped inspire the Selma to Montgomery marches only one month later. In the Selma-based effort, two more people, white folks from up north, would lose their lives supporting voting rights. Five months later, President Johnson signed the Voting Rights Act of 1965.

Since I had had my own personal experiences of discrimination in trying to register to vote and was sympathetic anyway, it was not surprising that I became involved. Today, my memory about the events, hobbled over the decades, has grown ever fuzzier. I knew I had been to Selma and was certain that I had not participated in either the Bloody Sunday march or the one that went all the way to Montgomery. History has documented three Selma marches that shameful year in Alabama. I now know there were four Selma marches, the first one overshadowed by the subsequent marches.

I will tell the story of the first march as I rediscovered it.

Until recently, I wasn't even sure of the year of this other march. I re-learned in 2018 that the orphaned march was the day before the infamous Bloody Sunday. Thus, in this account, I call the March 7 Bloody Sunday march the second one. It got its name after state troopers bloodied the unarmed Black marchers with tear gas and billy clubs. The world soon saw the photograph of Amelia Boynton, an organizer, lying bloody and unconscious on the Edmund Pettus Bridge. The subsequent outpouring of documents on Bloody Sunday dampened the first march, rendering it barely recorded. Not forgotten by Scott and me were the activities of another organizer of the Bloody Sunday march, James Bevel from Birmingham, which touched our lives later that year but not in a positive way.

Americans, outraged by what they had seen in the news on March 7, began demonstrating across the country. Martin Luther King Jr. appealed to clergy everywhere for support and participation. More than three hundred ministers quickly made their way to Birmingham, including fifteen Unitarians. Our church housed the latter. The third march, now with about two thousand demonstrators, occurred on March 9, led this time by Dr. King. They got far enough across the Pettus Bridge to be stopped by the wall of state troopers on horseback holding guns. Dr. King called on the marchers to pray and turn back. There had been no bloodshed yet. That evening four white men attacked four of the Unitarian ministers, leaving them beaten on the ground. One, James Reeb, was rendered barely conscious from severe head trauma. The white hospital in Selma refused him, and the Black hospital did not have adequate treatment facilities. Finally, he was taken to the university hospital in Birmingham, where he died on March 11. Our church was in crisis. The membership was afraid, and no one knew what to do. Finally, our church released a one-page statement supporting the protests and voting rights and deploring the killing of Rev. James Reeb.[1]

The fourth march, the best known, began on Scott's birthday, March 21, with around eight thousand people gathering at Brown Chapel African Methodist Episcopal Church in Selma. By then, President Johnson had federalized the Alabama National Guard and ordered that guardsmen ensure the marchers could march and were protected. By March 24, several thousand, having covered the fifty miles, set up camp at the City of St. Jude complex, comprising a hospital, church, and school.[2] The history on this final march is detailed in many accounts, some of which I drew on to summarize these events. The facts still didn't mesh with my memories.

Several Selma memories I have never doubted have stayed with me over the years. One was being on a field teeming with people and knowing that a number of celebrities were there. A friend had pointed out James Baldwin's tiny trailer. Of that, I was sure. Now, I know from recent reading that that was from the City of St. Jude rally held March 24, when celebrities arrived to support and entertain the marchers. Obviously, I was there. I remember the killings before and after the marches. I knew I had not been on any of the three marches detailed in newspaper accounts and history books. What had I been on?

~

This puzzle has haunted me for decades. I am certain in the beginning I assumed I could never forget the details. A few decades ago, something triggered thoughts of the mystery march. Searching my recollection for the particulars and finding them stretched to oblivion over the decades, I asked those who might have been involved. It was too late. No one knew anything. Not even Scott. He remembered I had been on a march supporting Black voting rights but could offer no details, much less a place or date. Possible fellow marchers had died. I researched civil rights marches in Alabama extensively and found only the usual three.

More years passed. Sometimes I doubted my memory, yet I never questioned the three episodes that stayed with me about that mystery march: the linoleum-floored basement of an African American church where we were trained in nonviolent resistance, the frisson of terror when I thought about the march, and the feeling of warm, slimy spittle hitting my cheek. By now, it was over a half century since these things had happened. Any further details were scrimmed by my long life, now punctured by sorrow at losing this piece of my life. Then, a small miracle.

~

I have had moments even before working on this book where the universe connected, pulling together somehow in that magical way quantum physics particles are said to be entwined. This time, this sparkling fallout gave me exactly what I did not have and what I would be needing the following year when I began this book: the march mystery solved. In the summer of 2017, I was headed to Maine to spend time with cousin Marion, Toby's sister. I stopped to see a dear friend at her family's weathered, century-old Craftsman island cottage. Perched only feet from huge granite outcroppings, it seems to serve as a bulwark against the ocean's waves as well as life's sorrows. I've been there a number of times. Polly, with her wisdom and hope and joie de vivre, and the cottage, with its views and timelessness, were always restorative. Polly and Rob Wright had become close friends of Scott's and mine in Birmingham. They attended the Unitarian Church during the years Rob taught history at Birmingham-Southern College. They moved away before we did.

The sun was setting as Polly and I chatted on the porch, catching up since our last time together. Because the cottage had no electricity, I soon went upstairs to my bedroom to settle in before darkness. I heard footsteps on the stairs. Polly entered my room with a sheaf of papers and said, "I thought you might like to see this. It is a chapter along with the epilogue of the book Rob was working on when he died." I knew Rob had been conducting interviews and doing research for a book on the Civil Rights Movement in Birmingham. I did not know he had gotten that far with it. I thanked her and went to bed with the papers in one hand and a flashlight in the other, eager to peruse what he had written.

Not believing what I was seeing, I read and reread,

> Saturday, March 6, 1965, seventy-two very nervous and frightened white Alabamians took a momentous step by marching to the county courthouse in Selma to demonstrate their support for black voter registration in Selma, Alabama. Calling themselves Concerned White Citizens of Alabama. . . . Feeling vulnerable to physical attacks, the marchers proceeded uneasily . . . down Broad Street to the Dallas County Courthouse. . . . They followed Reverend Joseph Ellwanger, the white pastor of a black Lutheran Church in Birmingham. In groups of four, spaced some 30 feet apart to avoid breaking Selma's parade ordinance . . . the men dressed in suits and neck ties, the women in dresses. A few carried placards.
>
> It was reported in the *New York Times* March 8th, 1965. Hundreds of whites lined the streets near the courthouse including one of the men later accused of killing Reverend James Reeb. Today few remember this courageous and unprecedented demonstration by white Alabamians. During the past three and a half decades historians of the civil rights movement have completely overlooked or ignored this effort.[3]

Then I saw, at the end of the epilogue, "A Letter from Alabama." The letter followed. It was a shock. My letter, entirely forgotten until I reread it, lost to me, both in physical form and memory.

I lay there in disbelief. I don't think I had ever talked to Polly about this march. She certainly did not know I had been searching for information about it. With tears in my eyes and galvanized amazement, I got out of bed and went to find her. "Polly," I said, "You cannot imagine what this means to me. You have just given me back part of my life." And there it was, the half-century-long mystery solved. A forgotten piece of history restored. Bits and pieces of memory returning, Martin Luther King Jr.'s "Letter from Birmingham Jail" had probably helped give form to my letter when a further killing caused desperate despair in my very being.

The day after the rally I had attended in Montgomery, the third killing in two months occurred. On March 25, 1965, Viola Fauver Liuzzo from Detroit, mother of five, was murdered by Ku Klux Klan members because she had participated in the final march and helped drive fellow activists to the airport in Montgomery. She was thirty-nine years old. At that point, my disgust and horror set further ablaze, I wrote my letter. Reading it now, I see I did not mention her name. Why, I don't know. I wrote the letter on March 26, 1965. Clearly, I gave the letter to Rob Wright. It is reproduced in his appendix.

~

Now that I knew what the mystery march was and the date, I was able to find out more about it. It turns out that the *New York Times*, the *Birmingham News*, and the *Birmingham Post-Herald* each published one small article before the news was overtaken by the enormity of Bloody Sunday and subsequent events in Selma. The *News* article, published on March 7 in the "Late Final" edition, was written by Tom Lankford, the reporter mentioned in a previous chapter. He detailed the violence: a Student Nonviolent Coordinating Committee worker was knocked down trying to photograph the crowd watching us, at least two of our group were shoved and hit, three of us were struck from behind as we lined up at the courthouse. While we were dispersing to return to the church, more happened. "'Hey, Lou Ellen, come here,' a member of the Sheriff's mounted posse shouted at the man. The man walked up to the posse members and struck another demonstrator on route. The helmeted officers laughed and clapped him on the back. As taunts from the crowd of about 300 persons grew louder and tension mounted, Public Safety Director Wilson Baker worked his way through the mob and ordered it to disperse."

The March 8 issue of *Post-Herald* had an article titled "'Concerned

White Citizens' Work to Continue, Says Member." It was on the front page, with its main headline, "Teargas Routs 600 Negroes," and the subtitle, "Law Men Use Clubs, Whips to End 'Walk.'" The article about our march began "Activities of the Concerned White Citizens of Alabama, a group of about 70 which staged its first demonstration march here Saturday, will continue, a spokesman for the organization said today. Dr. Frederick Kraus, a professor at the University of Alabama Medical Center in Birmingham, said Saturday's march was only a beginning for his group which is aiding the Negro in his drive for equality."

The article went on for another column and a half, ending with, "The Rev. C. T. Vivian, a leader in the [Southern Christian Leadership Conference], told the group that [the march's] action had done as much for the civil rights cause as would 25 marches by Negroes. 'Those wanting to suppress the Negro and continue the southern way of life fear you much more than they would ever fear any Negro,' he said." The *New York Times* article on March 8 had a quote from Dr. Kraus, "We have remained silent for a long time, trying to give moral support to Negroes. I personally felt it was time to show that a group of demonstrators can have a face other than that of the Negro."

The key phrase in the *Post-Herald*, the "southern way of life," is still with us all these years later. Most of us know it as code for white supremacy. The momentum for this march was built out of the frustration caused by continual witnessing of violence and lack of progress for "Negro rights." Scott's and my dear friend Frederick knew it was time for white people to take visible action themselves. Because we knew Frederick and we believed in the cause, we readily decided to participate. It made sense for me to go and Scott to stay with the children and get some work done.

Between a jarred memory and recovered sources I can now relate what happened. Over some weeks, the planning occurred, transportation was arranged, and eventually participants, all white, from Birmingham, Auburn, Tuscaloosa, Tuskegee, and Huntsville made their way to Selma that Saturday morning in small groups of individual cars. I probably rode down with Frederick. The day was cloudy and chilly as we filed into the basement of the African American Reformed Presbyterian Church on Jefferson Davis Avenue, where we were trained in nonviolent resistance. We were to march twelve blocks to the Dallas County Courthouse to present our statement supporting voting rights for Black people. We were terrified but determined; it was a very long twelve blocks going and even longer returning.

Rev. Joseph Ellwanger of Birmingham was our leader. Because we did

*Figure 15.* White marchers facing the sheriff at the courthouse in
Selma, Saturday, March 6, 1965, at the Concerned White Citizens
of Alabama march. I am the first woman in the second row.

not have a parade permit, we walked in lines of four spaced thirty feet apart
to avoid violating the ordinance. I happened to be on the outside of one of
the rows, which increased my sense of vulnerability. I did not know yet at the
time, but I was pregnant. If I had known, perhaps I would have decided not
to participate. As it was, reflecting on it now, I cannot imagine what I was
thinking. I had two children. Any of us could have been hurt or killed.

Hecklers were lined up jeering at us as we got close to the shopping district. The taunts grew louder, full of curses, and more violent. My heart was
beating fast, my body tense. Suddenly, a woman leaned toward me, and I
heard her spit a fraction of a second before I felt the wetness hit my cheek,
slick and dribbling. As we had been taught, I did not react but kept walking
forward. Another heckler knocked some pamphlets out of the hands of one
of our group. Someone else was shoved. Finally, we arrived at the courthouse
and lined up.

Recently, people from the Birmingham Unitarian Universalist Church,
as it is now called, researching activities in the 1960s as part of the *Bending
the Arc* documentary project, unearthed photographs and movie footage of
that march that none of us had known existed. The materials are housed at

Washington University in Saint Louis. In one photo, I am standing third from the left, wearing a scarf around my head and a dark coat, my expression solemn. More men than women seem to be present. Everyone is dressed warmly. There are small signs spaced evenly in front of us, with the words SHERIFF CARS ONLY. At the time, we did not know how fortunate we were that Sheriff James G. Clark was not there. He was the one that had previously arrested hundreds of African Americans at an earlier demonstration. We were surrounded by twenty other sheriffs and deputies and other law enforcement agents in addition to the hostile crowd.

Reverend Ellwanger read our statement aloud. Someone from law enforcement whispered in the ear of one of our leaders. When it was time to leave, as we turned to head back to the church, our leaders told us to disperse and walk back using a different route. Later we learned that law enforcement had reason to think we would be physically attacked and so suggested a different route to thwart the attackers' plans. Apparently, in contrast to their lust for Black blood, they did not want too much white blood on their hands. Changing our route going back worked because we arrived at the church safely. We never marched again; we didn't need to, or we thought so at the time. A few weeks later, the Selma to Montgomery march ended with tens of thousands of people gathering in front of the state capitol making their demand. On August 6, President Johnson signed the Voting Rights Act. Little did we know that now, fifty-five years later, African Americans would still not to be able to easily exercise their voting rights in many states.

———

At home, with the final Selma to Montgomery march about to take place, more people started coming to Alabama from all over the United States, especially the Northeast. The often-summoned specter of the "outside agitator" was true. Thousands of people were flocking in to participate. Our church again called on members to house and feed as many as we could. Since Scott and I had an unfinished upstairs, we had room for many pallets and sleeping bags. Neither of us remembers details about all the men and women who passed through our home. A few of the ones staying the day of Scott's birthday may have joined us for cake. Some were Unitarian ministers, others were college students, and others, who knows. How we coped with only one bathroom we cannot imagine. At least we had an iron and ironing board. That we had a request for this surprised me so much I still remember this detail. Several of the young white women passing through our home had long hair, and every morning they asked me to iron it to make it smooth. I can still picture one standing close to the ironing board, arching her back and flicking her long hair over the width of the board, slowly un-arching to expose a new section of hair as I ironed.

Spring flared into summer as it can only do in Birmingham. Some of our friends flared as well, burning through the long-established one-way sexual boundary between African American men and white women, it being highly legislated against, feared, volatile, and dangerous. On the other hand, the behavior of white men with their rape of Black women, enslaved or free, was tolerated, even expected. The skin color of African Americans today demonstrates the commonness of the latter. Stories arose as civil rights work continued: some fabricated accounts as ugly and salacious as possible, some prurient chronicles of certain biracial sexual episodes, some sweet stories of consensual and daring relationships.

Many inflaming accounts about civil rights participants were likely not true and were rightly denied. However, I knew from episodes in my own circles, sometimes these relationships did occur. And why wouldn't they? People thrown together in common cause and intense work will find others they are attracted to. At this time, in the 1960s, unlike in the days of slavery where white men were abusing Black women who could not give consent, it was usually white women with Black men. These African American men often had more status than the white women they took up with. Some of the men were prominent figures in the Movement. One of our white friends dallied for a while with James Bevel, an attractive and charismatic Black civil rights leader. She sought our help with arranging their rendezvous. That was more than we wanted to be involved with.

There were others. The interracial relationship clearest in my memory involved another white friend, a lithe and charming woman who almost died at the hands of her lover. I never met him, nor do I know his name. I'm not sure of the exact timing of events, but at some point, after she and her husband were in the process of divorce, she had begun an affair with an African American man. What precipitated the event, I have no idea. That he was Black did make the whole episode dangerous should the authorities find out. Around two o'clock one morning, she called me saying she had been badly hurt and needed help.

Scott stayed with our children, and I drove to her house, which, under the circumstances, seemed impossibly far away even though it was only a few miles. I found her prostrate and her skin, cooling fast, as pale and dry as translucent tracing paper. She was barely able to tell me her boyfriend had knocked her off her porch during an argument. I wondered whether more had happened because the emergency room found that her spleen had ruptured and most of her blood had spilled into her abdomen. Emergency surgery and multiple transfusions saved her life. It should be obvious why we had to make up a story about what happened.

Birmingham was not peaceful either. In late spring, bombings and bombing attempts picked up again. Fortunately, for two of these, one involving a Catholic church and the other A. D. King's home, the fifty sticks of dynamite placed by the Klan were either disarmed or failed to explode. The third bombing, on Dynamite Hill, left a six-foot crater and injured a family's thirteen-year-old son. Thirty-eight sticks of dynamite were left at the home of Nina Milglionico, a fairly liberal white attorney whom I got to know later. They were disarmed before exploding. The last bombing that year was against another white target, Mayor Albert Boutwell, who had displeased the Klan. Those sixty sticks of dynamite were disarmed by police.

At home, an afternoon visit from my mother added yet another minacious event to our own immediate sphere. My third pregnancy had just been confirmed. Mother was sitting on a settee in what should have been our dining room, except we had no dining room furniture. I can still see her sitting there. When I told her I was expecting again, a look of disapproval flushed across her face, and she said, "Can't you get rid of it? You should have an abortion."

—

In late spring, I received a query from the American Ethical Union asking whether I would participate as a teacher in an early childhood education program it was supporting in Tuskegee. How the union got my name may have had to do with Project CAUSE. I don't think I had heard of this group, an outgrowth of an early 1900s humanist movement known as the ethical culture movement. It focused on building human goodness and ethical relationships. One of the group's efforts in the sixties was racial justice.

The opportunity sounded interesting. I was familiar with Tuskegee, and I would earn a little money. It fit in with my yearning for new experiences and challenges. An old résumé of mine describes the position as, "Teacher, community program for disadvantaged children." I explained, "I worked with the group in planning a 'Head Start' type program for rural Black children and had full responsibility for the designing and implementing of my own program for my classes." So, in the early summer of 1965 I was back in Tuskegee, this time pregnant, both of my children in tow, and with our Volkswagen bus. Since we had only one car, Scott agreed to bike or walk to work. As always, he was so supportive of my various efforts. Somehow, he managed to get groceries and do other things that required a car.

Just outside the town of Tuskegee I found a simply furnished, small clapboard house for rent. I have forgotten the name of the African American woman I hired to look after the children while I was teaching. They were too young to accompany me. I was not picky about housekeeping or other chores. The main thing I cared about was her taking good care of Greg and Marcus.

Obviously very capable, she took on more for herself than I asked for, keeping the house spotless in addition to keeping the children contented and happy. I remember a scene, so touching to me. When coming home one day, I found her ironing my sheets and pillowcases. That was the only time in my entire life I have had ironed linens in my home. I felt cared for and pampered so I know my children must have as well. Scott would come on weekends. My father was kind enough to lend him his 1956 Ford Fairlane. All Scott

*Figure 16.* With my students in Tuskegee, 1965.

remembers about the house was lying in the bed on Saturday nights reading computer manuals. He was always working hard.

I was assigned the class of eight- and nine-year-old children, all of whom were Black. Integrated classrooms were still some years away in much of the South, despite the 1954 *Brown v. Board of Education* Supreme Court ruling. We teachers, however, were a mixture of Black and white. The children in my class and I spent much of our time outdoors. I taught games, songs, and appropriate lessons. Often, we got together with other classes. Some days we went to a swimming pool. There would be a dozen or more children in my Volkswagen bus. In the days with no seat belts and no rules for safe transportation, having twelve or more children in a vehicle was not an issue. It used to amaze me how many children could fit in that bus. I'm pretty sure I once counted sixteen.

One day, one of the children had a minor injury needing medical care. I packed my whole class into the bus as I had no one to leave them with. We drove to the John A. Andrew Memorial Hospital on the campus of Tuskegee Institute. The children and I sat in chairs lining the main hallway, waiting for the injured child to be seen. It was probably a learning experience for all the children. Now I think about how we might have seen syphilitic men in the infamous Tuskegee Syphilis Experiment passing in front of us as we waited.

Records for this episode of my life are mostly nonexistent. All I have are two photographs and my Social Security wage and tax statement, the latter thanks to Scott, who recently found it. I was paid $325 that summer, which is worth a little more than $2,600 now. One photograph is of me beside a picnic table with ten happy-looking youngsters. I look rather plain, my hair parted in the middle and shoulder length. The other photograph shows a nicely coifed African American teacher standing with thirteen younger looking children in front of her, all with big smiles. A residential home shows in the background.

From my current research, I learned that the goal of the program must have incorporated some of the activities designed by the Chicago Ethical Society's Commission on Race and Equality. The society was working to eliminate bigotry in the South by having African American and white people interact in social settings. What we now all know as Head Start programs were just getting underway in certain areas of the country, under the direction of the Office of Economic Opportunity's Community Action Program, a section of the overall War on Poverty.

~

When my children and I returned home, we were greeted by a shadowy green over almost everything in the house: the rugs, furniture, leather goods, and especially books. There were mildew-free areas where Scott had spent the most time. I could tell his routes through the house. It took a long time to get rid of that pre-air-conditioning fungus, especially on the books. I knew that Scott had been too busy and hard at work to even notice.

We had a new neighbor and a new newspaper in Birmingham. The *Southern Courier* was the idea of two undergraduate journalists at Harvard College.[4] Participants in the 1964 Freedom Summer in Mississippi, the two noticed that white-run papers in the South were not accurately reporting African American events. So, they got together some money and a few friends and founded the paper. One hundred and seventy-seven issues were published, one a week from 1965 to 1968. We learned about the paper sooner than our friends did because of an employee of the paper.

Clay Musselman moved into our neighbor's tiny garage apartment one lot down on the left of our backyard. The entrance was onto the alley. The other end was held up by brick pillars four or five feet high set on the edge of a terrace carved out of the steep decline below. The whole thing looked like it might topple over, but it held out, at least while we lived there. Clay was to be entwined with our life for many years to come. One of these tendrils involved his obsession with the writer Alice Walker, whom he knew, which affected Scott and me later. His subsequent replacement brought a new charming and helpful entwining decades later: both proverbial small-world stories soon explained.

Clay was fun, but also work and worry. He was a handsome young man with an angular face, bold features, and dark hair falling in a V over his forehead. He sounded like my beloved Lancaster County because he happened to be from there. It turned out he was from Ephrata, the birthplace of my father. It didn't take long to discover Clay's grandfather had been a teacher of my father's when he was a boy. So, there they would be, Papa and Clay, perched on the edge of one of our backyard terraces taking themselves back to their glorious green homeland by the sharing of old stories.

Clay had been hired on by the fledging newspaper as a reporter and distributor. The paper turned out to be another one of those "damn northern troublemaker" efforts, a much-needed one. Clay was twenty-three years old and had already been involved in a project helping African Americans get access to books. He had dropped out of Lehigh University, anxious to do things in the world, to make a difference. Clay took right to us, and we to him. He soon became part of our family. He kept us informed about what was going on in Alabama, gave us copies of the newspaper, and often joined us for meals. It was extra fun when his wife, Peggy, visited.

Together, we shared dreams. All this was tragically cut short on October 17, just a few months into his new career. Clay was returning from Lancaster County after visiting Peggy. He fell asleep driving and crashed into a bridge abutment. He amazed everyone by emerging six months later from a coma and, with years of struggle, becoming somewhat functional. Sadly, he was never able to leave what we now call assisted living. He had to relearn everything.

Meanwhile, the young man sent to replace Clay moved into the garage apartment for a short time. We connected with him as we had Clay, the three of us gathering tightly together in a hostile environment, seeking comradery and solace. This young man passed through our lives so quickly we did not remember his name. We know it now and will not forget Jim Willse again.

—

On August 8, we had a birthday party for Greg, who was turning four years old. It was our first of many parties through the years with our soon-to-be three children. Helen's and Sidney's boys came, as did the children next door. It was a nice day so we set up the party on the picnic table on the patio that overlooked the city. The table had come with the house, and we used it a lot. I made newspaper hats for the children and a cake with chocolate icing, four candles, and store-bought sugar letters to spell out Happy Birthday. Scott sat on one end and Marcus on the other in his high chair. There were games and presents. We gave Greg a cowboy outfit, which he was so proud of he wore it practically the entire rest of that year.

Another memory from that time has stayed with me. On a lovely afternoon a couple of months later Greg and I were on the patio watching the autumn leaves swirling down. A city brush collection truck pulled up. There were already piles of leaves in the gutters. Men emerged from the truck with rakes as the driver got out, stood beside the truck, and watched the men as they worked briskly, his arms crossed over his ample belly. Greg studied the scene, then turned and looked at me. "Mama," he said, "why are the Black men doing all the work and the white man is just watching?" Hard moments with my thoughtful little boy.

Thanksgiving arrived along with my advancing pregnancy. The baby was supposed to arrive around that time, but nature had another thought. Day after day nothing happened. Finally, eleven days later, I went into labor. Scott needed a haircut so we hurriedly accomplished that before he took me to the hospital. I had cut his hair ever since high school to save money. We made it to St. Vincent's in plenty of time. Neither the doctor nor the hospital had changed. Still no fathers in the delivery room. The baby finally emerged, and the nurse placed it all warm and wiggly and wet on my newly shrunken abdomen. The feeling that gave me was so wondrous, so magical and marvelous, I had completely forgotten that I had resigned myself to having another boy. All of a sudden, I heard a voice, "It's a girl!" Our beautiful daughter, Melantha.

Christmas soon came to our now family of five. Papa gave the boys a cowboy set they badly wanted that we could not afford. An early plastic toy, it had two horses, a cowboy, a cowgirl, an American Indian boy and girl, and all sorts of accessories: saddles, reins, chaps, weapons, down to mess kits

*Figure 17.* Scott and me with newborn Melantha, four-year-old Greg, and Marcus, who was almost two, December 1965, in Birmingham.

with cutlery and a tiny coffee pot. The tumble of all this out of the boxes was thrilling to Greg and Marcus. They played with it for years, later joined by their sister. What remains of it is now with Marcus, who has just become a grandfather. These much-loved toys will give new joy to the next generation.

—

The year ended peacefully, in contrast to the voting rights events that inspired my Birmingham letter. Here is my rediscovered letter, written after the third killing over voting rights in a short span during the spring of this year.

March 26, 1965

March 1965 in Alabama was the longest month of my life. On Saturday, the 6th, I marched with 71 other whites to the well-known courthouse in Selma to read our statement protesting voter discrimination, police brutality, and suppression of dissent. We were answered the next day, that horrible Sunday, by what our governor termed the "fine work" of our state troopers. Already before that, a trooper had shot and killed Jimmie Lee Jackson as he was trying to protect his mother and grandfather from being beaten. Then came the death of Rev. Reeb, beaten not by the communists or outsiders as the people of this state like to say, but by Alabama racists. And after that the marches came, all over Alabama, all over the nation. There were more marches and more beatings and more police brutalities always answered by more marches. Then, finally, Martin Luther King and his marchers left Selma and walked to Montgomery and joined by thousands, they marched—some with fear but all with their heads high to stand under the Confederate flag and Alabama state flag flying from our capitol. Alabama does not fly an American flag.

Then last night a woman was shot in our state, not by outsiders, but by Alabama Ku Klux Klan members. Our people will soon forget it as they have forgotten all the other killings. This morning our governor said, "I still commend all the people of Alabama . . ." I suppose he meant the latest murderers, too.

This month has been long and the years have been long here in Birmingham. This is my home. I grew up here. My parents, my friends, all my childhood memories belong to Birmingham and to Alabama. I loved it once. It is hard to watch my home die, but I am sick of it. I am sick of Birmingham, sick of Alabama and Gov. Wallace, sick of the desperate racists, sick of the silent "moderates," and sick of myself for not doing more to try to help. As I look back now, the month was a whirlwind of meetings, letters, telegrams, telephone calls and calling, of marchers passing through our home for the night, of hopes and broken hopes, of worry and fear and anguish.

My hope is gone. I am tired and weary. But my children still cry to be fed. I have hardly seen them or my husband all month. Now I am crying, too. In Alabama it is a sickness unto death.

I wrote this letter exactly fifty-eight years ago to the month, as I am writing now at the end of 2019. I was twenty-four years old. Viola Liuzzo, a white Unitarian woman, had just been shot and killed by Alabama racists while driving in a car with a Black passenger soon after the Unitarian minister James Reeb and Black activist Jimmie Lee Jackson had been killed. It was more than I could stand. The church bombing that killed four young girls had occurred two years before, on September 15, 1963. Before that, in May 1963, under Bull Conner's orders, Black children marching were pushed back by water from fire hoses with enough pressure to shred clothes. and police dogs were used against adults and children alike. There were countless other atrocities. The despair and the terror during this time are seared into my being. We were afraid. We wanted our children to have a normal life.

~

It was time to leave.

~

Now, two decades into the twenty-first century, the shadow of the Cotton Kingdom floats over us still.

*Chapter 15*

# Burrowing into Cotton

## THE COTTON PAPERS

When I was little, the route to Florida followed roads through Alabama and Georgia bordered by acres and acres of cotton. Passing the fields made me feel I was floating on a frothy ocean or, if the weather was cold, snow. Fields were often still white in December, from either unfinished hand pickings or bolls the machines had missed. When a sea of white loomed ahead, I would beg Mother to stop. I wanted to creep unseen to the edge of the field and pick a branch with open bolls to study the white, fluffy fibers spilling out. It seemed like magic. I did not know that though the cotton was soft, its history was hard and brutal. The real story is embodied in the rough brittle stems, tiny burrs and spines that would tear fingers, the sticky seeds, stinging insects, hot and cold weather, sharp briars in the rows, mosquitoes, no shade, not enough to eat, dust in every breath, and cries for water. An enslaved child might scurry to the picker with a bucket and dipper. The overseer on his horse keeps his whip ready. All this with the pickers' backs bent over from dawn to dusk as they drag sacks weighing eighty pounds and more.

Now at the other end of my life, I see that cotton must be attached, wanted or not, to my very DNA. On my mother's side, I am a product of cotton, enhanced by a sprinkle of sugar produced by ancestors on Louisiana plantations, soaked with Harmony Hall's turpentine, and seasoned with salt procured from the Caribbean for the Civil War: all from generations of these enslaving planters behind me. I am only just now figuring this out.

Cotton may be soft, but its edges will stick you until you bleed. So wrote W. E. B. Du Bois:

> Then came the black slaves. Day after day the clank of chained feet marching from Virginia and Carolina to Georgia was heard in these rich swamp

lands. Day after day the songs of the callous, the wail of the motherless, and the muttered curses of the wretched echoed from the Flint to the Chickasawhatchee. . . . Twenty thousand bales of ginned cotton went yearly to England, New and Old; and men that came there bankrupt made money and grew rich. In a single decade the cotton output increased four-fold and the value of lands was tripled.[1]

Perhaps some of the bitterness my mother held on to stemmed from her growing up amid her father and grandfather's efforts to recover money from the Union for their "stolen cotton." Her affected grandfather, Henry Choice Price, sowed resentment, even anger, about the episode onto his only known child and his grandchildren. He never gave up. In some ways, this has even lain on my first cousins and myself. This is especially true for Marion and Toby, the children of my Aunt Beth and Uncle Kenneth. None of us cousins knew our great-grandfather, but Beth knew him well: from 1909 at the age of two she was raised by Henry Choice Price and her step-grandmother, Lucy Banks Price.

Henry was born in Newton County, Georgia, in 1833 and died in 1916 in Miami, Florida. His father, Zaccheus, a name with such variable spellings it didn't help me in finding the few records there might be. Zaccheus married a Browning, bringing the McAlpins and other slaveholding lines into the family. Zaccheus had nine children, with Henry in the middle. Zaccheus also had enough money, cotton money, to send all his children, even the girls, to good schools, including Emory College and the Male and Female Seminary.[2]

Zaccheus came from a line of three John Prices of Welsh origin that came to America about 1650 with other Quaker families and settled the Welsh Tract in Pennsylvania. My line soon went on to the Shenandoah Valley. In four generations, these Quakers, who took refuge with William Penn to protect their religious freedom, became Methodist enslavers.

Based on censuses and other records, it seems my maternal ancestors were all caught up in the heat of cotton, increasing their numbers of enslaved people to grow even more. The invention of the cotton gin in 1794 allowed the cruel, feverish kingdom to flourish, though not without economic issues involving booms and crashes, credit, mortgages (of which enslaved people were often the collateral), bad debts, and more. Those issues must have played some small role in the fact that I grew up with a mother whose family was still in angst over the loss of cotton money to the Union in the Civil

War. The story is known to our family as "The Cotton Papers." Their pursuit of money from "stolen" cotton finally ended in 1934, only seven years before my birth.

Two years ago, I began reading books about slavery and the rise of cotton in the South. Cotton, in use for seven thousand years, is a member of the mallow family; the fibers are almost entirely pure cellulose. Most of us take *Gossypium* ssp. for granted. World production is about 110 million bales a year. India is the largest producer, and the United States the largest exporter.[3]

The labor from enslaved people allowed the United States to ascend in this world. The "cotton is king" era, though dampened by the Civil War, lasted from the early 1830s into the 1920s, with sharecroppers replacing those formerly held in bondage. England and New England were completely dependent, thus complicit, on the cotton economy as their textile industries needed the South's product. My ancestors and thousands of other white folk peopled this landscape, becoming ever richer, many becoming more debased and crueler in their efforts to maintain dominion over their human chattel.

⁓

Before my great-grandfather Henry Choice Price was born, his father, Zaccheus, already held seventeen enslaved people.[4] Given information in censuses and laws at the time, aspects of the conditions under which my great-grandfather grew up can be parsed. With more than ten enslaved people, an armed overseer was required. His father and older brothers—even his mother, for a few years—were required to ride armed in slave patrols biweekly, inflicting punishments, invading slave quarters, and more. Henry would have participated when he turned sixteen. Patrols and associated laws suggest enslavers' fear pushed increased subjugation of chatteled people and may offer a glimpse into the ongoing presence of fear that rules the South to this day.

Family notes indicate that Henry was about seventeen when the family moved to Marion County, Florida. By then, Florida was a "slave state," which allowed Zaccheus to bring his enslaved people and begin growing Sea Island cotton, a variety of higher value. With the American Indians subjugated, some referred to the urge to move to Florida as a "fever." In the next ten years Zaccheus prospered. Two daughters married and moved away. The eldest child, John Wesley, after finishing at the Medical College of Georgia, returned to the family, so the household then comprised four grown sons and Zaccheus. All the children were likely helping with management of the enslaved people they held and the large amount of land under cultivation.

By 1860, my great-great-grandfather's property value was recorded as $18,000 for real estate and $25,000 for personal property, more than doubling from the previous ten years. His personal property would have included the value of his then thirty-seven enslaved people, who ranged in age from three months to one hundred years. The "slave censuses" marked the color of each person with a "B" for Black or "M" for mulatto. I startled when I saw that the only mulatto among these people in 1860 was a three-month-old girl. Zaccheus was sixty-six years old. The June census included seven females in their late teens or twenties. With six young women already, would he have purchased a young mother and her newborn only a few months earlier? It seems unlikely. Or was he already enslaving seven young women, one of which was the mother? This would mean rape by a white man.[5] Could that baby be a Price?

It must have seemed to my great-grandfather that life with a lot of land worked by enslaved people was the norm and had always existed. He clearly embraced that way of life because later in the Civil War, when a Union prisoner, he escaped rather than signing the Union Pledge of Allegiance.

Henry grew up steeped in cotton, pricked with fear and loss. By the time he was fifteen, several siblings and his mother had died. Stress probably honed his losses until they were brittle. As with others who held people in bondage, he and his family must have been ensconced in anxiety about their safety, especially as "enhanced methods" of forcing enslaved people to increase their workload came into practice. At the same time, white people had to have been affected by the brutality of practices and laws that developed to keep control of enslaved women, men, and children.[6] White people must have been demeaned and debased by this. Did these practices instill harshness and the ability to inflict cruelty without much thought in my great-grandfather? Did his attitudes soften over time? Certainly, they did not lessen with regard to his "stolen" cotton.

One formal photographic portrait of Henry exists. He appears to be in his thirties. His face is of an oval shape defined by high cheekbones, which, studying the portrait, I note for the first time, I have inherited. His broad forehead is surrounded by thick, dark hair. His expression is serious and determined, his lips narrow, his face with finely drawn features. He looks straight into the camera. I know from a later snapshot that he was tall and slender and stood carefully upright.

*Figure 18.* My great-grandfather Henry
Choice Price (1833–1916). Photo from my
family trunk, date and origin unknown.

Remarkably, as I develop his "Cotton Papers" story 163 years later, I
hold in my hands an original letter written to Henry by his older brother
John Wesley, mailed from Tampa on June 21, 1857. In it, John tempts Henry
to join him in the Florida military, writing "wages are good, about $800 for
six months." Especially interesting was John's mention in closing, "George
[their brother] has just landed here from home. All well. Has gold aplenty.
I have been pocketing some of Uncle Sam's money. And hope to get $1,000
more before long." Henry did not follow his brother into Florida military
service, but it was not long until he found himself in the militia anyway.

The Cotton Papers themselves have had a peripatetic life and are remarkably well preserved given their age and quarters. In years prior, they
were in Uncle Carle's moldering trailer in Florida. After he died, they were
shipped north to the sea captain's house, which, on the edge of a little bay,
is close enough to be doused if the waves get high. The island house, en-
during 217 years of ocean spray, random descents of thick gray fog, and

heavy snows in those far north winters, nonetheless managed to protect these papers.

The papers now in my possession were extracted by my cousin Marion and me in 2017 from a trunk in the dusty, silverfish-infested attic eaves of the old house. She and her brother came into possession of the house when their mother, Aunt Beth, died in the early 2000s. The papers, now sorted and strewn carefully about on several tables in my house, comprise family letters, cotton brokers' reports, bills and receipts, affidavits, and Henry's handwritten draft about why the federal government owed him money for cotton. It is titled "Provides Data That May Be Useful in Preparing Claim." In addition, there are letters to and from attorneys, investigations into people who would remember the event or have related documents, mentions of telegraph operators consulted and detectives hired, letters to and from both branches of Congress, affidavits about purchases of various lots of cotton and from witnesses to the "theft," pertinent newspaper clippings, and letters from family members with related information. When Marion and I extracted that box, I had no idea I would be writing about this.

It has taken many hours of reading and rereading, some of the penciled script being highly legible and some not, taking notes, organizing and sorting, researching questionable points, and thinking to get the Cotton Papers story straight in my head. Finally. It had never seemed quite right the way I heard about it. Nor when I read the account that Beth wrote after she discovered the papers in her brother's trailer. Writing for a Florida historical publication, she covered the three-part story thoroughly but not in sequence.[7] One section was an account of Henry's service for the Confederacy; the other two related to cotton. Before the internet, there were a few points she could not know or confirm. With gratitude to her and appreciation for all her work, I proceed.

~

Great-grandfather Henry, a participant in the King Cotton culture, was twenty-seven years old when Florida seceded from the Union. The year before, 1860, he describes, "George and I were farming in partnership part of my father's plantation and keeping bachelors' hall." In 1861 younger brother George was mustered into Confederate service. Slightly later Henry signed up as a cavalry orderly sergeant with the Marion Dragoons. Before Henry left, his father agreed to "superintend and advise the negroes in the management of the crops, etc." This line is Henry's only mention of their enslaved people in the entirety of the documents. I read that sentence several times. The benignly euphemistic description of the actual situation was jolting.

Soon Henry, along with many others, contracted typhoid fever. Seriously ill, he ended up under the care of the surgeon and Confederate general Willis Westmoreland. Westmoreland needed citrus to prevent scurvy among the troops, so he worked out a deal with Henry. With Henry's questionable health, he could not serve as a soldier again; instead, he would procure citrus for the troops. Over time, Henry, at his own expense, made several challenging deliveries of lemons and limes to Savannah using the war-impaired railroads and later being paid in Confederate money.

While conducting his antiscurvy activities, he noticed that goods coming in from Nassau and other islands were being exchanged for cotton. He decided to help the war efforts by becoming a blockade runner. He wrote, "I crossed over to Nassau and engaged in the blockade business regularly, importing such articles needed by the people and impossible to secure at home . . . mostly powder and salt. Most of the salt went to people from the 'backcountry,' who came in with teams to collect it." Usually, he exchanged his imports for cotton and cork. In this manner, by 1863 he ended up with about one hundred bales of cotton. This was the cotton for which he later sought compensation. His blockade running lasted over two years, ending abruptly after his capture.

With his first ship wrecked, and with the hundred bales hidden inland near the town of Glencoe, Florida, Henry decided to make another run to Nassau in his new schooner, the *Clotilda* (not to be confused with the slave ship by that name).[8] On April 15, 1863, he left New Smyrna with thirteen new bales of cotton and 720 pounds of copper. He was captured the next day on the lower coast of Florida by the *Transport SS McClellan* and towed to Key West. Henry was "placed in a good hotel under the charge of the US Marshall and given full range of the city under his own reconnaissance." There he was to remain for two weeks until his trial. When a friend let Henry know he would have to take the oath of allegiance to the United States or else be imprisoned in Fort Taylor, he managed an escape with a captain of a Nassau schooner.

The story picks up again when he learns that Union brigadier general David B. Birney and his soldiers had found his hidden bales. Great-grandfather wrote, "affidavits of several reliable citizens living there, state that the cotton was seized . . . during a raid down the east coast of Florida in the spring of 1864." Henry soon began his quest to be compensated for the cotton's value, which he estimated at that time was $4,000, approximately $120,000 today.

Henry was not without hope. Numerous Cotton Claims bills over many

*Figure 19.* My great-grandmother Lavinia Hickson Price (1844–73),
wife of Henry Choice Price. Date and origin of photo unknown.

years were introduced into Congress to reimburse those whose cotton was
seized during the war. Meanwhile, Henry carried on with his life. Around
1866, now about thirty-three years old, he married Lavinia Prothro Hickson, thus connecting the Prices with large numbers of Hicksons and Pro-
thros and the enslaved people held in their families. My great-grandmother
Lavinia Hickson was a mystery to Beth and has remained an enigma, though
I know a good bit of her lineage now and fewer blanks remain on her page in
the genealogy book. Lavinia has always loomed large in my mind, especially
after I saw her tintype image. She looks like she could have a trace of American Indian or African lineage or both. I continue to wonder about this, although nothing shows up in the few of her descendants' DNA tests, except
for a trace of sub-Saharan ancestry in myself, one of my grandsons, and a
Hickson cousin. There could be more undiscovered as most family members
have not had their DNA done.

My great-grandfather took up business after his marriage. Several letters
and account sheets from 1866 to 1869 indicate dry goods and continued
cotton sales, the latter shipped to Liverpool. Henry's son, my grandfather
Carleton Hickson Price, was born in Barnesville, Georgia, in 1869. I have
recently learned via DNA that Carleton had either a half brother or half

first cousin, perhaps related to his father's Nassau trading as this family line is mixed race and based in the Caribbean, another mystery yet unlocked.

Lavinia died in early 1873. Three years later Henry married Lucy Banks, and he soon took her back to Marion County, establishing an orange grove with the help of their formerly enslaved people. After the Great Freeze of 1895 wiped out the groves, Henry and Lucy moved to Miami, built a grand house at 227 NE Third Street they called the Marion, and joined the ranks of the "Miami pioneers."

In 1909, my grandmother sent Aunt Beth, then two years old, to Miami to be cared for by Henry (her husband's father) and his wife. M'Wese was overwhelmed with supporting and caring for five children. My grandfather had been unable to work steadily for years due to his lifelong tuberculosis. Seven years later Henry died, leaving a grieving nine-year-old granddaughter. Beth was too young to understand that her grandfather being uncompensated for his cotton surely added an extra burden to his ruminations as he lay dying. His circumstances were already difficult enough. His death certificate lists the causes as "general debility and a gangrenous left foot."

But the story does not end there. This proud and stubborn man known for his handsome black alpaca suits passed his quest for reimbursement for his "stolen" cotton on to his son, my grandfather. Dutifully, Carleton Hickson Price continued the cause, adding more documents to his father's records, including several yet again from Congress. Finally, on February 17, 1934, a letter to my grandfather arrived. Senator Duncan Fletcher stated, "unless Congress in some future date passes legislation restoring the jurisdiction of the Court of Claims, in such claims it would appear useless to try to secure the payment of any claims going out of the Civil War." My grandfather finally recognized the futility of further attempts at compensation for his father's confiscated cotton. After that, the long saga finally ended.

Those sixty-four years of effort wink at the gauze of cotton, gained by slavery and stained by money and terror, that has covered my family for more than three hundred years.

## OUR LOUISIANA COTTON

Having been to the boggy, slithery areas of Louisiana at various times throughout my life, I can attest that the bayous and swamps of Natchitoches on a gray day heavy with clouds could be frightening. The mist would exude a hinting whisper that it could open up and swallow evil and spit it back if given the chance. I have already alluded to the shock I felt upon my discovery of the disturbing story of Robert McAlpin Jr., my third great-granduncle. On Christmas night 2017, as I sat sickly and sad, idly searching names on my laptop after a canceled family event due to illnesses, up popped a 2002 *Washington Post* article: "down the river lay the [Natchitoches Parish] plantation of Robert McAlpin, alleged to be the prototype for the villainous Simon Legree in *Uncle Tom's Cabin*."[9] I had known nothing about this.

In a curious coincidence, a few weeks earlier, I had finished Frederick Law Olmsted's 170-year-old book *The Cotton Kingdom*, about his southern travels. It was the mid-1850s when Olmsted heard that the story of Simon Legree and Uncle Tom was thought to be set in Natchitoches Parish.[10] I continued researching. Within two weeks I learned how the story of my murdered fourth great-grandfather, *Uncle Tom's Cabin*, and the evil Simon Legree are braided together.

—

Robert McAlpin Sr. probably bought the Red River property to gain a holding where land was rich and inexpensive and slavery legal. The Port of New Orleans would soon be able to ship cotton. The sale closed on June 21, 1804, with "that certain tract . . . known as Ecore Cache, 10 Acres X 40 Acres."[11] Robert Sr.'s murder on the way home (chapter 4) prevented his namesake, the youngest son, from ever knowing his father, but Robert Jr. certainly knew the land.

By 1827 Robert Jr. had moved there, as evidenced by a legal notice regarding an enslaved man.[12] Robert Jr. appears in the 1830, 1840, and 1850 censuses, living alone, except for the enslaved people he had acquired, the only McAlpin listed in Natchitoches Parish. His 1850 "slave census" lists twenty-four males and twenty-three females, including three mulattos. Robert died on the property in 1852, likely during one of his frequent drunken spells, according to local records. He was well known by his neighbors.[13]

*Uncle Tom's Cabin*, the 1852 antislavery book by Harriet Beecher Stowe, was set in the area encompassing McAlpin's and his neighbors' plantations on the Red River. The gentle bondsman Uncle Tom, used to kindly owners, is sold to Simon Legree. Uncle Tom responds to his cruel keeper with tolerance and forgiveness, maintaining his Christian faith until his brutal death at the hands of Legree.[14] Although "Uncle Tom" has become a byword for Black complicity in the milieu of white oppression, Tom's virtues positioned him as the novel's chief moral example. Stowe's book followed the 1850 Fugitive Slave Act, which "made it illegal to give aid to a runaway slave." Released in March 1852, it soon sold three hundred thousand copies.

I looked for other evidence on a Legree/McAlpin link. In 1892, a Texas judge, Daniel B. Corley, documented the McAlpin/Legree connection. A "sworn statement" to the district clerk in Natchitoches Parish by Lamy Chopin, son of the man who bought the plantation after McAlpin died, was one of many in Corley's small book.[15] Chopin stated he knew the place as the Legree Plantation and a particular cabin as Uncle Tom's. The still available book by Corley contains numerous other sworn statements attesting to McAlpin's reputation as an exceptionally cruel enslaver and a periodic drunk. Corley's motive for these statements was to establish Tom's cabin as legitimate and acquire it for an exhibit in the 1893 World's Columbian Exposition. That story, detailed in the November 20, 1892, edition of the *Chicago Tribune*, is available online.[16] This article stated that Stowe's brother Charles Beecher suggested the character of Simon Legree, which Stowe confirms in her closing chapter. My research confirmed her brother was a clerk who traveled from New Orleans into McAlpin's area, collecting overdue bills for his mercantile employer.[17]

Though many consider the story about the McAlpin/Legree connection a legend, there is more historical information supporting it. The most interesting to me is the parallel between the two mulatto women in Stowe's novel and the two mulatto women McAlpin had in his house, at least one of whom was his unwilling "mistress." My third great-granduncle had at least two children by the enslaved woman, I was to learn, so their descendants are my cousins. Stowe and her novel are an interesting side story.

The more I researched, the more vines in the bayous sprouted and grabbed me, until there was no doubt I had to go there. At last, I looked up Natchitoches Parish's history and whereabouts. My efforts to understand the area were not helped by the ebbs and flows of the unpredictable channelings of its rivers. The more I learned, the more there was to learn.

—

Just as investigations into my African American McAlpin lines led to the 2019 trip to New York City to meet some cousins (chapter 4), this 2017 discovery called for another trip, this one to see a man named Robert Gentry. It turned out my intersection with Mr. Gentry had begun sixty years earlier.

Within two days of researching this topic, I stumbled across an intriguing Facebook entry. An online news column published in 2015 by a Robert Gentry detailed his decades-long association with the possible link between *Uncle Tom's Cabin* and McAlpin. I was soon able to contact Mr. Gentry, who turned out to be, among other things, a local editor and newspaperman. A few days later I had in my hands his notebook titled, "Writing about *Uncle Tom's Cabin*, June 25, 1959, through June 10, 1960." Amazing! A few years prior, he had given all his papers on this topic to the Cammie G. Henry Research Center at the Watson Memorial Library, Northwestern State University, in Natchitoches. After our contact, he went back to the center to retrieve some papers and photographs to send to me.[18]

Gentry's papers described all the documentation he had found a half century earlier about the supposed McAlpin/Legree relationship, his involvement in the question of whether the cabin was genuine, and his visits to their graves. The graves and their location have also been described in a few nineteenth-century accounts. Mr. Gentry, born and raised in this area, had visited the lonesome cemetery a half century ago and had revisited it, machete in hand and accompanied by grandchildren, in 2015. This, in itself, seemed a remarkable story.

Among his fascinating documents, now back at the Cammie G. Henry Research Center, was the story of a Deacon Thomas C. Parry of Shreveport, Louisiana, who, after reading Gentry's newspaper articles, wrote to the Natchitoches Chamber of Commerce in March 1960, explaining he was a grandson of Robert McAlpin Jr. The chamber shared the letter with Mr. Gentry. Parry related several happenings pertaining to the cabin and plantation. An investigation by the chamber showed that "Deacon Parry might well be a grandson of McAlpin since many things he remembers correspond with what is known about McAlpin." The report goes on to state:

> Living with Parry is his brother Robert McAlpin [Parry] who is named after the original McAlpin. Deacon Parry goes on to say that his grandmother was an Indian slave belonging to McAlpin. Her name was Lucindy Harrison, she was from somewhere around Memphis, Tennessee.
>
> McAlpin and Lucindy Harrison had two children: Carrie McAlpin and Cora McAlpin. It seems they kept the name McAlpin.
>
> Robert McAlpin, according to available information, died in a drunken spree in 1852. After his death all the slaves were freed and Lucindy and her two daughters left Chopin (the plantation then having been

bought by Dr. J. B. Chopin) and went, first, to Logansport, then to St. Augustine, Texas, and finally settled in Jefferson, Texas, where they operated a rooming house.

In 1873 they all moved to Shreveport and Lucindy Harrison helped care for the yellow fever epidemic victims of that year. Here Carrie McAlpin married George Parry. They had 12 children, six of whom died in their infancy. Among their children living today [1960] are Deacon Parry, Robert McAlpin Parry and Mrs. Cora V Hall of Los Angeles.

The 76-year-old Deacon Parry said that he remembers hearing his grandmother tell how mean McAlpin was and that he was a heavy drinker. According to Deacon Parry the whole neighborhood honored McAlpin because they were afraid of him. He said that his grandmother told him many times about how mean McAlpin was to her.

"My grandmother was kind of like the mistress of the plantation," he relates. "Although McAlpin was very mean to her, she and McAlpin told

*Figure 20.* Deacon Thomas Parry (*left*) and Robert McAlpin Parry, grandsons of enslaved house servant Lucindy Harrison and Robert McAlpin Jr. Photo taken by Robert Gentry at their shotgun-style house at 1630 Milam Street, Shreveport, April 1960. He interviewed them there for a story that ran in the *Shreveport Journal*. Courtesy of Robert Gentry and the Northwestern State University of Louisiana, Watson Memorial Library, Cammie G. Henry Research Center.

the slaves what to do." Both Deacon Parry and Robert McAlpin Parry display racial characteristics of the Indian.

Neither remembers hearing of Harriet Beecher Stowe, who wrote the book, *Uncle Tom's Cabin*. Although they have no proof, both think that the plantation was the setting for Mrs. Stowe's controversial book.

Deacon Parry looks upon the restoration of Uncle Tom's cabin as the will of Jesus Christ. He said that his prayers ascend nightly for those connected with the restoration of the cabin that "the will of God be done."

My research found that the enslaved people were not freed but all sold at the succession sale after McAlpin's death in 1852. The succession papers follow.

With some added investigation on my part, dates and census entries lend credence to these two men's statements that they are the grandchildren of Robert McAlpin. In the censuses their grandmother, McAlpin's enslaved woman Lucindy, is listed as "mulatto" rather than "Indian." She could be part

*Figure 21*. Carrie McAlpin (Parry), daughter of Robert McAlpin Jr. and enslaved house servant Lucindy Harrison, about 1900. This photo was loaned to Robert Gentry by her son Deacon Thomas Parry in 1960, when Mr. Gentry was reporting on her sons, McAlpin's grandsons. Courtesy of Robert Gentry and the Northwestern State University of Louisiana, Watson Memorial Library, Cammie G. Henry Research Center.

American Indian as census data was known to be loose with racial designations at that time. The census data also verifies Cora and Carrie, the latter being the mother of these grandsons of Lucindy.

The Parry brothers went on to have correspondence with Robert Gentry. He went to Shreveport to meet them, taking a photo during the visit. Gentry went back to the area in 2018 to search for them and found the old houses gone and no trace of the brothers.

All of this seemed so remarkable, so awful, and so brimming with unwonted coincidences I was in a kaleidoscope that needed sorting out.

—

Christmas soon passed, and anticipation of a lovely springtime in New Orleans and Natchitoches took hold. Mid-March was a good time to visit my new friend and colleague Robert Gentry. Much to my delight, when I mentioned my plans to my elder son, Greg, who had read what I had written so far about the whole McAlpin/*Uncle Tom's Cabin* story and who had lived in New Orleans, he indicated he would like to come along. We flew to New Orleans and rented a car. In Natchitoches, our hotel management provided happy hour goodies and wine in its lovely little lobby, where we entertained the Gentrys for several evenings. Robert, a tall, sturdy man about my age, and his young wife, Laurie, were the epitome of classic southern graciousness, warmth, generosity, and friendliness. Laurie, pretty and lively, was an accomplished musician among her many other talents. Both had lifelong histories in the area and knew just about everything we asked about.

The next morning Robert and Laurie picked us up. We noted tools and a broom in the back of their van. Laurie drove while Robert was on his cell phone talking to a former governor. It was obvious Robert and Laurie had a lot going on. The weather was cool and clear, the sun bright. Soon, we arrived at the tiny community of Chopin, named after the family that had purchased McAlpin's plantation, known locally as Hidden Hill, in February 1854. The site of McAlpin's former holdings alighted by bright budding leaves seemed cleansed by the sunshine, with most of the anticipated spookiness having fled under the tender green colors.

I had seen Judge Corley's 1892 photographs and drawings of the large cut through the bluffs by the Red/Cane River, made so the 1883 train tracks could lie flat. One photograph showed my third great-granduncle's house with its missing wing, which had been removed for the rail bed. There we were, 125 years after those photos and drawings: the gleaming tracks, the huge

FRONT VIEW OF LEGREE'S RESIDENCE.

*Figure 22.* An illustration of Hidden Hill from D. B.
Corley's 1892 book *A Visit to Uncle Tom's Cabin.*

earthen cut, woods on the rise above the river, and flat land to the northwest
now covered with pecan trees. Suggested by the succession papers, there had
been acres and acres of cotton, perhaps as many as 2,500 on those flat fields
worked by McAlpin's enslaved people. Their cabins had pressed up against the
rise of the bluff just across from Robert's house. A small creek and a bayou glis-
tened in the sun as they must have all those years ago, the landmarks that fit
details of the two freedom seekers' escape route in Stowe's book.

Robert Gentry, with his warm smile and machete, was a man on a mission.
Laurie, with her large, sparkling eyes, looked like she might be about to take us
to a hovering netherworld on the broom. We crossed the tracks, the beds now
wider and thicker with gravel than they would have been in 1883, and made
our way up the bluff between the tracks and river to the old burial grounds.

Peering through the trees as we reached the top, I could see one of the
wrought iron fences that had been put around Uncle Tom's and Robert
McAlpin's graves in the 1960s by people interested in the Uncle Tom/Legree
connection. Even though I assume from my research that the grave is unlikely
the "real" Uncle Tom's, I still felt a heavy heart. Robert McAlpin's grave was
the real thing, having been well described from the time he fell dead and was
summarily buried among his departed enslaved people.

The enslaved people's graves were marked by rocks that once must have seemed to be emerging from the ground like large mushrooms, now partly sunken with the frost and heaves of many bygone years. Still the rocks remained, struggling to do their jobs as markers, some angled by large trees grown up over the 168 years since the ground had been disturbed by a burial. Robert and Greg hacked the little trees emerging inside the fence around Uncle Tom's grave, and Laurie swept the plaque clean. I found some spring beauties, a tiny, early spring flower, and placed a few on an ancient moss-covered brick at the fence's edge.

My third great-granduncle's grave was twenty or thirty feet away. I stood looking down at his marker, thinking could all this really be, could he have been so cruel, so evil? Robert suggested more flowers. I felt reluctant, but in a moment a bouquet was thrust into my hands so I knelt at the fence, placing them with a prayer for healing and forgiveness. The men did more tree hacking and clearing, Laurie did her sweeping, and we slowly began to make our way back down the hill. Handmade bricks, so large and old, were scattered everywhere. I pictured the enslaved people bringing bricks to supplement the rocks marking the graves of their dead companions. Robert McAlpin lived at Hidden Hill for only twenty-five years or so. Even though he had held many people in bondage, my impression was of too many graves for such a short period of time. It is possible that the next owner of the property continued to use the burial ground, still . . .

The feeling was heavy as we walked back through the rough burial ground. The spring growth of mayapples, fuzzy gray-green mulleins, and delicate ephemerals moved gently in the breezes as if to sweep away our somber mood. Back at the tracks we stood with a copy of Corley's 1892 book and compared its drawings of the old tracks, McAlpin's house, the trestle, and other landmarks with what we saw now. It all fit. Robert Gentry knew where the enslaved people's cabins had been. He remembered last seeing a 1960s replica of Uncle Tom's cabin in 1980.

Back at the car and with our feelings lifted, we chatted and looked for a picnic spot as we drove along the pecan orchard road named after the Little Eva character in Stowe's book. Greg and I spent the rest of the day with Robert and Laurie as they showed us the many historical sites in the area. Natchitoches's Creole history is as exotic, rich, confusing, and layered as a well-loved and mended crazy quilt. The Gentrys were the perfect tutors.

The next morning, our last, Greg and I walked to Northwestern State University's campus, where Laurie and Robert had arranged a visit to the

Cammie G. Henry Research Center archives. The Gentrys had already contacted the archivist. We could have spent many hours with the maps of McAlpin's land and other related documents she found, but we had to get to the courthouse that afternoon. Robert introduced Greg and me to the clerk of court, who came to the rescue by finding the two ancient records I wanted the most: the deed for the 1804 land purchase, and the record of the sale of Robert Jr.'s enslaved people, land, buildings, and their contents. Though Greg and I had found other related records, those had been misfiled. The succession papers are what all this has been leading up to. The ancient script was challenging.

—

These papers are a painful, even hideous, illustrative document of the horrors of slavery, and that is why I decided I needed to transcribe them here exactly. And, that is why they need to be read.

## The Robert McAlpin Succession Document, Begun February 9, 1854

I have transcribed this handwritten twelve-page document to the best of my ability. I altered some punctuation and capitalization to increase readability. Otherwise, I have recorded it exactly. Note that several people are named multiple times across the document, sometimes (as with Culberson/Culverson) with different spellings.

It will be noticed that John McAlpin, Robert's brother, purchased some of the enslaved people and property. John and his wife had moved to this area from Mississippi by the 1840s. John, eighteen years older, was named estate administrator. John was late in life (he died in December 1854), so his son William T. McAlpin and son-in-law James D. Scott came from Texas to represent John's interest in Robert's estate.[19]

> Of sale, recorded March 4, 1854. The original of which this is the record delivered to the clerk of court at the request of the administrator. March 17, 1854.
>
> State of Louisiana, Parish of Natchitoches
>
> Be it remembered that on this ninth day of February 1854 and pursuance

of an order of the Hon. District Court in and for the Parish of Natchitoches and state of Louisiana, and after, notice to that effect given by advertising for more than 30 days in the English and French languages, in the Natchitoches Chronicle & News, a paper published in the town of Natchitoches, the first insertion of which was made on the 31st day of December 1853 and like notices in the English and French languages, hosted for a ___ space of time on the door of the courthouse of the Parish of Natchitoches.

___ H. Butts, an auctioneer in and for the Parish of Natchitoches and State of Louisiana proceeded to offer at Public Auction to the highest bidder, at the late residence of Robert McAlpin situated in this Parish on that part of the Red River called Cane River below the town of Clouterville. The following describes the property, belonging to the succession of Robert McAlpin deceased, upon the following terms and conditions "to wit." For all sums up to $20 cash for the movables, for all sums above that amount payable on the first day of May 1854. . . . For the land and slaves, one third cash, and one third in two years from the day of the Sale. Purchasers to give their notes with approved security in solid payable to the administrator or bearer being 8% per annum after maturity until paid and secured by vendors privilege and a Special Mortgage retained on the objects solved for which the notes are given, the Lands and Slaves to be sold subject to the clause of non-alienation "de non." To the prejudice of the vendors privilege, and Special Mortgage retained of them and the deferred installments for the tract of land, where the deceased resided being divided into two notes for each installment at which time and place I proceeded to adjudicate the said property on the said terms and conditions to the persons having after maintained at the last and highest bidder ___. A tract of land situated in this Parish of Natchitoches on the right descending bank of Red River called Cane River above the mouth of Bayou Barbue, being two thirds of the original confirmation to Michael DeRoy, containing 226 acres, more or less bounded above, by lands belonging to Victor Rachal, and below of those of Valerie Gainnie, sale from boundary to boundary for the quantity it may contain with all the improvements there as was adjudicated to Adam Carnahan for the sum of $1,300 all that tract of land on which the deceased resided, on both sides of Red River in the Parish of Natchitoches composed of several contiguous tracts of land belonging

to the deceased above on both sides of the Red River by lands of John
Carnahan.

Amount brought over $1,300

and below on both sides by lands of Emile Bast containing about 4,367
acres more or less to be sold from boundary to boundary and in accor-
dance with a plat to be exhibited on the day of sale, with all the improve-
ments thereon, consisting of a fine two-story dwelling (brick) Kitchen,
Hospital, Negro Cabins, Rooms, Stables and Gin, and a mill house driven
by waterpower, and running two gin stands, to sash saws, cotton press
(___ screws), corn mill. There is on this tract about 2,500 acres of bottom tillable land and the balance in pine hills was adjudicated to John
McAlpin for the sum of $28,000. A tract of land situated in the Parish
of Caddo, about one half a mile from the town of Greenwood, being the
northwest quarter of section 23, Township 17, Range 16, entered in the
name of Michael Wood, containing about 160 acres, more or less was adjudicated to G. H. Culverson for the sum of $400.

$400

All the deceased right title and interest to a claim of Land in Arkansas near
the Hot Springs, was adjudicated to J. F. Culverson for the sum of $35.

Amount Over $1,735

At this point the listing of the enslaved people is made.

Jack Barnes, a Negro man aged 37 years, a runaway
Lucy, a woman aged 35 years
Westley, a Negro age 17 years, sickly and subject to bleeding at the nose
Alfred, age 11 years
Adolph, age 9 years
Louisa, age 5 years
Frank, age 3 years
Nancy, age 35 years, rheumatic
All sale with guarantee of title only, to Mrs. Mary F. Colver for $6,110.

$6,110

Abraham, a Negro man aged 35 years, crippled in the hips
Mary, a Negro age 23 years
Lucy, a Negro girl 8 years, crippled in ankle
Mahala, 4 years
Virginia, 6 months
All sale with guarantee of title only to J. F. Culverson for the above
$3,000.

$3,000

Yellow Andrew, age 38 years, fistula in the urethra
Mary, 25 years, prolapsed ut[er]in
Robert, 7 years
Violet, 5 years
Jackson, 3 years
All sale with guarantee of title only to J. F. Culverson for $2,505.

Ephrain, aged 50 years
Big Caroline, 35 years
Sarah, aged 17 years
All sale with guarantee of title only to John M. Stewart for the sum of
$2,780.

$2,780

Tom, aged 18 years
Justin, aged 16 years
Sale with guarantee of title only to J. F. Culverson for $2,825.

$2,825

Several of the next set of names were known to me from a deed describing McAlpin's joint purchase of enslaved people and land from Simeon Rachal in 1850. This was one of many deeds in Robert McAlpin's name for purchases of land and at least one house that I found in the Natchitoches courthouse in 2018. McAlpin was an active buyer and seller of human and real property. The Rachal purchase was described as, "also the following named and described slaves, to wit Rose, a negro woman aged 36 years, and her children Reuben age 12 years, Nat age 10 years, Bob aged 5 years, [also] Millie aged 37 and Alexander aged 2 years, Charles a negro man age 30 years, Paszite a negro woman age 20 years, Justin a negro girl age 15, all slaves for life and guaranteed against the vices, maladies, and defects declared inhibitory in law."

One can see below that Rose still had her children Ruben and Nat with her. One wonders about Bob. Also noted is that four years later at this succession sale there is no Millie, Alexander, Charles, Paszite, or Justin. Some may have been sold or died.

Little Jack, 40 years
Rose, 39 years
Ruben, 15 years
Nat, 12 years
Ben Burton, 7 years
Alec, 4 years
All sale with guarantee of title only to John M. Stewart, for the sum of $5,200.

$5,200

Amount Brought Over $21,650

William, aged 36 years, crippled in the hand
Nancy, 22 years
Alec Jesse, 5 years
Billy, 3 years
Amanda, 2 years
Holland, 1 year
Kimbell, infant
All sale with guarantee of title only to Charles A. Stewart for $3,250.

$3,250

Ted 39 years, syphilis
Aspasie, 19 years
Sale with guarantee of title only to B. M. Luckett, tutor for Mary Jane and Alfred Thurston Luckett for the sum of $1,950.

$1,950

Millie, aged 75 years
With title guaranteed only sale to Sam M. Hyams [?] for $750

A note is written sideways on the document across Millie's name—"The mortgage retained on the slave Millie is this day canceled by filing of the receipt of the administrator, August 2, 1857, L. Williams, Recorder."

Israel, 28 years
Henry, 25 years
Justin, 6 years
Richard, 2 years
All sale with title only guaranteed to B. M. Luckett, tutor for Mary
Jane and Alfred Thurston Luckett for the sum of $3,600.

$3,600

Alec, age 36 years, sore eyes and one thumb off
Ellen, 37 years, thumb off and crippled
Sale with the title only guaranteed to John H. Boling for the sum of
$910.

$910

Black Andrew, 46 years, runaway
Rosetta, 35 years
Black Lucinda, 20 years
Cyrella, 6 years
Jane, 15 years
Ellen, 5 years
Charlotte, 2 years
Oscar, 4 months
All sale with guarantee of title only to John H. Boling for $4,605.

$4,605

Amaka, aged 40 years, diseased and unsound
John, 10 years
Joshua, 7 years
Henrietta, 6 years
Adeline, 5 years
All sale with guarantee of title only to John M. Stewart the sum of
$2,650.

$2,650

Sam, 41 years, crippled and diseased
Sarah, 38 years
All sold with title alone guaranteed to J. F. Culberson for the sum of
$1,500.

Amount Carried Over                                  $39,365

Sarah, aged 38 years
Sale with title alone guaranteed to John McAlpin for the sum of
$1,200.

                                                      $1,200

Rhoda, a Negro woman 70 years old
Sale with title guaranteed to Mrs. Eliza Williams for the sum of $140.

                                                       $140

Here, a note is written perpendicularly to the document: "The two notes
given for slave Rhoda described in this account filed this day as paid and
mortgage canceled. May 13, 1857."

Sarah, aged 35 years, diseased and crippled
Susan, 13 years
Sale with title alone guaranteed to Jerome Messi for the sum of $825.

                                                       $825

Here, another perpendicular notation: "The two notes given for the slaves
Sarah and Susan described in this account filed this day as paid and mortgage
canceled. February 21, 1859."

Andrew, aged 50 years
Clarisse, 43 years, prolapsed uterus
Sale with title only guaranteed to John Carnahan for the sum of $2,360.

                                                      $2,360

Charles, aged 48 years, blacksmith, two fingers crippled
Maria, 46 years, rheumatic
Thom [?], age 3 years
Sale with title only guaranteed to John Boling for the sum of $2,020.

                                                      $2,020

Jim, aged 21 years, chronic sore leg
Matilda, 16 years, and

Moses 7 months
All sale with title alone guaranteed to John H. Boling for his minor
children Lucius, Sam, Maryann Bowling for $2,475.

$2,475

Nelson, aged 56 years, rheumatic
Jenny, 40 years
Francis, 9 years
Elizabeth, 7 years
All sale with title alone guaranteed to Pense Collomb for the sum of
$2,475.

$2,475

Henry, age 12 years
Isaiah, 6 years
Sale without a guarantee except as to title to Alexander McAlpin for
$3,046.

$3,046

Amount Carried Over $53,906

Joe, aged 40 years
Sale without guarantee except as to title to B. M. Luckett as tutor of
Mary Jane and Alfred Thurston Luckett for the sum of $1,380.

$1,380

Betsy, age 30 years
Crippled infant
Sale without guarantee except as to title to Pense Collomb for the sum
of $910.

$910

Easter, aged 55 years
Sale without guarantee except as to title to W. G. Coxfield for the sum
of $185.

$185

Phyllis, aged 18 years with her child,
Rosanna, 6 months

Sale without guarantee except as to title to Cary H. Blanchard for sum
of $1,000.

$1,000

Below, Lucinda (Lucindy) appears with her two children fathered by Robert McAlpin. Their names and ages fit well with the grandsons' account
given to the Shreveport Chamber of Commerce in 1960. Lucinda's age was
not exactly known. She could have been as much as ten years younger. The
1850 federal "slave census" for McAlpin lists one sixteen-year-old mulatto
female. This could be Lucinda. Postbellum censuses show her as being born
around 1835. This same "slave census" also lists several young mulatto children. In later documents, Carolyn appears as Carrie. One wonders whether
John, Robert's brother, knew that the four- and seven-year-old girls were his
nieces and, thus, his reason for purchasing this family group, three of the
five enslaved people he bought?

Lucinda, aged 28 years
Carolyn, 7 years
Cora, 4 years
All sale without guarantee except as to title to John McAlpin for the
sum of $1,400.

$1,400

Dary, age 62 years, sore eyes, rheumatic and runaway
Sale without guarantee except as to title to John McAlpin for the sum
of $600.

$600

Bill, aged 45 years, crippled arm
Sale without guarantee except as to title to J. M. Stewart for the sum of
$680.

$680
———————
$60,161

The section above was followed with signatures by all purchasers. Some were
represented by attorneys-in-fact. Many names I recognize as Robert McAlpin's
neighbors. Then begins a long list of tools and other items.

| | | |
|---|---|---|
| 1 crosscut saw | N. Frediece [?] | $3 |
| 2 crosscut saws | E. L. Hyams | $5 |
| 4 cans & contents | J. H. Deplin | $5 |
| 1 box & contents | " | $1 |
| 1 lot sundries | M. Carnahan | $1.50 |
| 1 bag shot & files | P. Collomb | $4.75 |
| 1 box medicines | E. L. Hyams | $4.00 |
| 1 lot Sweet oil | F. F. Metoyer | $1.25 |
| 1 lot Porter [?] | F. Racbecca [?] | $1.00 |
| 1 cotton mark | N. Garcia | $1.00 |
| 1 lot bottles | M. Carnahan | $2.50 |
| 1 keg powder & lanterns | McKenny | $4.00 |
| 1 stack & die | N. Garcia | $5.00 |
| 1 double corn sheller | E. L. Hyams | $2.00 |
| 1 pair stocks | N. Garcia | $1.00 |

At this point I stopped listing names and prices except where of interest.

1 stillard [?]
3 mortars
3 cans & contents
3 demijohns & jar
1 keg & irons
2 pairs scales
1 lot medicines
1 lot medicines
1 lot medicines
1 lot sundries
1 lot medicines
1 lot medicines
1 lot medicines
[?] mash brush
1 set cupping glass
1 lot jars
1 lot scales ___
1 bay ointment
Amount Over $60,167.45

1 lot pipes & keys
1 keg nails
1 lot paper & black ___
1 scale
1 lot pots traps & ___
1 lot tallow
1 lot sacks
1 wagon     $119
1 cart
1 jackscrew

Mules

| | |
|---|---|
| ___ | $100 |
| Mare Bett | $100 |
| Sam | $54 |
| Marianne | $75 |
| Sophie | $105 |
| Lyon | $110 |
| Susan | $127 |
| Paul | $128 |
| Mamselle | $100 |
| Jim | $130 |
| Milly | $134 |
| Jenny | $138 |
| Kate | $140 |
| Mary | $142 |
| Jane | $110 |
| Liger | $30 |
| Selly | $39 |
| Eliza | $100 |
| Peyen | $90 |

[Horses]

| | |
|---|---|
| Horse Snip | $77 |
| Pony Gray | $35 |
| Horse Ball | $40 |

| Horse Tom | $152 |
|-----------|------|
| Horse Fox | $80  |

Amount Over $62,641.45

Following this are 153 more lines of animals, tools and batches of other goods. Items that have not appeared before include twine, demijohn and cradle, steel scrapers, coils of rope, window blinds, bagging, gates, cattle in the woods, oxen yoke, several cribs of corn, lot of hogs, a ferry flat, a grindstone, wheels, a cistern, a lot of timber, several lots of lumber, pots and kettles, milk cans, wash kettle, wheelbarrows, shoats in pen, and one lot of fodder. That list is followed by more script.

> One military land warrant No 31 g 58 for forty acres date 16 Dec 1851 in favour of Eucaine Alexander, sale to Gen. LaPlace for $35.

This is followed by three more "military land warrants" to different people, for 40 acres on April 13, 1852, 160 acres on June 12, 1852, and 160 acres on February 14, 1851.

> The tract of land including the homestead, represented on this ___ verbal as having been adjudicated to John McAlpin for the sum of $28,000 and he having declined to comply with the

Amount Over $65,890.12

conditions of the sale, the same was at the request of the administrator and consent of the said John McAlpin by me offered a second time at public sale to the highest bidder at the same place and upon the same terms and conditions at the risk of John McAlpin, the former purchaser. When Dr. J. B. Chopin being the last and highest bidder became the purchaser of the same for the sum of $22,000.

The negroes Abraham aged 25 years, cripple in hand, Mary aged 23 years, Lucy aged 18 years, crippled ankle, and Mahala, aged 4 years represented in this by process verbal as having been adjudicated to J. F. Culberson for the sum of $2,050 and he having declared to comply with the conditions of the sale, the same was at the request of the administrator if he offered a second time at Public Sale to the highest bidder at the same place and upon the same terms and conditions at the risk of J. F. Culberson the former purchaser, when Mrs. Margaret Smith being the last and highest bidder became the purchaser of the same for $2,050.

The negroes Andrew aged 38 years, fistula in urethra, Mary, age 36 years, falling of the ut[er]in, Robert, aged 7 years, Violet, age 5 years, Jack, age 3 years, represented in this by process verbal as having been adjudicated to J. F. Culberson for the sum of $2505 and he having declared to comply with the conditions of the sale the same as at the request of the administrator, by me offered a second time at Public Sale, to the highest bidder at the same place and upon . . .

Amount Over $89,940.12

Here, the copy of the long account of the succession sale ends. It appears one or more pages are missing. It would have been impossible to transcribe this document without Robert Gentry having sent an enlarged copy, for which I am grateful.

~

For the two years between the death of my third great-granduncle and the succession sale, I have not found any records about the enslaved people at Hidden Hill. It is likely that John supervised them and the property. Examining this tragic list of people auctioned after McAlpin's death, I offer certain observations and speculations. The enslaved people totaled eighty-nine. Quite a few were children. From the groupings it appears that most of the young children were kept with their mothers, to be expected because Louisiana law at the time forbid separation of mothers and children under ten.

Four of these stolen people had been used to secure mortgages. Evidently, older age or infirmities were not an impediment for use as collateral. The mortgages on the two oldest were paid off some years after the succession sale. Millie, age seventy-five, brought $750 at the sale. Rhoda, age seventy, brought $140, approximately the same amount each of three mules with the names Millie, Jenny, and Kate fetched on the bidding block. Sarah, diseased and crippled at age thirty-five, also served as a mortgage security, along with thirteen-year-old Susan, possibly her daughter.

A large proportion of McAlpin's enslaved people were sick, crippled, or suffering from chronic problems. It seemed too many. Sure enough, I found a 1998 study on Natchitoches Parish slavery.[20] At McAlpin's time, with Natchitoches Parish being one of the richest areas in Louisiana, 6 percent of enslaved people in the study were found to be infirm. Almost 41 percent of McAlpin's enslaved people aged eighteen and over were unwell or had physical deformities. Might this support the accounts of McAlpin's cruelty? Most chilling was that two of his enslaved people were missing thumbs. What are the odds of accidents causing thumb amputations to two? Could amputations have been punishment for serious infractions such as running away or learning to read? Slave codes allowed for mutilation including amputations as punishment. Possibly related to the cruelty issue, I also noted in the 1850 "slave census" that two twenty-two-year-olds were listed as "fugitives from the state," meaning they had run away within the year so were still counted as his property. I checked six census pages before and after McAlpin's listing. No other slaveholders had fugitives.

Information may continue to emerge about Robert McAlpin Jr. and Hidden Hill, a forced labor camp shrouded with mystery and encased with stories of evil; an unmarked burial ground for enslaved people, their cruel owner lying in their midst; and a site alleged to have inspired the fictional monster Simon Legree. Hidden Hill is noted to this day on occasional maps. More references about the McAlpin/Legree connection continually come online.

As for McAlpin as a model for Legree, there are several competitors. Perhaps more than one figure served as a model for Harriet Beecher Stowe to aid her in crafting her evil character. Some are listed by Stowe herself in her nonfiction *Key to Uncle Tom's Cabin*. Others have been self-appointed. Oddly, the Harriet Beecher Stowe Center in Connecticut, which is dedicated to preserving and interpreting her Hartford home and collections and to "promot[ing] vibrant discussion," has only one document related to the McAlpin/Legree issue: the D. B. Corley book. According to the center's collection manager, the center has none of the many related documents held in the Robert Gentry collection at Northwestern State University.[21]

Another surprise in all this, a welcome pleasantness, was discovering that two women of renown are associated with Hidden Hill. The first is the artist Clementine Hunter, who was born at Hidden Hill after it was sold to the Chopins. As a lover of folk art, I had heard of her but had no idea she had sprung from land my ancestors had owned. After leaving Hidden Hill she worked as a field hand at the two-hundred-year-old Melrose Plantation. Her artistic career took off when she was in her sixties.[22] It is not surprising that many of her almost five thousand paintings over her 101 years had to do with a life of forced work.

The second, Kate Chopin, an early feminist writer of Creole descent, spent time at Hidden Hill after marrying Oscar Chopin, son of Dr. J. B. Chopin, who purchased McAlpin's Hidden Hill at the succession sale. Her writings made use of the stories about McAlpin/Legree. Although she is best known today for her 1899 *The Awakening*, her first book, *At Fault*, published in 1890, has a well-crafted description of Hidden Hill, including a young couples' visit to the burial site of Robert McAlpin and enslaved people who had been forced to work his land. A large amount of material on Kate Chopin is available online.[23] Discovering her writing, some scandalous for the times, has enriched my understanding of the cultural complexities of Natchitoches Parish, and provided a fascinating offshoot to the painful story of my third great-granduncle.

Here at the end of this saga, I find myself considering whether I have benefited somehow from even the smallest bit of wealth Robert McAlpin Jr. accrued on the bodies of the people he kept in bondage. His estate was worth about $2.3 million in today's money. Since Robert had no direct heirs, his siblings divided his estate. His sister Isabella, my third great-grandmother, died years before Robert. Her daughter Mary Cosby Browning, my great-great-grandmother, had died four years prior to the death of her uncle Robert McAlpin Jr. Being that Mary was the wife of my great-great-grandfather Zaccheus Price, could he or their children have received her portion? Could this account for his having afforded so much land, the purchase of human beings, and the education of his six living children? Could it be related to how my great-grandfather Henry Choice Price was able to acquire (and lose) two ships and build two large houses? That so many of my ancestors were well educated, unusual in those days, was undoubtedly a benefit to me. Conjecture without certainty.

—

Since that March 2018 visit to Natchitoches Parish, a large moss-covered brick sits at the edge of my garden. Robert Gentry thrust it in my hands when Greg and I were saying our goodbyes. Robert was given it by the men tearing down the last McAlpin enslaved people's cabins around 1960. The workmen claimed it was from McAlpin's house. How I got the brick through the airport and onto the plane is another story. This chapter is already too long.

Robert McAlpin's 4,700 or so acres are now part of an 11,000-acre pecan orchard known as Little Eva, the largest in the United States. As for the brick, at first, I thought I would not like such a visible reminder of this surely cursed ancestor. Now I have grown to appreciate it. It reminds me to think, to be grateful, to consider prejudice, and to grow.

—

Even after all this, Louisiana is not finished. Sugarcane and more bayous remain. And leaving Birmingham.

*Chapter 16*

# Leaving Birmingham, 1966

Alabama started the new year true to itself. The January edition of the *Southern Courier* did not find a chastened state.[1] Three federal judges said they would not rule against the poll tax unless the Justice Department could prove discrimination. Attorneys for the state said it was "simply a test to see whether a citizen is really interested in voting." State attorney general Richmond Flowers started a campaign to change the Alabama Democratic Party logo from a crowing rooster under a fluttering banner that contained the words "White Supremacy" to the same rooster under a banner with the word "Democrats." Below the rooster were the words "For the Right." That part stayed. I suppose the change was small progress, but the attorney general also sued to overthrow the Voting Rights Act of 1965, not that the act was doing any good. Demonstrations for voting rights were being held around the state, sometimes with violence from white authorities. As usual, the *Southern Courier* was the best source of information regarding civil rights and the African American community.

At home, things were settling in as we learned how to be a family of five. Scott continued working hard, and I developed a new routine as I learned how to care for two young children and a brand-new baby girl. The January cold and snow kept us inside a good bit, which didn't seem to matter since I was figuring out how to nurse Melantha as often as she liked and still manage to keep her brothers safe and entertained. Greg and Marcus soon became "the boys," and Melantha "your little sister." The boys loved to amuse Melantha and to get her to smile and laugh, which was their treasured reward.

One of my most precious memories during that period was watching the boys gleefully finger-painting at our breakfast table, with my beautiful baby girl nestled in my arms. In late January we received welcome news when we learned that Clay Musselman, our friend who had suffered the wreck, had regained consciousness. The city lay quietly below us for a change. Our brief period of tranquility did not last long.

Later in January, I was asked to be on the Child Development Committee for the local Office of Economic Opportunity to help with planning integrated childcare centers in the city. The initial center, for children ages three to six, was in a Catholic facility on Eighth Avenue North, a section of Birmingham northeast of us. With the center funded by a federal grant, white parents needed to be identified who were willing to have their preschool children attend. Not surprisingly, Scott and I were approached about sending Greg, then four and a half years old. We hesitated. The hours of the school were long. Greg was getting adjusted to a new baby sister. He was shy. He had never been in a program away from home. After Scott and I discussed, and Greg expressed interest and willingness, we said yes. At first, he was homesick and intimidated by the strange children and adults, but typical of his personality, he forced himself to be brave.

After a couple of weeks, Greg was conquering his fears and enjoying going, for the most part. Soon he was telling us he liked his teacher and his new friends. He was excited when it was a school day. However, he was also asking us what phrases like "paddling" and "I will skin you" meant. Greg told Scott and me that the teachers would say this to the children while calling them bad, and that some Black children were being hit. I was shocked. We did not use corporal punishment and did not want our child in such an environment, especially where Black children were specifically being targeted. Further, in my role with the Child Development Committee, I did not feel corporal punishment was an appropriate policy for the fledgling integrated centers.

A few days after we heard these questions from our little boy, he came home quite upset. His teacher had told him if he cried anymore she would "whip him." I doubt he would have understood what "whip" meant unless he had seen it. Or maybe he just knew from the teacher's tone of voice that whatever whipping was, it was frightening. The next morning, I went to the center to talk with the director. If I didn't know who she was, I found out. Katherine Blackford is beside me in my sixth-grade school picture. She was in the debutante crowd, and we had never been friends. Her response to the "whipping" threat was that the children needed it, especially the "colored" children ("that is all they know"), and the practice would be continued.

That evening, I called one of the teachers who I knew slightly. She confirmed that "spanking" did occur and was frequent. She also thought it necessary and described the objects used for hitting the children: wooden paddles, rulers, and broomsticks. She told me children were "spanked" in the presence of all the children. Parents were not asked for permission. Finally, she said using corporal punishment followed the orders of Father Foster, the priest who oversaw the facility.

By then it was early February, and Marcus turned two. We had a small birthday party. Soon after, the center director called and asked whether I would volunteer part-time as an assistant teacher. I agreed to two hours a week. This seemed promising, but I soon saw there was no intention of pulling back on the corporal punishment policy. I also observed that, indeed, it was being used almost entirely on the African American children. My next step was to send a letter to the Birmingham Office of Economic Opportunity. The letter arrived on February 21. Four days later Greg was sent home with a letter on the letterhead "St. Vincent's Nursery, Child Development Center, Component No. 701," signed by my former classmate.

The letter stated, "after careful consideration for the past several weeks, I feel that, for the reasons outlined below, we can no longer accept your child as a pupil in the school." The reasons included her opinion that "he was unhappy there, asked the teachers too many questions, and doesn't participate in an activity if it is not to his liking." She further stated many of the children came from deprivation and needed a learning environment that our son did not since he already knew colors, letters, and numbers. Scott and I struggled to find the words to tell Greg why he could no longer attend the school for which he had worked so hard to overcome his initial fears.

This wasn't the end of the whole sad saga. I was summoned to meet with Father Foster and explain my concerns. I wore my nicest dress. I was nervous. I hoped he would consider my points. I never knew whether the meeting made a difference. I have spent my life in professions concerning children. I am aware that disciplinary practices among social, racial, and ethnic groups differ and that questioning them is often fraught. I still think I was correct to expose and question the nursery school's use of corporal punishment. Hitting children for discipline, especially with objects, is no longer considered acceptable by childcare professionals, and even then was not acceptable to many. Hitting only members of one group of children while another looks on is barbarous, especially when they are only three, four, and five years old. And the group being hit was African American.

~

Following Greg's dismissal from the nursery school, I looked at some other schools, all white, of course, since he now missed nursery school. I remember one where the teacher bragged that they taught the four-year-olds to stay within the lines in coloring books. After that, Greg stayed home with his siblings, until kindergarten, following our move from Birmingham.

The months flowed on, dotted by frequent morning get-togethers with Sidney and Helen, with our intense discussion of issues in our lives and the world while our children played. The city stayed quiet as far as bombings or major demonstrations were concerned. Plenty was happening in the state, however, and in other southern states. We were not involved in any of those events.

My father visited on weekends, played with the children, and puttered in the yard as he loved to do. We kept attending the Unitarian Church and the recorder group, the latter thanks to Papa babysitting. Influenced by Papa's interest in what was then called "health food," I was reading about nutrition and organic foods. We discovered Walnut Acres, a farm in Pennsylvania, started by a young couple selling their organic products by mail order. There were no markets like Fresh Foods or Whole Foods, local organic markets, or even organic sections in grocery stores back then. It was a happy day when an order came. A five-gallon bucket of natural peanut butter was our favorite. The oil sat on top, and it was hell getting it stirred in but worth it. I started baking bread after discovering their delicious flours. When we could afford it, we ordered honey, canned vegetables, and more. Poring over their catalog and ordering was a treat. The Krauses taught us how to make yogurt, a skill they knew from Europe, and gave us starters. In southern stores yogurt could not be had. In fact, I did not know commercial yogurt was available anywhere until a grocery store visit during a trip up north. It was the perfect time to be learning how to cook for a family with three growing children.

Sooner or later, I suppose it was inevitable that there would be another problem with my mother. We had a mixture of nuts left from the holidays in a bowl. Mother came to visit, spotted the Brazil nuts, and referred to them with a racial slur, laughing. I must have lost it, so to speak, rather like the time in high school when I left home. I pushed her out the door and told her to stay away and never to say those words in my presence should I ever see her again. After four months I relented because by then we were about to move. I felt badly for her as I began to realize that she would probably not see the children more than once or twice a year. Papa would see them more because of his Pennsylvania visits.

In the spring of 1966, Scott left the University of Alabama at Birmingham and went to work for a rayon plant, Beaunit Fibers, in Childersburg, Alabama. His new job with its major salary increase made the ninety-mile round-trip commute worthwhile. He learned the processing of wood into rayon. The cellulose, dissolved in sulfuric acid, was squeezed out of tiny openings in extruders. Computers were new in textile mills. They could be programmed to adjust the gauges that set the size of the extrusions, according to the specified fiber. The job was offered with the understanding that the company would transfer Scott to the Research Triangle area in North Carolina after six months. Instead, when the time came, the company sent us to Gastonia, North Carolina, for a year, due to the company's space and equipment availability. Greg went to kindergarten there, and I stayed home with Marcus and Melantha.

⁓

In June, shortly before we left, our dear friends Polly and Rob Wright and their three children, playmates of ours, left Birmingham. Several other families had already moved, either because they'd lost employment due to their civil rights involvement or because they'd had so many threats, sometimes even cross-burnings, that they feared for their lives. Some experienced both. By then, we knew we were moving, too. Now, I can see how sad it must have been for my parents, but with our youthful energy and hope to make a better life for our children we were excited.

On August 15, 1966, we took off in our Volkswagen bus for a large, colonial-style rented house in Gastonia. Beaunit Fibers paid for our move, including packing household goods. I still remember the packers exchanging glances as they wrapped up our jelly jar glasses, our gas station giveaway dishes, and the assorted goods we had cobbled together. The orange crates that served as toy boxes and bookshelves gave the packers pause, as did the boards and concrete blocks. I was not used to people doing work I could do and felt embarrassment both from that and from the silliness of their careful wrapping of jelly glasses and even plastic forks. All we had to do was get ourselves to the Gastonia house and receive the movers.

The day we left was ghastly hot and humid as August days in Birmingham were. Perhaps we didn't notice. Between our excitement and relief to be leaving and three small children in a vehicle pre–car seats, we had plenty to occupy us. Scott and I drove east, then slightly north, watching the despised red clay with its permanent stains in clothing disappear and morph into darker, more hospitable soil. Our hopes for better circumstances for our children swelled with every mile. Goodbye, Birmingham. Now, five-plus decades later, that future is our past. I have lived in North Carolina ever since that August trip in a packed Volkswagen bus. My mind still pictures the cracks in the sidewalk in front of my childhood house, the thrill of skating down a nearby hill and of being able to roam all over downtown Birmingham at such a young age, my father puttering in the backyard with his beautiful hollyhocks and four o'clocks, and so much more.

—

In Gastonia, we soon learned about its dark 1929 Loray Mill strike history, with the killing of a leader, Ella May Wiggins. She was an unlikely hero, a single mother of nine children, four lost to whooping cough. As they grew, their mother became a folk song writer and singer, using her talents to help lead the strike. Instead of renting a house from the mill, she chose to live in a wooden shack with her children, the only white people in the tiny village "Stump Town."

The 1929 strike seemed a long time ago. Scott and I felt safer and elated to be out of Alabama. We started attending the Unitarian Church in Charlotte and made a few friends. In less than a year, however, Scott was recruited by a Beaunit colleague who had gone on to Duke University Medical Center. When we went house hunting, our drive through Durham felt and looked too much like Birmingham, so we chose Chapel Hill, despite its twelve-mile drive each way to Duke.

In June 1967 we bought a small house on the east side of Chapel Hill, staying only a year and a half before moving to a larger place. There, as the war in Vietnam was raging, we became foster parents to a war-injured five-year-old girl named Huong Pham. She returned to her parents in Vietnam after almost two years with us. Close to two decades later, at her request and with a trip to Vietnam and a lot of interaction with government agencies on our part, she returned to the United States. We adopted her, and she remains close by. Our lives were profoundly affected both positively and negatively.

Scott thrived in the Duke community, starting out as a consultant in the Biomath Division, soon joining the Department of Pediatrics as a system analyst. In another few years, he was asked to teach introductory computer science. Scott went from instructor to lecturer to research assistant professor, teaching courses in biomedical engineering, the Duke evening program for adults, and computer science. As always, he worked hard and long. Outside consulting and serving as a student adviser added other demands. I was so proud of him and the Medical Center. Scott had not been able to finish college, but Duke realized his value and talents, nonetheless.

Being close to the University of North Carolina campus, I began taking courses to add to the one year at St. John's while working part-time in the Department of Botany. Eventually, I switched to Duke University, where I took a bachelor's degree in health sciences and obtained certification for what was then called a physician associate. I joined the Department of Pediatrics and for most of the time there was the assistant director of the Pediatric Clinic as well as the medical director for the child abuse team. In the early 1980s, I returned to the University of North Carolina for my master's in public health, and in 1994, I received a doctorate in public health. After I left Duke later that year, I continued child-related research and public health work for many years. My professional life has been rich and rewarding.

I will be forever grateful to Scott for helping me continue my education while sacrificing his own, and to my mentor at Duke, Thomas Eliot Frothingham, the finest pediatrician and wannabe parasitologist I have ever known. Much of my success (along with its unexpected notoriety) in conducting and publishing research, all within the field of pediatrics, was due to Tom's support, advocacy, and belief in me. After Scott left Duke, he started his own consulting firm. He served Chapel Hill for years in the political realm and as a board member for the county water authority. Our family life was full of rich experiences and adventures. The children got to grow up in a 1920s clapboard house with a porch across the front, an attic, a basement, lots of books, and nooks and crannies nestled all over. It was surrounded by woods yet was only two and a half blocks from downtown Chapel Hill and the University of North Carolina campus. After thirty-five years together of mostly love and wonder, Scott and I went our separate ways. We have five precious grandchildren and two great-grandchildren. With the passing of more years, we each remarried, and after more time we are good friends again.

I have returned to Birmingham several times in the last two decades: a fortieth and fiftieth high school reunion, several funerals, and most recently a research trip for this book. I continue to marvel at how mountainous Birmingham is, at the varied soils, some set with flinty sharp chips of rock that were anathema to my father, and the lovely, varied architecture of the nicer homes. Parts of the city swell with beauty, and some are still ugly. The air is cleaner. Large trees in the center of Twentieth Street and the revitalized downtown are remarkable. The university has grown tremendously. Last time I was there, my eyes were treated with a rainbow of happy, friendly people as I walked around my old haunts in Southside.

—

Clay Musselman continued to be part of our lives for many years. He had managed to visit us, somehow sneaking away from his assisted-living placement in Lancaster, twice before we left Birmingham. It must have been during the time that we now see as his golden period. Clay surprised everyone by regaining some of his abilities after emerging from his coma; then, after about six years, he deteriorated, becoming incapable of traveling on his own anymore. Even at his best, it was painful to watch him bent and crippled, hobbling along with a cane, struggling to eat with a utensil, even laboring to talk. But he retained his basic intelligence and sardonic witty personality. He loved being around our children. During the years we received letters from him they were always addressed to all five of us. Eventually, encouraged by Clay, he and his wife divorced. He knew she had no future with him. She wanted children, and his temper strained their relationship.

Clay didn't visit us in Gastonia, but he did make it a couple of times to Chapel Hill. He was not supposed to be traveling at all, so we viewed his visits as an escape from whatever facility he was in at the time. He had to scheme and save money to make it happen. We would pick him up at the bus station. One visit was especially memorable as, unknown to us, Clay had an additional plan. When it was time for him to go back, we thought we were putting him on the bus to Lancaster, but in actuality, he had figured out how to get to Jackson, Mississippi, where he was determined to visit Alice Walker, with whom he was still infatuated. Eventually, we learned he arrived at her house with his cane and crooked stance, knocked at the door, and was greeted by her husband, who threw him off the property. About twelve years later, she used the sad episode as the basis of a short story, "Laurel." The quotes from Laurel's letters in the story sound precisely like how Clay communicated after he came out of his six-month coma, so much so it is tempting to suspect Walker may have used his sentences verbatim. Some express his love and desire for her. Others are not flattering as to his character. Did these emerge in his letters because he was like a stroke victim in having lost that part of his brain that gave him judgment, a social sense, the ability to inhibit his hurtful, inappropriate thoughts? "I hope you know how I lost part of my brain working for your people in the South." Or, "You married a jew . . . I guess you have a taste for the exotic."[2] Statements like these did not emerge from his precoma self.

I was upset when I saw the story because it was so thinly disguised any-one who knew Clay would know the story was about him. As fate would have it, I had a subscription to the magazine that published it. The story is excellent but seemed, with my fondness for Clay, exploitive at the time. Now, with the tincture of time and experience, I realize he was a stalker and ha-rasser, brain damage or not. Eventually, there was no more sneaking out of assisted-living centers for Clay, and he came no more to either of us.

For years, his two-page single-spaced typed letters arrived on a regular ba-sis. From reading the Alice Walker story, clearly autobiographical to an extent I cannot know, I suspect she received even more letters than we did. I cannot imagine how long it took Clay to type them with his one shaky finger. We al-ways answered his letters. They were a mixture of normal back-and-forth news, stream of consciousness, and uncensured comments, sometimes crude and sometimes profound. Always, they were raw with the pain of his loss of brain-power and physical ability, of which he was all too aware, loss of his wife, and loss of any chance of wooing Alice Walker, for whom his obsession remained, or any other woman for that matter. His letters made it clear that he missed the sexual companionship of a woman. In one he wrote, "I still think I need the gentle touch of a woman, but this might be socially induced. 'Do not forget to masturbate,' said one shrink to me in the nuthouse. I thought that if that is how he calms himself and he has several degrees, it must be the way for me, too."

The last letter we received from Clay was dated August 31, 1980. He wrote of still missing his ex-wife. We never heard from him or anything about him after that. We waited for months, and then it was too late. Both parents had died. Pre-internet, we used old-fashioned methods to determine he was probably not in Lancaster County but remained unable locate him. I used to visit him whenever I was in Lancaster County visiting my family. It was al-ways painful to see him in his constricted condition, so lonely and impaired, and then to have to say goodbye. Recently I looked for him again. I finally found an obituary on the internet. I was astounded to learn that he had lived thirty-one more years. Those years must have seemed endless and full of suf-fering. Clay died on July 2, 2011, in a rehabilitation home near Gettysburg. It pains me that we lost contact and that he must have had years away from his beloved green homeland.

—

When Scott and I thought of Clay, sometimes we would think of his brief replacement, even though soon we could not remember his name. Years later, we realized we didn't know what happened to Clay's replacement or the *Southern Courier*. By then, we were in a new phase of life in North Carolina, being parents of schoolchildren and getting involved in new friendships, new activities, and social issues around the Vietnam War.

I now know that Clay's replacement, Jim Willse, left Birmingham for Tuscaloosa only a few weeks after his Birmingham arrival. The *Southern Courier* stopped publication in 1968. Jim went on to have a renowned career as a prizewinning journalist and editor of the *New York Daily News* and then the *Star-Ledger* in New Jersey until he retired in 2011. We learned this in June 2016, when I went on a Baltic Sea cruise and tour of Norway with my husband, Doug Berg, a trip of special interest because of Doug's Norwegian heritage. The universe had conspired for Clay's mysterious replacement and me to get back together. Jim, having the lifelong habit of a reporter, kept a small notebook and pen in his shirt pocket to be ready to record events of interest. Thus, it was that he wrote the words below, words more accurately crafted than my memory and ability allow. With the ship docked, Doug and I had disembarked and were with some fellow cruisers in a restaurant at a long table. Chatting comprised the typical as one does with strangers. "Where are you from?" "Birmingham." The man across from me explained he had been there for a short time working on a small civil rights paper. Later he wrote in his public blog:

> Oh, she says, did I know someone named Clay Musselman? I sure did, I say, I was his replacement for a few weeks in Birmingham before I went to Tuscaloosa for the paper. I'm remembering as I talk—he was in an auto accident, fell asleep on his way back to Alabama from New Jersey, he had a box of my LPs in the back of his car, I stayed at his place on a hill in Birmingham, next to great neighbors who were very kind to me, a young couple with an unforgettable name—Scott and Marcia Herman-Giddens.
>
> And there it is. She holds up her blue-and-white Duke name tag—Marcia Herman. She was the kind and generous young woman who with her husband [Scott] and their young son made me feel welcome—a New York carpetbagger about to venture into some tricky Southern waters. We are both somewhat thunderstruck—what are the odds of a chance meeting, a *re-meeting*, like this 50 years later, on a rainy day in Oslo, Norway.

Jim Willse is now in this writing phase of my life as a new mentor, and I am forever grateful.

# Chapter 17

# At the End

*Also I give to Zachariah Nettles three Negroes (viz) Peter, Titus and Joe*
*... to be enjoyed by Zachariah Nettles and his lawful heirs forever...*
Zachariah Nettles, will, signed November 1, 1803

The genealogy book that began as a thread tugging me when I was young
has turned into a heavy cord. It still raises questions and has family branches
unexplored. Now, nearing the end of these explorations, I have learned that
most, perhaps all, of my maternal great-grandfathers of an age to serve in the
American Revolution fought in that war for freedom while holding people
in bondage at home. The Stygian irony of this has woven itself through my
family and the history of this country.

M'Wese, my mother's mother, Louise Gibson Richardson Price, born
nine years after the end of the Civil War, was the only grandparent still living
when I was born and was responsible for my first name. She spent her early
childhood in Jeanerette, Louisiana, near her great-uncle's sugar plantation,
Bayside-on-the-Têche, previously worked by enslaved people. Coming from
two slaveholding Richardson lines, she married a Price from Georgia, joining another long line of enslavers. One branch of the line I am named after
has been here for almost four hundred years, all but one holders of people in
bondage. The progenitor, Amos Richardson, was a slaver, trading along the
coast from New England to the Caribbean. Though I had known from childhood that my ancestors held enslaved people, to learn that there was also the
trafficking of humans shocked me. Neither had I realized that I was named
after slaveholders before all this exploration. This sits heavily on me now in
2020, in the winter of my life.

A name bestowed on a child is one of the few real powers parents have. My first name, Marcia, put me under the penumbra of M'Wese's father, my great-grandfather William Marshall Richardson, and his mother, Catherine Marshall. My middle name, Edwina, was after my father's first name, Edwin: straightforward and not with the exigency of Marshall, as I well knew my father and what family he had left.

There can be a destiny in naming. Some cultures believe a newborn's name should reflect their purpose in life. They have shaman and elders to discover the suitable name. Much has been written about this. There is even a hypothesis called nominative determinism: some people gravitate toward activities defined by their name. I always smile when I see examples. It is surprisingly common. I have read about an orthopedist named Dr. Bone, a park ranger named Forrest, a city planner named Street. My friend who had been a public defender discovered in her sixties that her Dutch name meant the equivalent. Names do more than this. For me, the effect included an attachment.

Carrying the female version of Marshall made me seek knowledge about my great-grandfather and piqued interest in that branch of my ancestors. Never mind that my name was spelled wrongly thanks to my grandmother. Being under his shadow influenced my allegiance, my identity. One coincidence, with no intent to make it happen, is that I have ended up spending most of my life in the state where he was born and grew up. I also received degrees from the same university he attended, mine from graduate school, his from undergraduate school 132 years before my first graduation. We both went on to study medicine.

My great-grandfather was a handsome man. My favorite picture was taken about 1855. He is clean shaven. He had recently finished medical school. He gazes straight into my eyes. His face is finely chiseled, his eyes intense, his nose narrow and long, his chin strong, his lips full but not too full, and his overall proportions pleasing. His slightly oval face is framed with dark, curly hair. His demeanor is firm and confident. Later, he grew a heavy beard, making his face difficult to see. What a tragic life was before him. No inkling of a grievous future shows in his countenance. On the back of another photo, my grandmother wrote, "Our beloved Papa."

Why I left him and M'Wese's maternal branch, which includes the other Richardson line, to the last is an unimportant mystery. Maybe I was afraid of what I would find. About forty years ago, curious about William, I went to the Southern Historical Collection at the University of North

*Figure 23.* My great-grandfather William Marshall
Richardson (1831–1929), posing for a wedding photo,
circa 1855. He is the ancestor after whom I am named.

Carolina at Chapel Hill to look up his records. I learned he had been one of
the speakers at his 1851 graduation. During that same visit, I unexpectedly
found records from my grandmother's maternal Richardson line about their
sugarcane fields west of New Orleans, the area of M'Wese's birth. I saw journal entries handwritten by one of this branch, my second great-granduncle
Francis DuBose Richardson, who owned the sugar plantation Bayside. The
entries noting trouble with the enslaved people made the whole ugly history
tangible.[1]

Growing up, I was aware that my great-grandfather was much admired
and beloved by his family. My grandmother was the oldest child from his
third marriage. I discussed her briefly in chapter 6. I knew she and her two
siblings were born and grew up in Jeanerette, Louisiana, a stone's throw
from her great-uncle's plantation. Bayside-on-the-Têche was a source of
pride in the family.[2] When I was taken there as a child, the mansion with
its white columns revealed itself to me through dappled sunlight coursing
through Spanish moss swaying off the live oak trees. The double row of majestic oaks, their branches bowing to the ground and rising again, lined the

*Figure 24.* Bayside-on-the-Têche, Jeanerette, Louisiana, undated photo from
my family trunk. My grandmother's parents met in this sugar plantation
house not long after the end of the Civil War. Source unknown.

driveway to the mansion. Its stateliness and grandeur enchanted me even
as the moist, heavy air added gravitas to the beauty. I am fairly sure no one
told me the mansion was built by enslaved people. As a child, I would sometimes stare at the large photograph of Bayside-on-the-Têche that hung in
our house.

William's third marriage would not have happened without him already
being in Jeanerette, in medical practice with his brother. Nor, if he had not already lost his first two wives and most of his children to malaria or tuberculosis.
He met my great-grandmother at a party at Bayside. Between his mother's family lines and his third wife's, many more ancestors joined my long list of those
who held people in bondage. There were Laniers, Gibsons, the second Richardson branch, Gauldens, Nettleses, DuBoses, and more. The DuBose name is
still carried in the family through my first cousin Marion, often mentioned in

Why did my great-grandfather end up in this area, such a long way from
North Carolina? And how did he bring another Richardson lineage into the
family? I never could find the answer to the first question. The second question was easy.

these chapters, and several of her grandchildren. These long-ago families had networks throughout the South, and west into Louisiana and Texas.

⁓

Few of my ancestors, aside from wills and succession papers, named individual enslaved people in their family records. If they were mentioned, it was by euphemisms such as "the help," "the hands," "the servants," or "the workers." I can only guess the reasons. Perhaps it was an attempt to soften and hide the sharp edge of owning human flesh. Most of my ancestors appeared, as far as records go, to pretend their human chattel were willing laborers. I especially noted the complete lack of mention of enslaved people by my great-grandfather. William's parents held fifty-four enslaved people, his nearby Marshall grandparents even more. It is striking that in all the records about him and letters he wrote that I have seen, he never mentions a childhood surrounded by enslaved people, much less any names. I can only imagine, perhaps hope, that the absence of mention and use of pseudonyms by so many of my ancestors was a cloak for shame.

Names often had to be given in wills and estate appraisals. Fifth great-grandfather Zachariah Nettles, who served in the Revolutionary War and whose will I quote under this chapter's title, had no trouble being explicit as he dispersed his enslaved people by name to his children and grandchildren; it was necessary, of course, to assign a certain Black person to a certain child. I should be used to such casual dispersal of human beings, having read so many ancestors' wills. Still, his addition of the words "to be enjoyed . . ." was disquieting. Nettles used this phrase twice in dispensing twenty-eight human beings along with goods and property. Another sentence is: "Also, I give to John Nettles [one of his sons] six Negroes (viz) Jack, Venus, Betsy and Nelly, her two children, with their future increase forever, the said property both real and personal to be enjoyed by John Nettles and his lawful heirs or his offspring." Interestingly, most of the document was worded in the usual manner, "I give and bequeath [child's name] the Negroes [their names]." He also gave to Mary, my fourth great-grandmother, by then married to Daniel DuBose, "one Negro girl named Dol."[3] Unsettled by "enjoyed," I was compelled to highlight it here. The enslaved people, the land, the mill, and the equipment were all from cotton money enabled by his human chattel as evidenced by further contents of Zachariah's will. Many more wills, stories, and intrigues emerged with further research on all these lines, too much to include. I must stop here.

—

Now that I am near the end of my quest, these explorations of so much ownership of human beings have made me feel evermore from a sea of whiteness supported by Black backs glistening with toil and sweat. I have learned that the wealth accumulated in the antebellum South by my ancestors was largely based on four white crops and one amber product: cotton with its muted whiteness, polished white rice with its hard dull glow, salt with its bright grains, refined sugar with its crystals sparkling like tiny diamonds, and pungent, piney turpentine with its amber gleam. Working turpentine was the second only to working sugar in its life-taking horrors.

Although my ancestors lost a good bit of their wealth right after the Civil War, and many never became as wealthy as when they had human property, as far as I know they all recovered reasonably well, some even continuing with the four white "crops."

I am awash with weariness and sorrow from the murk of my ancestors' lives and so little found to illuminate and define the lives of the people they held captive. All this searching seems to be as a water faucet opened as a trickle, now flowing ever harder. If I branch out to my pre–Civil War great-aunts and great-uncles, which I have done to some extent, the drip becomes a swelling sea. As bled as I am, I will gather what names I can of my ancestors' enslaved people as a dedication and as words to be spoken aloud: a prayer to their humanity.

It could take the rest of my life to explore further family branches and gather available records. Much is online, and quantities of documents are waiting in county courthouses. I stop here except to mention the story of my paternal great-grandmother Lavinia Hickson Price and her family lines. When I was a child, I knew only this about her: my mother disliked her appearance, known only by a few tintype photographs, which I did not see until I was grown. My curiosity about Lavinia was a phantom companion to my growing up because of the racial overtones in my mother's description of her: "coarse features, a large flat nose, high cheekbones, and a wide face." I pried the family stories about Lavinia from Mother when I was twelve or thirteen. They hinted at American Indian connections. To me, she looks more like she could have had some African blood.

—

Great-grandmother Lavinia was the first wife of Henry Choice Price of "The Cotton Papers," and the mother of my grandfather Carleton Hickson Price.

She died when he was only two years old. For all my life, the little box with her name in the genealogy book by Aunt Beth was another one that sat on a page empty except for her and her parents' names. The mostly blank page glared at my child's eyes, reflecting my unfulfilled curiosity. A few years ago, cousin Marion and I made a startling discovery. Searching for something under the eaves of the old captain's house on the Maine island, we found a labeled hank of her hair in a tattered, musty box. This disconcerting bundle took away Lavinia's shadow, yet her life remains a mystery but for the shocking finding that her parents were closely related.

Not that many years ago I found where Lavinia's parents, Levi Hickson and Susan Prothro, uncle and niece, are buried. Mother used to take me to Micanopy, Florida, when I was little. All that time, she had no idea these great-grandparents were buried just a few miles outside of Micanopy. I only recently learned that my other maternal great-great-grandparents, Zaccheus and Mary Cosby Browning Price, lived not far away, on their large cotton plantation in the adjoining county. A gravestone for Mary Price stands alongside some other Prices, including John Wesley and his son Zachariah, in the Micanopy Historic Cemetery. Where Zaccheus is buried may never be known, but not for lack of my efforts. Now, when I visit these cemeteries, knowing with some precision how these ancestors earned money and how many enslaved people they held, I feel conflicted standing before their gravestones and those of other ancestors, too.

My grandfather also spent a lot of time in Micanopy, and I gravitate to this quaint village even though I never knew him. Florida places in our family history have a certain magnetic quality. To this day, I am drawn to the area and go about once a year. I have close family members living around the state, and my oldest child now lives in Florida.

I bid farewell to all these ancestors. I think most of them thought they were good people and were in many aspects. The North Carolina Harmony Hall Richardson men were often ministers; their families were deeply religious, as told by records and obituaries. They gave land and money to help establish churches. The McAlpins, the South Carolina Richardsons, and other lineages contributed to their communities by donating land to help build towns, serving on juries, and holding political offices. One ancestor helped establish the then all-white "Louisiana Institution for the Deaf and Dumb and Blind," motivated by having a blind brother. Of course, the only reason the men could do these things was that they were white, and owned land. Perhaps they could not see their cruelty, their double standards, their cognitive biases, for if they could, they would have been tormented souls. Perhaps they were. Perhaps this carries over to this day, becoming ever more twisted.

For generations America's version of Christianity supported slavery. For generations people lived in, at first, the colonies, and then a country with state-sanctioned support of slavery. My ancestors held human beings in bondage for over two hundred years. Whether any of them ever had doubts or winced watching a Black body being shredded by a whip or wished they could not hear baying dogs chasing another desperate enslaved person running for freedom, I cannot know. There is no trace in any of their records that they did. Nor did I find mention in records of my ancestors or other enslavers of living under a constant state of fear. Perhaps they pushed their fear into the recesses of their minds and hearts as well. How could they not be in terror of the people they kept enslaved? The evidence was part of their daily lives: the "slave patrols," the sound of baying dogs, the Black codes, the stories of overseers and owners being killed, the need for constant vigilance to prevent behaviors made into crimes if carried out by enslaved people such as literacy or knowledge of poisonous plants. The venomous cloud of terror enveloped Black and white like. Sometimes enslavers' fear and anger were so great they killed their enslaved people despite the loss of valuable property. What did this do to them? To us, now? People suffering angst and terror generation after generation cannot thrive.

If I imagine myself as one of my ancestors, I surely would have been afraid. If I had any shame about what I was doing to my fellow human beings, perhaps it would have been so deeply repressed I would be unaware. Shame torments the soul. The humanity of the enslaved people was all too recognized despite its frequent denial, obvious by the suppression tactics that were used to keep so-called order. Shame may have erupted in violence at times.

The Civil War may have ended slavery, but it prompted white supremacists to develop new methods for enforcing continued subjugation and fear: the lynchings, the suppressive laws, the Ku Klux Klan, the police killings, and so much more. The net of violent suppression is still with us.

There must have been special suffering by my female ancestors. Generations of my great-grandmothers would have seen the occasional babies born of enslaved women, pale babies fathered by their husbands or their sons. These women must have had the extra burden of helpless fury, hatred even, and sorrow added to their fears.

That I have so many African American cousins is an ignominious testament to the behavior of my male ancestors and relatives who with their vile power used their license to force themselves on their female chattel, who could not refuse. Revealed by direct contact and DNA matching sites while I worked on this book, the number of African American cousins I have is likely in the thousands. These cousins bear witness to their and their enslaved forebears' incredible strength, resilience, intelligence, and ability to endure and forgive even when forgiveness is not required. Thanks partly to the process of writing this book I now am privileged to know many of these cousins and have come to love them. I marvel at their grace, their talents, their beauty, and their welcoming, forgiving arms. I am filled with gratitude for their presence and all I have learned from them. I stand in awe.

—

My struggle to understand my story, my background, and my torment, and to put down words has shown me a light, a telling. I suddenly realize from whence came my early anguish. In my memory even before I had words, I believe I heard my family's enslaved people's whispers. Why, I do not know. Their murmurings, dancing and swirling in my mind, have been as clouds pressing on me, billowing one moment and dark and gray at others. Their echoes, soft haunting echoes, have given me a voice. At last, I understand.

# Afterword

## Shame, Hope, and Discoveries

We think we know our lives. We don't. There is a vapor, a mist that overhangs. We get surprised. Even the sudden recent appearance of an unimportant event in my lawn reveals more shame and trauma.

—

Guineas brought on a childhood revelation. I arrived home one afternoon to find four guineas in my fenced yard. No one in the neighborhood claimed them. They went away and came back again. I put water out. They were cute despite their squawks so I began to think about giving them names. The counting rhyme I had heard so much as a child, "Eeny, meeny, miny, moe," previously forgotten, crept unbidden into my head as I watched the guineas pecking. The rhyme was followed by a slippery coldness and the sudden memory that I had heard that rhyme in its ugly version hundreds, perhaps thousands of times growing up.

> Eeny, meeny, miny, moe,
> Catch a n_____r by the toe.
> If he hollers, let him go,
> Eeny, meeny, miny, moe.

My mother said it sometimes. The children in my neighborhood did when we played our games of kickball, hopscotch, hide and seek, softball, tag, and jump rope. It was always abhorrent to me. I never said that version. I heard my mother say that repugnant, demeaning epithet enough that I grew up loathing it. I shudder at the ugly racial slur.

I looked up guinea fowl. It surprised me to learn that the term for a group of them is called a "confusion." In more recent times they come from sub-Saharan Africa, the same area from which so many African people were stolen and enslaved. Was this a message, albeit a message of confusion? Perhaps. Does this explain why, to my silent hidden shame, the racist word I despise still sometimes and for no apparent reason creeps into my head? With my hearing it so much growing up, did it harbor itself in a small corner in my brain only to struggle for an occasional release? This unbidden memory brought on by a confusion of guineas digs into my mind with a fury of denial. I sit with it as I contemplate the end of this book, this journey I tasked myself with.

Recently, reading Jacquelyn Dowd Hall's book *Sisters and Rebels*, I am struck by her quote from Katherine Du Pre Lumpkin, "White supremacy . . . handed on from one generation to another . . . begins . . . with the Southern child, before she is conscious of herself as a self."[1] I must have not been immune. It is a bitter thought.

—

According to popular attribution, Ralph Waldo Emerson once said that every man is a bundle of his ancestors. My pilgrimage and my bundle have revealed several certainties.

First, there is no doubt that my growing up in Birmingham's smog seeped with Jim Crow was shaped by my mother's racial proclivities, imprinted as they were on her from her ancestors who held people in bondage. She and they pushed me in the opposite direction, likely a result of my temperament and personality seasoned with the ghostly whispers I heard as a child. My early abhorrence of my mother's aggression toward me sealed it. I did not trust her. My father's tolerance and kindliness in his dealings with others was a strong and loving influence.

Second, I learned my maternal ancestors' bundle is tied and retied with transgressions, violations, and greed. My forebears' slaveholding, their histories seen through today's lens, represented a greater evil than I ever supposed. Some would say it is not just to view them with the polished magnifying glass of the present, but I must. For my ancestors it was normal to be an enslaver. Some even thought they were somehow saving the kidnapped Africans from themselves. But the condition of slavery was always evil, no matter the many cultures around the world that had this practice in the past. Though the ancestor bundle has also tied me in many ways, where I have been able to unknot the binding cords, great gifts presented themselves, many of which I have written about.

Third, my being haunted by the unknown and my need for explanations have been largely relieved. I have brought details of my maternal history with slavery to light and have gained a better understanding of the motivations of these relatives and ancestors, the paths they forged, and the way they led to me and my white and Black cousins.

Fourth, I now know my next challenge: to plan and accomplish a personal form of reparations for the benefits I inherited from my ancestors' enslavement of human beings. These benefits include social class, economics, education level, social capital, and a full sense of agency, all based on the substance gained through the accumulation of generations of holding people in bondage.

Fifth, I have an even greater appreciation of and gratitude for my life and all that has happened: the difficult times, the agonies, the searing moments, as well as the privileges, not the least of which is white privilege. I am surrounded with the richness of a large, loving family. I have had wonderful adventures and joyous periods that flowed like cresting ocean waves touched with sparkling heights. I am grateful to have had the privilege to participate in some civil rights events in Alabama in the 1960s. Nonetheless, there are enigmas in my life I will never be able to parse.

Sixth, I can see the remarkable patterns that caused me to be blessed with mentors just when I needed them, both as a child and as an adult. Without them, I would not be who I am and would not have accomplished what I have been able to do. I may not have even survived.

Seventh, I discovered and began participating in the national organization Coming to the Table.[2] I struggled with my history alone for many years, not knowing that good people—descendants of enslaved people and enslavers alike—had come together in 2006 to create this organization with its vision of healing. It is a safe and mending place and full of teachings. It is an honor to be involved.

—

Into the midst of my completing this book, three searing and startling events occurred and beg for recognition. Two of these were worldwide: a pandemic caused by a new, highly contagious virus named COVID-19; and roaring cascades of civil rights events, especially in the United States, the likes of which we have not seen since the 1960s. The latter resulted from the lynching in Minneapolis of George Floyd, a Black man on the pavement, hands cuffed behind him, his neck under the knee of a white policeman with a nonchalant facial expression for eight minutes and forty-nine seconds until he died. The video of the May 25, 2020, lynching, shot by a teenager with her cell phone, sped around the globe. Humanity has been shaken by the depth of racial hatred, the killing mirrored back to billions of human eyes. The third startling event, a personal one, is my being diagnosed with an invasive and aggressive breast cancer in the late spring of 2020. I cannot finish my story without denoting these three events; each grips me tightly and begs for scrupled reflection. The cancer, though found early, also brings with it the pressure of time, even though among the spectrum of women with this diagnosis, I have a better chance than most at a good outcome.

—

Ghosts, loosened by genocide and theft, have floated over this land since the beginning of our nation, our "land of the free." These hovering phantoms sometimes gain such clarity that I feel I can see them. With George Floyd's murder, the ghosts have coalesced into a new visibility. These apparitions are everywhere; they haunt our dreams and actions. They cannot escape and cannot cease because victim after victim continues to add to their numbers. Protests simmer with fury. Riots explode across our nation, along with the flash grenades for crowd control. Worldwide protests spread like the mist of tear gas. Each country, it seems, has its own version of oppression of people with darker skin or lesser means. White supremacists continue their violence. I thought back to August 2017, when a white supremacist in Charlottesville, Virginia, protesting the planned removal of a statue of Robert E. Lee, plowed his car into the counterprotesters, killing one woman and injuring others. This followed a Ku Klux Klan rally there a month earlier. Over a half century later, the Klan is still at it. Confederate flags are still being waved. A car driven by a white supremacist is again plowing into a crowd. In 1963, that happened on May 3 in Birmingham. At least no one died that time. The driver was arrested.

When I close my eyes and think of my ancestors, I see a direct line from enslavers and traders of enslaved people to the Black boy Emmett Till and the Black man George Floyd, their murders separated by sixty-five years, a line connecting all the people of African descent before and during and after who have been discriminated against and maimed, tormented, and killed. When Emmett Till was tortured and lynched in Mississippi in 1955 he and I were same age, fourteen years old. I do not even remember knowing about it when it happened. That was the mask of Birmingham and Jim Crow. Now, news about racism is impossible to suppress. That is progress.

I ponder why after the 150-plus years since the Civil War ended there is still so much racism. It began with the Black codes defining what it was to be white. Systemically embedded in our country, white supremacists are unleashed by thinly veiled political hat-tipping.

I ponder white fear; my introspection, informed here and there by scholars of slavery and racism, sits at the level of my own ability. My thoughts coalesce into what, if I were a woman among my forebears, would be my main dreads and fears: probably the threats of uprisings and the rapes of enslaved women and girls. Could they be shaping some of the racism today?

Enslaved men were special targets in attacks driven by white fear. Male slaveholders could be vicious in emasculating (sometimes literally) the men and boys they enslaved. White people allowed little to no control for the enslaved over the fates of their families. At times, enslaved men witnessed the rapes of their wives by their owners, helpless to protect their women at risk of all their lives.

How much of the white power structures' fear of Black men stems from a terror that the oppressed could rise up and retaliate? White attempts to dominate Black men are demonstrated by four hundred years of countless atrocities against African Americans, who yet remain courageous.

Could white men's bone-deep anxiety around Black men stem from the blinding truth told by the spectrum of light to dark skin among descendants of African enslaved women? The many shades of Black skin are living documentation of the past crimes of violation. Is this related to the white man's fear of Black men having sexual contact with white women, fear that led to miscegenation laws and thousands of lynchings? Is there an epigenetic guilt, a dread of revenge?

—

When discussing the history of this country, one often hears politicians and historians use the phrase "original sin" to refer to its foundation of slavery. To me, if we are ever to overcome the festering wound from our collective consciousness of evils committed, we cannot blind ourselves to our *two* original sins. This country is founded on the genocide of American Indians, enslavement of many, and theft of their land, then covered by the backs of African people held in bondage.

How can I celebrate this country based on principles of freedom, a nation that has so much potential, while at the same time I besmirch its beginning and seek to learn from the offenses of my forebears? Certainly, not easily.

I must speak the truth as I see it in all its glory and brutality and keep a vigilant examination of my own attitudes and motives flowing. Moving forward, I recognize my debt to the many hundreds of enslaved people who helped create the wealth and stature of my ancestors, which have, in turn, benefited me. I recognize and laud the incredible resilience of these people and their descendants and marvel at the degree of forgiveness they have found for the sins against them. I celebrate all the resplendent parts of American culture contributed by people of color. I recognize that the end of my journey that created this book is another beginning for me. There is still so much work I need to do.

Generations below me are showing welcome steps forward. My grandchildren support social justice with their actions. Portraits and statues and names of white supremacists are literally coming down from cities, courtrooms, universities, and other institutions across the United States as well as in some other countries. Laws and policies are undergoing review, with changes anticipated to establish equity and justice. Recognition of the contributions of the people held in bondage and forced labor toward the building of this country is starting to happen, along with discussions of reparations. The clarity of what more is needed is coming into focus.

This is hope made visible and glowing.

—

Thus is my story. It comes with the howls of wolves and the bleats of lambs, flows from me as a river of blood. I am indebted to my fortunate circumstances, which have allowed me the time and ability to study my life, its surroundings, and past. A life reflected on is a great privilege, coming as it does with swells of gratitude, new friendships, old ones expanded, remarkable coincidences and adventures, and a deep knowledge of where I have been and still want to go.

It is my chronicle of discovery and angst, sorrow and joy, a seeking to comprehend and to mend. Of uncanny adventures and synchronicities. Of the struggle to understand my ancestors who held enslaved people and the effect on me and, thus, my family. The ghosts and haunts have been lifted.

It is fitting to come to a close here in the summer of 2020 during a new wave of protests and examinations of our deeply embedded racism, full circle from where the early chapters started, with the civil rights demonstrations of the 1960s. That is familiar territory, at least. My now having to shelter from the pandemic with forced outings to the hospital for treatment is an unwelcome new phenomenon. Nonetheless, I must add these to my still-growing life experiences.

To my ancestors' thousands of stolen human beings kept in a torturing bondage, I say I am sorry. And, to my living African American cousins, I am sorry for what happened in the past and for your struggles and my struggles, still not over. I celebrate your survival. Where I have been welcomed into your families, I am loved and experience joy from having you to love. I have learned from your generosity, graciousness, and strength. The world is a better place for you and with you. Thank you for being.

―

We must not forget.

# Acknowledgments

This book has been forming in my consciousness for many years, occasionally bubbling through, but always seeping back into crevices postponed to another day. Once started, it would not have been possible without the enormous amount of support and help that was always there just when I needed it. The love and interest of my Alabama children Gregory, Marcus, and Melantha Herman-Giddens and my five grandchildren kept me going. They have graciously tolerated my frequent absences from their lives while I researched and wrote and rewrote. My husband, Douglas G. Berg, has also been tolerant of my attention being on all things book, taking time away from other aspects of our lives. His support, careful reading, and editorial comments have been invaluable. My former husband, G. Scott Herman-Giddens, met with me frequently to help fill in memories of our life together. He also looked through many old records he still had that were sometimes needed to provide certain dates and facts. I could not have done this without him.

My thanks to Libba Adams, who put me in contact with William R. Ferris, then at the Center for the Study of the American South at the University of North Carolina at Chapel Hill. At my meeting with him a half year after I had read about my third great-granduncle Robert McAlpin Jr.'s association with Harriet Beecher Stowe's Simon Legree character, he listened to my growing-up story and encouraged me to write it down. In fact, he said I must write it down.

Records and details of certain events and Birmingham memories would not have been possible without the help of Ingrid W. Kraus and Jeff Tiller, Annie Long, Pam Walbert Montanaro, Carolyn Maull McKinstry, Rosemary Downie Noel, Randall Jimerson, Marjorie Walz, and Margaret Whiteside, archivist at the Altamont School (Brooke Hill). Pam Powell, director/producer of the *Bending the Arc* project, helped with details of certain critical events. Polly Wright's remarkable contribution is a story in the text. The

Unitarian Universalist Church, the *Southern Courier* archives, and the Birmingham Public Library Archives added so much.

I could not have known the full Louisiana story of my third great-granduncle about whom I wrote were it not for Robert Gentry's trust, interest and support, and literal guidance up a rocky bank with his sparkling wife, Laurie, to McAlpin's slave cemetery, unmarked as it is in this big world. Robert generously shared his papers and research as well as himself. Here, I must acknowledge even the social media without which I would have never discovered him. Robert and Laurie also introduced me to Mary Linn Werner, archivist, Cammie G. Henry Research Center, and David Stamey, clerk of court, Natchitoches, both of whom aided this part of my research. In addition, Robert and Laurie generously read and reread the finished manuscript, offering helpful comments.

Other specialists far and wide who generously came to my assistance include Cheryl Ferguson, archival assistant, Tuskegee University Archives; Peter W. Patout, historic property specialist in New Orleans; and Nick Wynne, Civil War expert. Southern history professors and authors who provided encouragement at the beginning of this journey include Charles B. Dew, professor emeritus of American history at Williams College; Larry Powell, professor emeritus of history at Tulane University; and Edward Ball, author.

Several additional people read and reread the entire manuscript as it was growing. They stayed with me the whole way, providing their expertise. Jim Willse's editorial suggestions, encouragement, and observations always came just when I needed them most. He—until retirement, an award-winning newspaper editor—hung in with me for over fifty years, we just didn't know it until recently. Doug Mann's kind offer at the start to use his copyeditor skills was much needed and appreciated. Both Jim and Doug showed me I needed to learn a lot about writing and the placement of commas, among other, larger things. My first cousin Marion DuBose Breeze-Williams, was a constant companion, providing details for our many shared experiences and adding to memories and records of family history while also being skilled at spotting typos. Other cousins who provided support, information, and experiences include Christopher MacAlpine-Belton, Julia Gaines, Evelyn Lanoix, Kathy Lanoix, Karen Mann, PJ MacAlpine, Marilyn Monk, and Elizabeth Swearingen. Many friends provided ongoing aid and helpful encouragement, including Carlos Bourdony, Ed and Linda Brown, Nigel Chadwick, Jean Chapman, Linda Grimm, Jo Ann and Bill Hoffman, Susan and John

Pierce, Agalia O'Quinn, Stephanie Wenzel, and Kathy Whaley. Many more throughout these years who have helped remain unnamed. Then, there are the friends and family whom I never told about my work as I was writing and revising, through some peculiar notion of jinxing the effort were it not kept tightly around me. That group includes my inspiring book club members, from whom I learned so much about reading and writing over the twenty years we have been meeting. My deep appreciation and thanks to you all, dear Reading Ladies: Julian Bland, Shannon Bueker, Virginia Chambers, Suma Dunham, Anne Greer, Sarah Greer, Susan Strozier, and those who are out there but no longer able to participate for various reasons.

My editor, Claire Lewis Evans, at the University of Alabama Press, shepherded me the whole way, kept me going, and pulled me out of trouble more than once. She is ever patient, ever helpful, and so skilled; it goes without saying the book would not have happened without her. The book has also been greatly improved by the extraordinary skills and craft of my copyeditor, Jessica Hinds-Bond, and project editor, Kelly Finefrock. Thanks to you all and everyone at the University of Alabama Press who helps make a book happen.

Were it not for the thousands of enslaved people held in bondage by my maternal ancestors, I would not be who I am and this book would not have been written. Their presence, their contribution to my forebears' wealth, their effect on my forebears' behavior, is part of me as it is for all my Black and white maternal ancestors and relatives along with the DNA of many. I thank them all for my life, balanced as it is on my paternal side with its history and strengths.

In short, this book happened because of the loving support of my family, help and expertise from many, and a great deal of good luck. I am indebted to all of you.

# Appendix

PUBLIC NOTICES REGARDING MY ANCESTORS' ACTIONS
WITH PEOPLE HELD AGAINST THEIR WILL

I offer these notices from various ancestors that appeared in antebellum newspapers and legal documents. The notices are a sample. More are available. These events are no one's story or imagination. They record a real event at a point in time. One can imagine the suffering of the individuals being posted about. The oldest notice in my lineage is over three hundred years ago. One notice concerns white indentured servants. The rest concern enslaved people in the family or enslaved people affected by an ancestor.

## *1709 The ordering of arrests and whippings.*

Warrant issued by Edmund Jennings, my seventh great-grandfather, who at the time was the Virginia Colony governor's council president. He was born in 1659, in Ripon, Yorkshire, England, and probably died on December 5, 1727, in his Virginia Colony home he called Ripon. The warrant is for the arrest of four enslaved people. White colonial leaders were always fearful of a slave uprising, so the slightest questionable behavior called for them to be arrested and whipped. The Virginia Colony 1705 slave code decreed thirty lashes to "any negro, mulatto, or Indian, bond or free, [who] shall at any time lift his or her hand in opposition against any Christian, not being negro, mulatto, or Indian."

By the Honorable President

You are hereby ordered and required with the assistance of the guard ___, and such other as you shall find and ___ for the service (whom you are hereby ___ to myself) to apprehend and secure the several negroes here under named and to bring them forthwith before me and for ___ this shall be ___ warrant. Given under my hand this 20th day of March 1709.

To Jon Bentley & James Hubbard or others of ___

Negroes names

Angola ___ at the plantation of Albertus Warren
Pamba, his wife
Bumbara, ___ at ___ Bray's
Mingo at William Davis's
Robin at Mr. Lovert's

## 1743 An advertisement for (presumed) runaway indentured servants.

This advertisement was posted by Richard Taliaferro, my sixth great-grandfather, Caroline County, May 6, 1743.

> Ran away from the subscriber, on the 19th day of June, two English convict servant men, one named Thomas Butler, a plasterer by trade, about 23 years of age, pretty tall and slim, his face pale and much pock patterned & he has a sore on the inside of his left ankle. The other name Thomas Preby, a biscuit maker by trade, about 40 years of age, of middle stature, very round shouldered, brown complexion, a well-met fellow. The said Thomas Butler had changed his name to Richard Howe. They both have false passes, signed by several Justices of the Peace, and went from Suffolk County to Hampton about the 6th of April 1743 with the intent to get over to the Eastern shore, and were hence seen in Norfolk. Tis believed they are now conceal'd they are, by a shoemaker, and a woman of evil fame, who went out of this county and now lives at Norfolk. Whoever will apprehend the said servants, so that they may be sent home, shall be paid Five Shillings Reward, besides what the Law allows.
>
> By Richard Taliaferro

## 1807 An advertisement for an enslaved man seeking freedom.

The person being sought is the son of an enslaved mother who was held by my fourth great-grandfather Colonel James Richardson, of Harmony Hall, Bladen County, North Carolina.

20 Dollars Reward.

Ran away from the subscriber living in Bladen County, on the 20th April, a negro fellow called

QUASH,

About 20 years old, possesses a pleasant countenance, nearly 6 feet high, large over the shoulders, small legs, he has a scar on his left side which extends half around his belly, his father is hired to Mr. Williams. Williams near the green banks of Brunswick County. Col. James Richardson owns his mother—it is possible he may be about Fayetteville as he is acquainted with some of the Major James Owens negroes that are hired at that place—he is Outlawed. All reasonable expenses will be paid to any person apprehending said Negro in addition to the reward above. J. Bradley July 14.

## 1830 Petition for enforcement against "runaways."

While my ancestors were not signatories on this petition, they likely had neighbors who were and certainly lived in this atmosphere of needing to "control" the enslaved people and being in fear of them.

1830 Petition to the Gen. Assembly of the State of North Carolina in which 87 slaveholding residents of Sampson, Bladen, New Hanover, and Dublin Counties appeal to the courts for greater enforcement against runaways, noting in a handwritten document that the slaves "go and come when and where they please and if an attempt is made to correct them they fly to the woods and there continue for months and years . . . not long since three patrols, two of which for executing their duty, had their dwelling house and other houses burnt down and the other his fodder stacks burnt." Published by the General Assembly, Session Records, Miscellaneous Petitions, November 1830–January 1831.

## 1841 The purchase of a nineteen-year-old woman and her child.

The purchase was made by Clement Marshall, my third great-uncle.

John M. Allen to Clement Marshall, State of North Carolina, Anson County

Received March 1841 six hundred & seventy-five dollars in full payment of a Negro girl slave by the name of Lucy about 19 years of age, her child, Freeman about two years of age, the right and title of said negroes I do hereby warrant forever to the said Clement Marshall, his heirs and assignees forever and I also warrant said the girl to be healthy and sound given under my hand the date above written. Done in the presence of . . .

## 1843 The buying and selling of children.

Again, the transactions are by Clement Marshall, third great-uncle.

Edward Beard to Clement Marshall. Received 14th day of March 1843 of Clement Marshall seven hundred & seventy-five dollars in full payment of two negroes (viz) Jackson about twelve years of age and Betty about ten years of age. The title of said negroes we do warrant and forever defend to the said Clement Marshall ___ . Given under our hand the date written above. Signed and sealed Edward Beard and David Carpenter

## 1852 Ad for a missing hired enslaved man.

Posted by a cousin, John A. Richardson of Harmony Hall.

Wilmington, N. C., April 14th, 1852

$70 Reward,

$20 will be given to any person who will deliver at the Jail of this (Bladen) County, a Negro known generally as Tom Pridgeon, the property of Mrs. Hannah Pridgeon, from whom I hired him in February last.

I will also give $50 reward for evidence sufficient to convict any person of having harbored, assisted, "aided and comforted" Tom while lurking.

John A. Richardson.

Elizabethtown, April 16, 1852 (Herald copy tf.)

## 1857 Probate Court records for Alachua County, Florida.

For the estate of my great-great-grandfather Levi Hickson, who died intestate.

. . . and for one Negro boy Peter, said Peter to be the property of Levi Hickson until said notes are paid. Due bill on G. B. Payne.

# Notes

## Chapter 2

1. Birmingham was founded six years after the end of the Civil War. From the beginning, the founders made it part of their mission to continue control of Black bodies.

2. John T. Milner was the mastermind of the system to continue forced unpaid labor from Black men after slavery ended. During the Civil War he and his partner built iron ore mines and a blast furnace, all operated with the labor of enslaved men. By ten years after the end of the war, they were operated by forced laborers from the penal system.

3. By the end of 1865, Alabama had enacted ill-defined vagrancy laws that allowed Black people to be arrested unless they were under the protection of a white man. The men went straight from serving time in jail as "vagrants" to being leased to mining and steel companies that paid small amounts of money to the state or local governments for the right to use this free labor. The companies kept the men under guard, could flog and mistreat them, and often fed them as little as possible. Under this system, with no motive to protect the value of their human property, these men died in droves.

4. The first large steel mill, Sloss Furnace, was operating by 1882. The early steel mills were made possible by the free convict labor, a practice that went on for four more decades.

5. E. V. McLoughlin, *The Book of Knowledge: The Children's Encyclopedia* (New York: Grolier Society, 1946), 2295.

## Chapter 3

1. Rebecca Solnit, *The Faraway Nearby* (New York: Viking, 2013), 64.

## Chapter 4

1. Alexander McAlpin, born between 1720 and 1730, died in Wilkes County, Georgia, in September 1790. Alexander served as a captain in the South Carolina militia, later receiving a bounty land grant of 575 acres in Wilkes County. He took his family there and remained until he died. I could not find whether he enslaved people, but his children and grandchildren did. Among them, the US "slave censuses" list hundreds of human beings.

2. Alexander McAlpin's first child, Robert Sr. (c. 1757–1804), is my fourth great-grandfather. One of Alexander's grandchildren enslaved a man, Tom McAlpin, who was interviewed in 1936 for the Federal Writers' Project (FWP); see FWP, *Slave Narrative Project*, vol. 1, *Alabama, Aarons–Young*, 1936–37, pp. 268–71, available online in *Born in Slavery: Slave Narratives from the Federal Writers' Project, 1936 to 1938* (digital collection), Library of Congress, Manuscript Division.

3. Henry Wiencek, *Master of the Mountain: Thomas Jefferson and His Slaves* (New York: Farrar, Straus and Giroux, 2012).

4. Doris McAlpin Russell, *McAlpin(e) Genealogies, 1730–1990: Alexander McAlpin of

*South Carolina and Georgia and His Descendants Plus Other McAlpin(e) Families of North
America* (Louisville, KY: Gateway Press, 1990), 37–38.

5. Russell, 28.

6. According to Russell, Isabella McAlpin Browning had a cute nickname, "Ibly." She
began bearing children as her mother was having the last of her own. She married William Browning around 1800, and they had eight children. She gave birth to my great-great-
grandmother Mary Cosby the same year her father was murdered. Her last child was born in
1812; eight years later William died, leaving her with enslaved people to manage. She soon
followed her brother-in-law Solomon McAlpin to Alabama. After being widowed, she sold
her share of the Natchitoches land she had inherited from her murdered father to a brother-
in-law who soon sold it Isabella's youngest brother, Robert Jr. Ibly's daughter and my great-
great-grandmother Mary Cosby Browning (Price) was only twenty-four when her mother
died and was at the time already married to my great-great-grandfather Zaccheus Price. They
all held many enslaved people.

## Chapter 7

1. Harmony Hall, now owned by the Bladen County Historical Society with limited
assets, gets no support from the state. Somehow, the historical society cobbles together vol-
unteers for Harmony Hall, who struggle to provide upkeep and availability to the public.
Overnight camping is occasionally allowed.

2. The indictment against Lydia Gilbert reads: "Lydea Gilburt thou are here indicted by
that name of Lydea Gilburt that not having the feare of god before thy Eyes thou hast of late
years or still dust give Entertainment of Sathan the great Enemy of god and mankind and by
his helpe hast killed the Body of Henry Styles besides other witchcrafts for which according
to the law of god and the Established Law of this commonwealth thou Deservest to Dye."
Quoted in Homer Worthington Brainard, Harold Simeon Gilbert, and Clarence Almon
Torrey, *The Gilbert Family: Descendants of Thomas Gilbert, 1582–1659, of Mt. Wollaston
(Braintree), Windsor, and Wethersfield*, ed. Donal Lines Jacobus (New Haven, CT: n.p.,
1953), 19.

3. There are several sources for the history of these Richardsons. A major one is Rosell L.
Richardson, *Amos Richardson of Boston and Stonington*, 2nd ed. (New York: published by
the author, 1906).

4. *Daily Journal* (Wilmington, NC), October 31, 1853.

5. "'Black' Simon, Richardson's Friend," *Bladen Journal*, February 17, 1972.

6. The statute was passed by North Carolina in 1830–31 and was titled "An Act to
Prevent All Persons from Teaching Slaves to Read or Write, the Use of Figures Excepted."
It reads:

> Whereas the teaching of slaves to read and write, has a tendency to excite dissatisfac-
> tion in their minds, and to produce insurrection and rebellion, to the manifest injury
> of the citizens of this State: Therefore,
>
> *Be it enacted by the General Assembly of the State of North Carolina, and it is hereby
> enacted by the authority of the same,* That any free person, who shall hereafter teach, or
> attempt to teach, any slave within the State to read or write, the use of figures excepted,
> or shall give or sell to such slave or slaves any books or pamphlets, shall be liable to
> indictment in any court of record in this State having jurisdiction thereof; and upon
> conviction, shall, at the discretion of the court, if a white man or woman, be fined not
> less than one hundred dollars, nor more than two hundred dollars, or imprisoned; and

if a free person of color, shall be fined, imprisoned, or whipped, at the discretion of the court, not exceeding thirty nine lashes, nor less than twenty lashes.

II. *Be it further enacted,* That if any slave shall hereafter teach, or attempt to teach, any other slave to read or write, the use of figures excepted, he or she may be carried before any justice of the peace, and on conviction thereof, shall be sentenced to receive thirty nine lashes on his or her bare back.

III. *Be it further enacted,* That the judges of the Superior Courts and the justices of the County Courts shall give this act in charge to the grand juries of their respective counties.

## Chapter 8

1. For the names of the prominent families involved with establishing Brooke Hill and ensuring its ongoing success, see Carolyn Green Satterfield, *A History of Brooke Hill, 1940–1975* (Birmingham, AL: Altamont Alumni Association, 2002). In 1975, Brooke Hill joined its counterpart for boys, Birmingham University School (BUS), founded in 1922, to form the co-ed Altamont. Altamont continues to be a college preparatory school and is now committed to socioeconomic, ethnic, and religious diversity.

2. Diane McWhorter, *Carry Me Home: Birmingham, Alabama, the Climactic Battle of the Civil Rights Revolution* (2001; New York: Simon and Schuster, 2012), 2.

3. From 1947 until 1965, there were at least forty-four racially motivated bombings (or attempted bombings) in Birmingham. All but four were of African American homes, offices, or churches. Exceptions were the attempted bombings of the Jewish Temple Beth-el in 1959, the Jewish-owned Loveman's Department Store in 1963, and the homes of a white attorney and the white mayor in 1965. See "List of Racially-Motivated Bombings," Bhamwiki, edited November 10, 2021.

4. Judge Seybourn Lynne, born in 1907 in Alabama, attended the University of Alabama School of Law. He was named a federal judge for northern Alabama in 1946 by President Truman, hearing cases until shortly before his death at age ninety-three. Judge Lynne supported segregation during the time I knew him and made rulings accordingly. He gradually realized the necessity for change. He is known for ordering the integration of the University of Alabama by Vivian M. Jones and James Hood in 1963. Some feel he made a deal with President Kennedy to allow Governor Wallace to put up a fight and then step aside without being arrested. As years passed, he made rulings against the segregation of institutions such as jails and cemeteries. Douglas Martin, "Seybourn Lynne, 93; Ruled in Civil Rights Case," *New York Times*, September 12, 2000.

5. Camp Winnataska is still operating, having celebrated its hundredth year in 2018. Winnataska in native Creek language means "Land of the Laughing Water."

6. Ramsay High School originally opened in 1930 under the name Southside High School. The name was soon changed to honor Erskine Ramsay, an important industrialist who served as president of the Birmingham Board of Education from 1922 to 1941. Ramsay got a start in mining in Pennsylvania, showed promise, and was soon hired by Tennessee Coal & Iron. This brought him to Birmingham in 1887 to run the Pratt Mines, where he showed talent as an inventor. By then, Pratt Mines and other such sites relied heavily on convict "slave" labor. Pratt Mines was beset with labor problems and costly accidents. Though Ramsay engineered some safety features, an explosion in 1891 killed ten convict workers and one free laborer. A *New York Times* article ended, "Two life convicts worked faithfully with the rescuing party." In 1894, Ramsay was promoted to chief engineer of all the Tennessee Coal & Iron mines in Alabama. "Eleven Lives Lost," *New York Times*, May 23, 1891.

7. Not surprisingly, the churches I chose to "try out" did not fare well under further scrutiny. I attended Highlands Methodist Church for my Methodist "period." Just a year or two after my attendance, the Methodist Layman's Union met there and resolved that integration was "a betrayal of unborn generations and a monstrous crime against civilization." The *New York Times* labeled Birmingham the center of Christian racism. The Episcopalian church (St. Mary's on the Highlands) and the Presbyterian church (Highlands Presbyterian) I attended did not fare much better during these tumultuous years. Even when the leadership was progressive, the congregations were not. These churches were attended by important Birmingham families. Of course, I did not know any of this then. Now, according to their websites, these churches have become inclusive. The Methodist Layman's Union and the *New York Times* response are discussed in McWhorter, *Carry Me Home*, 141.

8. Dr. Frederick Kraus, born in Prague in 1910, received his medical degree and dental degree in 1934 and 1935, respectively, soon marrying Viennese Anny Weiner. Fluent in seven languages, Frederick was of Jewish heritage. Anny's parents were "free thinkers." Anny bribed Frederick's way out of Nazi imprisonment and her brother's release from a concentration camp. They were unable to save her mother, who died in the camp Terezin. Fleeing the Nazis in 1939 with their five-year-old son, Anny and Frederick went through Paris and crossed the Pyrenees to Lisbon. Their two-year struggle ended when a Prague friend, Margit née Morawetz, also fleeing, gave them her freighter tickets to the United States. Dr. Kraus obtained additional dental training at Tufts College and then volunteered for the US Army, serving in Europe as a dental surgeon in the Twenty-Ninth Infantry Division. Back at Tufts, their daughter, my dear friend Ingrid, was born in January 1946. In 1953, Frederick was recruited by Dr. Joseph Volker to head the dental service at the Birmingham Veterans Administration Hospital and was given an appointment in the University of Alabama School of Dentistry. He went on to have an illustrious career in microbiology. Having developed a social conscience during adolescence, he became active in the Civil Rights Movement, helping found the Birmingham Council on Human Relations. He and Anny were leaders and participants in numerous civil rights activities. They already knew what it was to risk their lives. Frederick and Anny were models for Scott and me in how to live. Anny died in 1993, and Frederick died in 2002.

## Chapter 9

1. Thomas Fell, comp., *Some Historical Accounts of the Founding of King William's School and Its Subsequent Establishment as St. John's College, Together with Biographical Notices of the Various Presidents from 1790–1894* (Baltimore, MD: Friedenwald, 1894).

2. St. John's College, *Bulletin of St. John's College in Annapolis: Official Statement of the St. John's Program, Catalogue 1958–1960*, September 1958, St. John's College Digital Archives. First-year readings from the catalog (p. 38) include:

| *Literature* | *Philosophy and Theology* | *History and Social Science* | *Mathematics* | *Natural Science* |
|---|---|---|---|---|
| Homer | Plato | Herodotus | Euclid | Hippocrates |
| Aeschylus | Aristotle | Thucydides | Nicomachus | Archimedes |
| Sophocles | Lucretius | Plutarch | Ptolemy | Harvey |
| Euripides | Epictetus | | | |
| Aristophanes | | | | |

## Chapter 10

1. Diane McWhorter, *Carry Me Home: Birmingham, Alabama, the Climactic Battle of the Civil Rights Revolution* (2001; New York: Simon and Schuster, 2012), 462.

2. McWhorter, 183.

3. UAB began with the University of Alabama's 1936 opening of the Birmingham Extension Center. In 1945, the Medical College of Alabama was moved to Birmingham from Tuscaloosa, thus founding the Medical Center.

4. McWhorter, *Carry Me Home*, 169.

## Chapter 11

1. W. Edward Harris, *Miracle in Birmingham: A Civil Rights Memoir, 1954–1965* (Indianapolis, IN: Stonework Press, 2004), 183.

2. Tuxedo Junction was an area in Birmingham known as the heart of social life for Black populations. The intersection of Ensley Avenue and Nineteenth Street in West Birmingham back in the trolley days was where two lines would stop to turn around. A small business district grew up with clubs, bars, and stores. Thus, it became a popular destination for commuters after work. Dancing and music were popular in the area.

3. The Alabama Council on Human Relations comprised white and Black community leaders. Its goals included improving racial relationships and working for equal opportunities. Harassment by the police and Klan forced some meetings to be held in the office of our dear friend Frederick Kraus as it was on federal property.

4. Randall C. Jimerson, *Shattered Glass in Birmingham: My Family's Fight for Civil Rights, 1961–1964* (Baton Rouge: Louisiana State University Press, 2014), 126.

## Chapter 12

1. "Segregation now, segregation tomorrow, segregation forever" would be widely quoted, becoming a rallying cry. Asa Carter later changed his white supremacist beliefs, adopted the pseudonym Forrest Carter, and wrote *The Education of Little Tree* (1976), a charming and supposedly autobiographical story about Cherokee and mountain culture. It was soon exposed as a literary hoax.

2. Scott Herman-Giddens recalled, "Sidney went to the state fair with a Black friend and it almost caused a riot (this was Alabama in 1963). It would have been seen as a protest even if it wasn't." Pers. comm., October 18, 2019.

## Chapter 13

1. See Carolyn Maull McKinstry with Denise George, *While the World Watched: A Birmingham Bombing Survivor Comes of Age during the Civil Rights Movement* (Carol Stream, IL: Tyndale House, 2011).

2. Betty Friedan, *The Feminine Mystique* (New York: Norton, 1963), 189.

3. The proportion of the US population then living in poverty was about 19 percent.

4. The first reference, President Johnson's 1965 *Manpower Report of the President* (Washington, DC: US Government Printing Office, 1965), 85–86, mentioned a critical need for trained counselors stemming from new federal programs. A second reference, James R. Galloway and Robert R. Kelso, "Don't Handcuff the Aide," *Rehabilitation Record* 7, no. 1 (1966): 1, contained a paragraph about Project CAUSE at the University of Colorado. A third reference, Invitational Conference on Government-University Relations in the Professional Preparation and Employment of Counselors, *Counselor Development in American Society, Conference Recommendations* (Washington, DC: US Department of Labor, 1965),

33 and 136, discussed Project CAUSE's goals and controversial aspects. And the 1964 Project CAUSE is discussed by John K. Harris, "CAUSE Points a New Direction," *Employment Service Review* 1 (December 1964): 43–45, but with nothing specific to the Tuskegee program. Nothing addressed the fingerprinting, diaries, and IQ testing requirements.

5. See Patrick J. Gilpin and Marybeth Gasman, *Charles S. Johnson: Leadership beyond the Veil in the Age of Jim Crow* (Albany: State University of New York Press, 2003); "50 Years/50 Collections: The Preston and Bonita Valien Papers, 1969," *Amistad Research Center* (blog), February 1, 2016. Dr. Valien collaborated with Preston Valien on projects concerning the desegregation of schools and civil rights, authored books, and interviewed important figures during the civil rights era.

6. Peter Buxtun fled the Nazis in 1939. At age twenty-seven, he became a venereal disease investigator for the US Public Health Service, there learning details about the Tuskegee Syphilis Experiment begun in 1932, which he likened to Nazi experiments. The *Washington Star* broke the story on July 25, 1972. Congressional hearings ensued and were eventually followed by new laws. See Derek Kerr and Maria Rivero, "Whistleblower Peter Buxtun and the Tuskegee Syphilis Study," *Government Accountability Project* (blog), April 30, 2014.

7. James H. Jones, *Bad Blood: The Tuskegee Syphilis Experiment—A Tragedy of Race and Medicine* (New York: Free Press, 1981).

8. The Julius Rosenwald Fund, established in 1917, supported education for African Americans in the South. From 1929 to 1931 the fund administered demonstration projects for syphilis control with the US Public Health Service, with Macon County being one of five sites across the South. This likely primed the Black population for the Tuskegee experiment.

9. Dr. Johnson detailed his Macon County work in *Shadow of the Plantation* (Chicago: University of Chicago Press, 1934). He describes the compliance of the poor Black residents with the syphilis demonstration project as related to effects of the plantation system and the learned behavior of obeying white people.

10. Preston and Bonita Valien Papers, box 30, folder 4, Amistad Research Center, Tulane University, New Orleans, LA.

11. According to Sidney Olansky, Lloyd Simpson, and Stanley H. Schuman, "Environmental Factors in the Tuskegee Study of Untreated Syphilis," *Public Health Reports* 69, no. 7 (1954): 693, "Patients with untreated syphilis were . . . primarily men with families . . . integrated into a community life." This makes it clear the experimenters knew they were sending untreated syphilitic men back to their families to infect their wives and children, even after penicillin became available. Eighty percent of 133 syphilitic men that were interviewed were married, and each had an average of five children. The total number of living children for this group was 453. Slightly over half of that number of children had died.

12. George Washington Carver grew up on the Iowa estate of the enslaver of his father. Carver taught more than forty years at Tuskegee Institute, having received a bachelor's degree and a master of science from Iowa Agricultural College. In 1938, five years before his death, Tuskegee built a museum to house his collections, paintings, and inventions.

13. *Let Us Now Praise Famous Men* (Boston: Houghton Mifflin, 1941), with words by James Agee and photos by Walker Evans, captured the Depression-era lives of white sharecroppers in Alabama.

14. Marcia E. Herman-Giddens, "A Case Study, A Seventeen-Year-Old Macon County Negro Girl," Project CAUSE field report, August 1964, Amistad Research Center, Tulane University, New Orleans, LA.

## Chapter 14

1. The statement from the Birmingham Unitarian Church on racial crisis in Alabama ended with "We will continue to dedicate ourselves to the eradication of this intolerable situation in our state and local communities." Later, it was learned four local white men were the perpetrators, not the police. One fled; the other three were acquitted. W. Edward Harris, *Miracle in Birmingham: A Civil Rights Memoir, 1954–1965* (Indianapolis, IN: Stonework Press, 2004), 162.

2. The City of St. Jude complex was founded in the mid-1930s by a Catholic priest to provide nondiscriminatory educational, medical, and social services to those in need, especially African Americans. The evening of March 24, 1965, celebrities arrived to offer support and entertainment to the marchers before their final march the next day to the capitol.

3. Winthrop R. Wright, "On the Road to Selma," unpublished manuscript, chapter 11. Dr. Wright, a historian, died before his book on civil rights events in Birmingham was completed. As it turns out, in 2021, another book on the Birmingham civil rights struggle would be published that discovered and detailed this first march, which would have given me another chance to solve my lifelong mystery. See T. K. Thorne, *Behind the Magic Curtain: Secrets, Spies, and Unsung White Allies of Birmingham's Civil Rights Days* (Montgomery, AL: New South Books, 2021).

4. On the *Southern Courier*, see The *Southern Courier*: A Weekly Newspaper Covering Civil Rights in the South 1965–68 (website), Southern Courier Association. The entire photograph collection has been digitized; see the Jim Peppler *Southern Courier* Photograph Collection, Alabama Department of Archives and History, Montgomery, published online January 2013.

## Chapter 15

1. W. E. B. Du Bois, *The Souls of Black Folk: Essays and Sketches*, 2nd ed. (Chicago: A. C. McClurg, 1903), 123.

2. What is now known as Emory University started in 1836 as Emory College, founded by the Methodist Episcopal Church. Then located in Oxford, Georgia, it was close to Zaccheus Price's plantation. A present-day school, Oxford College of Emory University, is still there. The Male and Female Seminary, founded in 1852 in Barnesville, Georgia, is now Gordon State College.

3. Cotton dates to prehistoric times. Until several centuries ago, cotton was grown in small batches and turned into textiles at home. India led in the development of fabrics. Today, the world supply of cotton is primarily produced by China, followed by numerous other countries. In all but the United States, cotton is still primarily handpicked, through systems of modern slavery.

4. Prior to 1850, the number of enslaved people was shown without detail other than gender on the regular census. By 1840, Zaccheus Price had twenty-nine people in bondage.

5. I have taken the position that white men having sexual relationships with enslaved women and girls was rape since the enslaved women had no power to refuse. They could never give consent, even if they may have appeared willing. They wanted to survive. Children often resulted from these rapes. Some assaults were deliberate in order to breed children.

6. Fear of enslaved peoples' resistance did not lessen, whether in Florida or elsewhere. The successful insurrection in Santo Domingo, known as the Haitian Revolution of 1791–1804, and other events added to slaveholders' fear for their lives and property. When white fear increased, the severity of the slave codes did as well. Codes forbade enslaved peoples' meetings, literacy, self-employment, certain types of work, and more. Punishments could

involve mutilation, branding, other forms of torture, and death. Added to this were techniques to force enslaved people to produce more cotton. Edward E. Baptist, in his controversial book *The Half Has Never Been Told: Slavery and the Making of American Capitalism* (New York: Basic Books, 2014), describes the "pushing system" of labor developed by cotton entrepreneurs to augment the invention of the cotton gin. While the gin decreased the number of workers needed to remove seeds from cotton fiber, it greatly increased demand for more cotton. For enslaved people, the whip was the exclamation mark at the end of their long list of punishments and "incentives," described in numerous scholarly documents including the *Slave Narrative Project* from the Federal Writers Project (1936–37). Indeed, when enslaved people were subjected to such measures, their productivity increased. Joseph Conan Thompson, in "Toward a More Humane Oppression: Florida's Slave Codes, 1821–1861," *Florida Historical Quarterly* 71, no. 3 (1993): 333, describes the inhumane slave codes in Florida:

> The penalties prescribed by Florida law were, by present-day standards, cruel and unusual; by any standard they were painful. The whip remained the preferred instrument of punishment. . . . Other forms of punishment proved less humane. A slave convicted of perjury, for instance, in addition to being whipped could have one of his or her ears nailed to a post. The slave would remain standing beside the post for one hour, at which time the mutilated ear would be severed from the head. . . . Other forms of non-lethal punishment dictated by Florida law included branding and nose splitting. Capital punishment was an extreme measure.

7. See the account by Elizabeth DuBose Price Breeze, "In the Land of Cotton," *Update* (Historical Association of Southern Florida) 13, no. 3 (August 1986): 10.

8. My great-grandfather's schooner *Clotilda*, which he procured in 1863, should not be confused with the infamous last known slave ship of the same name, which arrived in Mobile Bay on the Alabama coast sometime around 1860. It held 110 or more African captives even though the Atlantic slave trade had been banned by 1808. That schooner was burned and sunk to hide evidence of the illegal trade. What remained of it was found in May 2019.

9. Michael Toscano, "Melodrama Weakens Foundation of 'Uncle Tom's Cabin,'" *Washington Post*, September 26, 2002.

10. Frederick Law Olmsted, *The Cotton Kingdom: A Traveler's Observations on Cotton and Slavery in the American Slave States*, 1861, ed. Arthur M. Schlesinger, intro. Lawrence N. Powell (New York: Random House, 1984).

11. Doris McAlpin Russell, *McAlpin(e) Genealogies, 1730–1990: Alexander McAlpin of South Carolina and Georgia and His Descendants Plus Other McAlpin(e) Families of North America* (Louisville, KY: Gateway Press, 1990), 33. Gary B. Mills, *The Forgotten People, Cane River's Creoles of Color* (Baton Rouge: Louisiana State University Press, 1977), 104–5, 318n54, relates that a "Jean Baptiste Barthelemy Rachal and his half-French slave," having had six children, founded one of the three main families *de couleur* in the area. It is likely that McAlpin bought the land from this man, who was white. The rest of the Rachals were part African.

12. Henry W. Lewis and Jacob Lewis, petition 20882701, February 16, 1827, Natchitoches Parish, LA, Race and Slavery Petitions Project (online database), University of North Carolina at Greensboro. The database abstract for this petition reads: "Jacob and Henry Lewis of Mississippi request the court's assistance in recovering their slave named Nat, also known as Peter. The petitioners inform the court that they entrusted Nat to the

care of John Nugent. They accuse Nugent of clandestinely removing Nat from the state of Mississippi and disposing of him in Louisiana. Nat is now in the possession of Robert McAlpin. The petitioners ask that Nat be sequestered while they prove their claim to his ownership."

13. Lyle Saxon, *Old Louisiana* (New York: Century, 1929). See also D. B. Corley, *A Visit to Uncle Tom's Cabin* (Chicago: Laird and Lee, 1892).

14. Harriet Beecher Stowe, *Uncle Tom's Cabin; or, Life Among the Lowly*, 2 vols. (Boston: John P. Jewett, 1852). Chapter 32, "Dark Places" describes the plantation home: "The wagon rolled up a weedy gravel walk, under a noble avenue of China trees.... The house had been large and handsome. It was built in a manner common at the South; a wide verandah of two stories running round every part of the house, into which every outer door opened, the lower tier being supported by brick pillars" (2:179–80). In chapter 35, "The Tokens," Stowe describes one mulatto woman, Cassy, who lived in Legree's house with him and who had some influence over him, even sassing him. The other mulatto woman is Emmeline. Chapter 39, "The Stratagem," describes a garret in the attic with a small window. Stowe refers to Cassy as Legree's mistress.

15. Corley, *A Visit to Uncle Tom's Cabin*.

16. "Not His Real Home: Uncle Tom's Alleged Cabin Coming to Chicago," *Chicago Tribune*, November 20, 1892, reprinted at Uncle Tom's Cabin & American Culture (website), University of Virginia.

17. See the letter from Stowe's brother, Charles Beecher, dated November 29, 1892, in reply to a query from Judge Corley, reprinted in his book. Corley, *A Visit to Uncle Tom's Cabin*, 41. In addition, in the Beecher-Stowe family papers at Harvard, I found letters from Beecher to his cousin Catharine A. Foote in Cincinnati dated between March and September 1839. These letters document his travels to collect bills from plantation owners, as far up as Natchez and the Red River area. The last letter was sent from New Orleans on September 26, 1839. In it, he describes being on the riverboat *Merrimack* going to New Orleans. From his route, it seems clear he had been in the area of the McAlpin plantation. See Charles Beecher, six letters to Catharine A. Foote, his Cincinnati cousin, March–September 1839, A-102, Beecher-Stowe Family Papers, 1798–1956, Beecher-Stowe Family Papers Digital Collection, Schlesinger Library, Radcliffe Institute, Harvard University, Cambridge, MA.

18. Robert Gentry collection, Cammie G. Henry Research Center, Northwestern State University, Natchitoches, LA. On the collection, see David West, "Gentry Collection to Enhance Watson Library," Northwestern State University News Bureau, September 18, 2014.

19. According to Doris McAlpin Russell, in 1937 a letter surfaced written by a relative of John McAlpin's, suggesting that his death during the estate process was due to drowning while checking on a salt mine on Avery Island that may have been part of McAlpin's estate. See Russell, *McAlpin(e) Genealogies, 1730–1990*, 43.

20. Rachal M. Lennon, "The Slave Trade in Microcosm: Natchitoches Parish, Louisiana, 1850–1855" (PhD coursework seminar paper, University of Alabama, 1998), copy in Elizabeth and Gary Mills collection, Cammie G. Henry Research Center, Northwestern State University, Natchitoches, LA. Interestingly, in Lennon's paper, she refers to McAlpin's death as possibly a poisoning (17). In 2018, I contacted her about her source and never got a reply.

21. Elizabeth G. Burgess, pers. comm., February 20, 2018. See also the website for the Harriet Beecher Stowe Center; and Harriet Beecher Stowe, *The Key to Uncle Tom's Cabin:*

*Presenting the Original Facts and Documents upon Which the Story Is Founded, Together with Corroborative Statements Verifying the Truth of the Work* (Boston: John P. Jewett, 1854).

22. See the website for the Melrose Plantation.

23. See the biography by Emily Toth, *Kate Chopin* (New York: William Morrow, 1990); see also the website of the Kate Chopin International Society.

## Chapter 16

1. *Southern Courier* 2, no. 1 (January 1–2, 1966), available at The *Southern Courier*: A Weekly Newspaper Covering Civil Rights in the South 1965–68 (website), Southern Courier Association.

2. Alice Walker, "Laurel," in *You Can't Keep a Good Woman Down* (Orlando, FL: Harcourt Books, 1981), 113.

## Chapter 17

1. Francis DuBose Richardson memoirs, n.d., collection no. 03010; Bayside Plantation records, 1846–66, collection no. 00053; and Frank Liddell Richardson Papers, 1851–69, collection no. 00631; all at the Louis Round Wilson Special Collections Library, University of North Carolina at Chapel Hill.

2. Peter W. Patout, "Bayside Plantation, Jeanerette, LA—Property Information Packet," Peter W. Patout: Historic Property Realtor (website), Spring 2019.

3. Zachariah Nettles, will, signed November 1, 1803, South Carolina, Wills and Probate Records, 1670–1980, Ancestry.com.

## Afterword

1. Jaquelyn Dowd Hall, *Sisters and Rebels: A Struggle for the Soul of America* (New York: W. W. Norton, 2019), 177.

2. Coming to the Table supports the transformative work of undoing racism. There are several dozen local affiliate groups in sixteen states across the United States. The organization encourages and supports the establishment of such groups to provide spaces and opportunities for people to meet regularly together for truth-telling, deep dialogue, relationship building, healing, and action to dismantle inequitable systems and structures based on race. Coming to the Table is one of hundreds of organizations that foster the healing and justice needed given our fraught racial history and encourage people of all racial and ethnic groups to come together. To list a few others: the Equal Justice Initiative, based in Alabama, works to end mass incarceration in the United States, challenges racial and economic injustice, and strives to protect human rights for the most vulnerable in our society. The Beyond Kin Project was begun in 2016 to encourage and facilitate the documentation of enslaved populations, particularly by involving the resources and efforts of the descendants of slaveholders. The Slave Dwelling Project envisions a future in which Americans acknowledge a more truthful and inclusive narrative of the history of the nation that honors the contributions of all our people, is embedded and preserved in the buildings and artifacts of people of African heritage, and inspires all Americans to acknowledge their ancestors.

# Bibliography

Agee, James, and Walker Evans. *Let Us Now Praise Famous Men*. Boston: Houghton Mifflin, 1941.

*Amistad Research Center* (blog). "50 Years/50 Collections: The Preston and Bonita Valien Papers, 1969." February 1, 2016.

Ball, Edward. *Slaves in the Family*. New York: Farrar, Straus and Giroux, 1998.

Baptist, Edward E. *The Half Has Never Been Told: Slavery and the Making of American Capitalism*. New York: Basic Books, 2014.

Bayside Plantation. Records, 1846–66. Collection no. 00053. Louis Round Wilson Special Collections Library, University of North Carolina at Chapel Hill.

Beckert, Sven. *Empire Cotton: A Global History*. New York: Alfred A. Knopf, 2014.

Beecher-Stowe family. Papers, 1798–1956. Beecher-Stowe Family Papers Digital Collection. Schlesinger Library, Radcliffe Institute, Harvard University, Cambridge, MA.

Brainard, Homer Worthington, Harold Simeon Gilbert, and Clarence Almon Torrey. *The Gilbert Family: Descendants of Thomas Gilbert, 1582–1659, of Mt. Wollaston (Braintree), Windsor, and Wethersfield*. Edited by Donal Lines Jacobus. New Haven, CT: n.p., 1953.

Breeze, Elizabeth DuBose Price. "In the Land of Cotton." *Update* (Historical Association of Southern Florida) 13, no. 3 (August 1986): 10. Available online at the History-Miami Museum website.

Chambliss, Prince. *Prince of Peace: A Memoir of an African American Attorney, Who Came of Age in Birmingham during the Civil Rights Movement*. Morrisville, NC: Lulu, 2010.

*Chicago Tribune*. "Not His Real Home: Uncle Tom's Alleged Cabin Coming to Chicago." November 20, 1892. Reprinted at Uncle Tom's Cabin & American Culture (website), University of Virginia.

Corley, D. B. *A Visit to Uncle Tom's Cabin*. Chicago: Laird and Lee, 1892.

Dew, Charles B. *The Making of a Racist: A Southerner Reflects on Family, History, and the Slave Trade*. Charlottesville: University of Virginia Press, 2016.

Du Bois, W. E. B. *The Souls of Black Folk: Essays and Sketches*. 2nd ed. Chicago: A. C. McClurg, 1903.

Dunn, Mitchell. "History of Natchitoches." *Louisiana Historical Quarterly* 3, no. 1 (1920): 26–56.

Eskew, Glenn T. *But for Birmingham: The Local and National Movements in the Civil Rights Struggle*. Chapel Hill: University of North Carolina Press, 1997.

Federal Writers' Project. *Slave Narrative Project*. Vol. 1, *Alabama, Aarons–Young*. 1936–37. Available online in *Born in Slavery: Slave Narratives from the Federal Writers' Project, 1936 to 1938* (digital collection), Library of Congress, Manuscript Division.

Fell, Thomas, comp. *Some Historical Accounts of the Founding of King William's School and Its Subsequent Establishment as St. John's College, Together with Biographical Notices of the Various Presidents from 1790–1894.* Baltimore, MD: Friedenwald, 1894.

Friedan, Betty. *The Feminine Mystique.* New York: Norton, 1963.

Galloway, James R., and Robert R. Kelso. "Don't Handcuff the Aide." *Rehabilitation Record* 7, no. 1 (1966): 1–3.

Gentry, Robert. Collection. Cammie G. Henry Research Center, Northwestern State University, Natchitoches, LA.

Gilpin, Patrick J., and Marybeth Gasman. *Charles S. Johnson: Leadership beyond the Veil in the Age of Jim Crow.* Albany: State University of New York Press, 2003.

Hall, Jacquelyn Dowd. *Sisters and Rebels: A Struggle for the Soul of America.* New York: W. W. Norton, 2019.

Harris, John K. "CAUSE Points a New Direction." *Employment Service Review* 1 (December 1964): 43–45.

Harris, W. Edward. *Miracle in Birmingham: A Civil Rights Memoir, 1954–1965.* Indianapolis, IN: Stonework Press, 2004.

Hedrick, Joan D. *Harriet Beecher Stowe: A Life.* New York: Oxford University Press, 1995.

Herman-Giddens, Marcia E. "A Case Study, A Seventeen-Year-Old Macon County Negro Girl." Project CAUSE field report. August 1964. Amistad Research Center, Tulane University, New Orleans, LA.

Invitational Conference on Government-University Relations in the Professional Preparation and Employment of Counselors. *Counselor Development in American Society, Conference Recommendations.* Washington, DC: US Department of Labor, 1965.

Isom, Chervis. *The Newspaper Boy: Coming of Age in Birmingham, Alabama, during the Civil Rights Era.* n.p.: Hewlett House, 2013.

Jimerson, Randall C. *Shattered Glass in Birmingham: My Family's Fight for Civil Rights, 1961–1964.* Baton Rouge: Louisiana State University Press, 2014.

Johnson, Charles. *Shadow of the Plantation.* Chicago: University of Chicago Press, 1934.

Jones, James H. *Bad Blood: The Tuskegee Syphilis Experiment—A Tragedy of Race and Medicine.* New York: Free Press, 1981.

Kerr, Derek, and Maria Rivero. "Whistleblower Peter Buxtun and the Tuskegee Syphilis Study." *Government Accountability Project* (blog), April 30, 2014.

Lennon, Rachal M. "The Slave Trade in Microcosm: Natchitoches Parish, Louisiana, 1850–1855." PhD coursework seminar paper, University of Alabama, 1998. Copy in Elizabeth and Gary Mills collection, Cammie G. Henry Research Center, Northwestern State University, Natchitoches, LA.

"List of Racially-Motivated Bombings." Bhamwiki. Edited November 10, 2021.

*Manpower Report of the President.* Washington, DC: US Government Printing Office, 1965.

Martin, Douglas. "Seybourn Lynne, 93; Ruled in Civil Rights Case." *New York Times,* September 12, 2000.

McKinstry, Carolyn Maull, with Denise George. *While the World Watched: A Birmingham Bombing Survivor Comes of Age during the Civil Rights Movement.* Carol Stream, IL: Tyndale House, 2011.

McWhorter, Diane. *Carry Me Home: Birmingham, Alabama, the Climactic Battle of the Civil Rights Revolution.* 2001. New York: Simon and Schuster, 2012.

Mills, Gary B. *The Forgotten People, Cane River's Creoles of Color.* Baton Rouge: Louisiana State University Press, 1977.

*New York Times.* "Eleven Lives Lost." May 23, 1891.

Northrop, Solomon. *Twelve Years a Slave: Narrative of Solomon Northup, a Citizen of New-York, Kidnapped in Washington City in 1841, and Rescued in 1853, from a Cotton Plantation near the Red River in Louisiana*. Buffalo, NY: Derby, Orton and Mulligan, 1853.

Olansky, Sidney, Lloyd Simpson, and Stanley H. Schuman. "Environmental Factors in the Tuskegee Study of Untreated Syphilis." *Public Health Reports* 69, no. 7 (1954): 691–98.

Olmsted, Frederick Law. *The Cotton Kingdom: A Traveler's Observations on Cotton and Slavery in the American Slave States*. 1861. Edited by Arthur M. Schlesinger. Introduction by Lawrence N. Powell. New York: Random House, 1984.

Patout, Peter W. "Bayside Plantation, Jeanerette, LA—Property Information Packet." Peter W. Patout: Historic Property Realtor (website). Spring 2019.

Peppler, Jim. *Southern Courier* Photograph Collection. Alabama Department of Archives and History, Montgomery. Published online January 2013.

Race and Slavery Petitions Project (online database). University of North Carolina at Greensboro.

Richardson, Francis DuBose. Memoirs, n.d. Collection no. 03010. Louis Round Wilson Special Collections Library, University of North Carolina at Chapel Hill.

Richardson, Frank Liddell. Papers, 1851–69. Collection no. 00631. Louis Round Wilson Special Collections Library, University of North Carolina at Chapel Hill.

Richardson, Rosell L. *Amos Richardson of Boston and Stonington*. 2nd ed. New York: published by the author, 1906.

Russell, Doris McAlpin. *McAlpin(e) Genealogies, 1730–1990: Alexander McAlpin of South Carolina and Georgia and His Descendants Plus Other McAlpin(e) Families of North America*. Louisville, KY: Gateway Press, 1990.

Satterfield, Carolyn Green. *A History of Brooke Hill, 1940–1975*. Birmingham, AL: Altamont Alumni Association, 2002.

Saxon, Lyle. *Old Louisiana*. New York: Century, 1929.

Solnit, Rebecca. *The Faraway Nearby*. New York: Viking, 2013.

South Carolina, Wills and Probate Records, 1670–1980. Ancestry.com.

The *Southern Courier*: A Weekly Newspaper Covering Civil Rights in the South 1965–68 (website). Southern Courier Association.

St. John's College. *Bulletin of St. John's College in Annapolis: Official Statement of the St. John's Program, Catalogue 1958–1960*. September 1958. St. John's College Digital Archives.

Stowe, Harriet Beecher. *The Key to Uncle Tom's Cabin: Presenting the Original Facts and Documents upon Which the Story Is Founded, Together with Corroborative Statements Verifying the Truth of the Work*. Boston: John P. Jewett, 1854.

Thompson, Joseph Conan. "Toward a More Humane Oppression: Florida's Slave Codes, 1821–1861." *Florida Historical Quarterly* 71, no. 3 (1993): 324–38.

Thorne, T. K. *Behind the Magic Curtain: Secrets, Spies, and Unsung White Allies of Birmingham's Civil Rights Days*. Montgomery, AL: New South Books, 2021.

———. *Last Chance for Justice: How Relentless Investigators Uncovered New Evidence Convicting the Birmingham Church Bombers*. Chicago: Lawrence Hill Books, 2013.

Toscano, Michael. "Melodrama Weakens Foundation of 'Uncle Tom's Cabin.'" *Washington Post*, September 26, 2002.

Toth, Emily. *Kate Chopin*. New York: William Morrow, 1990.

Valien, Preston, and Bonita Valien. Papers. Amistad Research Center, Tulane University, New Orleans, LA.

Walker, Alice. "Laurel." In *You Can't Keep a Good Woman Down*, 105–17. Orlando, FL: Harcourt Books, 1981.

West, David. "Gentry Collection to Enhance Watson Library." Northwestern State University News Bureau, September 18, 2014.

———. *Master of the Mountain: Thomas Jefferson and His Slaves*. New York: Farrar, Straus and Giroux, 2012.

Wilder, Craig Steven. *Ebony and Ivy: Race, Slavery, and the Troubled History of America's Universities*. New York: Bloomsbury Press, 2013.

# Index